Liberalism and its

C000244492

In *Liberalism and its Practice*, prominent scholars from Europe and North America contemplate the intriguing meeting between liberalism and practical politics at the end of the twentieth century.

This study focuses on two of liberalism's greatest emerging challenges: societies that are undergoing transformations in the liberal mould, and well-established liberal democracies that are becoming multicultural. Following a close examination of liberalism's current appeal, the contributors suggest a number of alternative theoretical perspectives and empirical studies which highlight the complexities that exist in the gap between liberalism and its practice. After considering whether liberalism can accommodate the pressures it is confronting, the study concludes by considering the viable alternatives.

This study provides an excellent insight into the meaning and practice of liberalism today. It will be essential reading for students of political science, political theory and for those studying multiculturalism, feminism and comparative politics.

Dan Avnon and **Avner de-Shalit** are both Senior Lecturers in Political Science at the Hebrew University of Jerusalem.

Liberalism and its Practice

**Edited by
Dan Avnon and
Avner de-Shalit**

London and New York

First published 1999
by Routledge
11 New Fetter Lane, London EC4P 4EE

Simultaneously published in the USA and Canada
by Routledge
29 West 35th Street, New York, NY 10001

Typeset in Baskerville by Routledge
Printed and bound in Great Britain by
Creative Print and Design (Wales), Ebbw Vale

British Library Cataloguing in Publication Data
A catalogue record for this book is available from the British Library

Library of Congress Cataloging in Publication Data
Liberalism and its practice / edited by Dan Avnon and Avner de-Shalit.
    p.   cm.
   Includes bibliographical references and index.
   (alk. paper).
   1. Liberalism.   I. Avnon, Dan.   II. De-Shalit, Avner.
 JC574.L519 1999   98–27628
   320.51–dc21

ISBN 0–415–19354–0 (hbk)
ISBN 0–415–19355–9 (pbk)

Contents

List of contributors

Dan Avnon
Hebrew University of Jerusalem

Ronald Beiner
University of Toronto

Frank Cunningham
University of Toronto

Lord Ralf Dahrendorf
House of Lords, London

Avner de-Shalit
Hebrew University of Jerusalem

Stephen Holmes
Princeton University

David Miller
Nuffield College, Oxford University

Susan Moller Okin
Stanford University

Bhikhu Parekh
University of Hull

Mario Sznajder
Hebrew University of Jerusalem

Edna Ullmann-Margalit
Hebrew University of Jerusalem

Acknowledgements

The preparation of this book was supported by a number of institutions. We would like to thank the British Council, the American Cultural Center (the Jerusalem branch), and the Department of Political Science at the Hebrew University of Jerusalem for their financial and moral support. Daniel Attas and Brian Barry were very helpful in their suggestions for revisions. We are also grateful to a number of individuals for their assistance: Anat Balkan, Susan Kennedy, Baruch Knei-Paz, David Ricci, and No'am Shapira. Finally, many thanks to Patrick Proctor, a skilful and efficient editor, and to Goober Fox of Routledge.

Although Susan Moller Okin's essay was originally written for this volume, it was first published in the journal *Ethics*, and we thank the University of Chicago Press for their permission to reprint it. We thank also the University of California Press for their permission to use material published in Ronald Beiner, *What's the Matter with Liberalism?*, Copyright © 1992 The Regents of the University of California.

These essays are written in honour of Professor Shlomo Avineri, our teacher and colleague. We present them to him with great respect and affection.

1 Introduction

Liberalism between promise and practice

Dan Avnon and Avner de-Shalit

At the end of the twentieth century two developments stand out as challenges to liberalism. First, within established liberal societies multiculturalism and multiethnicism have emerged as social realities that seek accommodation within the liberal framework. But at the same time, fighting for their autonomy as groups rather than as individuals, these claims for an even more inclusive theory and practice of liberalism undermine, at least *prima facie*, the very framework they wish to expand.

Second, in societies with a weak or non-existing liberal tradition, which have only recently emancipated themselves from authoritarian regimes, liberalism has become the rallying cry around which new political orders are being assembled. However, this mad dash towards liberal freedoms and individual autonomy is creating great tensions in states that lack the necessary preconditions for creating a liberal society. Calls for political freedom (based on liberal conceptions of individual rights) clash with the call for a very quick move towards economic prosperity (based on the free market principle). In these cases we find a tension between individual liberty that assumes a weak, non-interventionist state, and the need for strong and stable institutions that can 'deliver' what is expected of liberalism.

Consequently, liberalism is challenged both from within and from without. The common characteristic of these challenges is that both want to change existing social orders, but to do so without having to necessarily discard liberalism (in the case of liberal societies) or to disregard it (in the case of non-liberal societies). Ultimately, this is a challenge to the homogeneity that characterised the original liberal society. Thus liberalism has been under pressure to considerably revise itself. It is self-evident that if liberalism accommodates itself to these pressures it will become yet more complex, incoherent, and fraught with inner tensions and ambiguities than ever before.

So why continue to address social tensions and apparently insurmountable difficulties in terms of liberal discourse? Why not simply acknowledge that liberalism is an incomplete, limited social philosophy that was very useful for addressing the contingencies of its historical and cultural origins, and that ought to now be dismissed in favour of new frames of reference? What is the appeal of liberalism that holds sway over the imagination of individuals and of nations, and causes them to fight for a liberal order (against liberalism's opponents) and about the meaning and practice of liberalism (when arguing with one another)?

Some people would immediately reply that liberalism's appeal lies in its being the most successful economic regime. Even though this is no doubt a very strong case for liberalism, we believe that it is not enough to explain liberalism's appeal in terms of its potential to generate material well being. The fact is that the most heated debates about liberalism – its assumptions, values, institutions and social carriers – are taking place in the affluent societies of the industrialised West. Had economic benefit been the primary reward for establishing a liberal way of life, we would have expected that in these societies empirical reality would have made such questions less central. But the fact is that it is precisely in the economically most advanced societies that the direction and future of liberalism is being questioned and criticised. In other words, those who are the primary beneficiaries of liberalism's apparent appeal are in many cases its most eloquent critics from within. Which means that they expect something more, something beyond economic prosperity and security. What is the basis of this expectation? What is the root of the desire to perpetuate liberalism, while at the same time transform it? What is the unfulfilled promise that liberalism has yet to deliver?

The creative multiple self: between external and internal pluralism

By asking these questions, we assume that there must be a latent psychological element that would explain the varied attempts to redefine liberal values or practices. In this section we are claiming that the key to deciphering liberalism's appeal is to be sought through a rethinking of the complex reality that is referred to by the innocuous term, the 'liberal individual'. While there is widespread acceptance of the individual as liberalism's basic social unit, when contemplating the liberal individual one must note that liberalism does not postulate that persons are solely monolithic 'individuals'. In other words we wish to focus attention on the background assumption of liberalism: that the liberal individual implies also the idea of a person who enjoys a rich and varied inner life. We would like to call this plural conception of individual the 'creative multiple self'.

Stated simply, the notion of a 'creative multiple self' alludes to the idea that persons create their own lives. Even though it may be argued that persons are constrained by the circumstances that they encounter in their social and cultural settings, still each person *is* a unique human being, endowed with a potential to change his or her 'settings' as he or she changes him- or herself. This is the creative dimension of personhood: each person is gifted with innumerable potentialities. Therefore, if not constrained by others, a person will be inclined to develop in more than one way, changing his or her external life circumstances as he or she experiments with the potentialities available to them. This ability of single persons to create diverse forms of life is the external expression of one's immanent creativity. The notion of 'multiple' in the expression 'the creative, multiple self' refers to the fact that the 'self' is not a monolithic entity, but rather a cluster of different 'I's, each manifesting different combinations of creative expression.

In what follows, we wish to point to the relation between the conception of the creative multiple self and liberalism's emphasis on political pluralism as a *sine qua non* of political order. We suggest that the emphasis on pluralism between persons (what we may call external pluralism) reflects and seeks to ensure liberalism's latent upholding of the pluralism within the person (what we may call internal pluralism). Hence the assumption guiding our essay is that liberalism's deep founded appeal goes beyond economics, and is rooted in the acknowledgement of one's multiple self.

It is easy to see why liberalism can be pictured as a response to the wish to foster and protect internal pluralism, or the multiple self, if we recall that liberalism's origin is all about plurality: liberalism emerged as a strong, long-suppressed reaction to superficial beliefs in the authority of transcendent orders and their human and institutional agents. By reacting to and rejecting the authority of external power, liberalism expressed a strong desire of individuals to be emancipated from external dogma, and thus to be autonomous and free to fulfil their desire to become creative expressions of their complex selves with their hesitations, doubts and scepticism. So the liberal 'individual' is in fact much more complex than the flat image that is often associated with this concept.[1]

Note our emphasis. Our argument is that in both the historical and ontological roots of liberalism, there is a desire to live in social and political contexts that acknowledge, respect and even foster persons' inner complexity and creativity. The call of liberals that the state/church/society let them choose freely is in fact an expression of this psychological need. 'I', says the liberal, 'have diverse potential selves, and I want to choose among them according to my own wishes, every time I think I should make this choice.'[2] Thus the social order that the liberal person wishes for is one that would reflect and respect his or her personhood as a creative multiple self.

Someone who is cognisant of the multiplicity of self would therefore desire a social and political environment that would be supportive of the innate desire to move freely between spheres of expression and relationship. This free flow enables one's complexity to manifest itself in diverse forms under different circumstances. 'Yes' declares the person, 'I can be deontological in my relations to other persons and consequentialist in my judgement of politics';[3] 'Yes, I am an individual when I want to possess, but I am embedded when I want to relate'; 'Yes, I am "calculated" in my business relations and "spontaneous" and carefree in my relationships with friends.' Thus, the person aware of the multiplicity of self that seeks expression would be attracted to liberalism rather than to any other theory. Why? Because rather than taking an apologetic stance toward the paradoxical features of human realities, liberalism takes a sanguine view. There is a neat fit between life's ambiguities and the ambiguities of liberal discourse and practice. Therefore, innate in liberalism is the promise that one may experiment with the paradoxes of one's inner life: rather than criticising consciously creative persons for being incoherent and inconsistent, liberalism harbours the potential for addressing their behaviour as expressions of their immanent multiplicity, projected onto relationships.

Thus in this idealised[4] expression, liberalism's promise is to enable one to manifest different facets of self in relation to multiple circumstances, to feel good about it and to not experience discomfort with apparent inconsistencies in the process. Institutionally, liberalism at its best should ensure that the world 'outside' of us would reflect and respect the world 'inside' of us. In both dimensions we are addressing worlds of multiple selves and multiple social contexts. This is the promise of liberalism: to enable external pluralism to enhance, and thereby respect, the internal pluralism of the multiple self.[5]

Pluralism and the multicultural society

Having discussed liberalism's latent promise, we now want to move on and raise the following question: if liberalism can be so self-fulfilling, and if *this* is its appeal, why does it face so many difficulties? We suggest that the reason is related to the two-fold development noted in our opening paragraphs: (a) the move from the more or less homogeneous societies in which liberalism originated to the increasingly multicultural societies in which liberalism finds itself nowadays; and (b) the attempts of previously non-liberal societies to adopt willy-nilly political and economical frameworks of liberal states without undergoing the necessary period of psychological and cultural adjustment.[6] At this point we should note that just as in our depiction of liberalism's promise we focused on what we think is a neglected aspect of liberalism, so in our discussion of liberalism's shortcomings we do not intend to develop a comprehensive explanation – this we leave to the other essays in this volume – but rather to highlight two liberal features that are responsible for the difficulties that liberalism faces in the move from promise to practice.

Liberalism is *the* theory of the modern individual. Let us imagine, then, a person, who for his or her own interest, wants to create the social and political environments which will allow him or her to flourish, or, as in our definition of flourishing, to realise the creative potentiality of the multiple self. She or he will require autonomy and political liberty because autonomy ensures personal responsibility for one's movement in life and liberty ensures continuous choosing among various options immanent in the multiple self. And she or he will need a state that equally respects as many ideas of the good as possible, because this enables the exploration of life's opportunities to take place without external hindrance.

This is where the multiculturalism in established liberal societies and introducing liberalism into illiberal societies enter our analysis, as posing a challenge to liberalism's theory and practice. Let us start with autonomy and liberty. It has long been argued that both autonomy and liberty are worthless in circumstances in which they cannot be exercised.[7] Thus in order to enable people to enjoy liberty and autonomy, the state – or any other political association capable of it – must provide the proper conditions. Such an intervention is not problematic in societies in which there is already an established liberal culture, where all people tend to accept the moral principles of liberalism and its psychological promise. These societies would be homogeneous in this sense of a shared liberal culture, even though they may be comprised of many different cultural groups. In such societies people would understand and allow for temporary suspensions of liberal values and their political practices, in order to ensure liberalism's continued existence. For example, in the case of an ecological or environmental crisis, these people would accept temporary limitations on their freedom of mobility (free use of private cars) in order to re-balance ecosystems and thus to ensure long-term prosperity, which is a precondition for the practice of autonomy and liberty.

But the status of autonomy and liberty is different in societies lacking a strong liberal political culture which attempt to adopt all or some liberal features in an effort to 'catch up' with established liberal states. That is because autonomy and liberty seem irrelevant, not to mention valueless in circumstances of extreme economic scarcity, political instability and physical insecurity. The most obvious examples that come to mind are the non-liberal societies of contemporary Eastern Europe or South America. [8]

The case becomes more complicated in established liberal societies which have only recently become multicultural (e.g. the UK).[9] In such societies it is very likely that there will not be proper conditions – *within the sub-cultural group* – for the practice of autonomy and liberty offered by the dominant liberal political culture. Consequently, in such societies there is a danger that the sub-cultural group will misuse liberty and autonomy, misinterpreting the intentions underpinning liberal culture.[10] Thus some temporary limitations or restrictions must be placed on liberty in order to safeguard its future proper use. But unlike the case of homogeneous societies, where members understand and accept these limitations (or even better, when it is not necessary to pose any limitations because the tradition of liberalism is so stable), in liberal societies with a recent tradition of multiculturalism such understanding is not taken for granted. To examine why, let us begin with an example, Britain in 1988, which was at the time a multicultural society in the making.

British society wanted to assimilate the newly arrived immigrants from non-liberal societies, and offered them liberalism as the great promise: it was the framework within which they would be able simultaneously to hold and practise cherished convictions and become members of the assimilating (liberal) community. But some of the proper conditions for fulfilling this promise were missing: first, some of the newly arrived immigrants had not yet internalised liberal values; moreover, some of them were impoverished and suffering economic hardship. Consequently, many of these immigrants misinterpreted freedom of expression, for example when they burnt Salman Rushdie's books and called for changes to the law of blasphemy. They did this as an expression of their outrage as Muslims, yet assumed that their conduct was legitimate as a personal act of freedom of expression (even though they did not act autonomously in the liberal sense of expressing individual, rather than group, sentiments and beliefs). Therefore, when the government rejected their demand that Rushdie's books be taken off the shelves of bookstores and libraries, the Muslims considered this a paradoxical bind. They asked the British society: 'Where is your great promise? You told us that we could be both Muslim and live as equal members in liberal societies. But now you are restricting us on the basis of our Islamic beliefs in the name of liberalism. Why should we assimilate into your liberalism without you expanding the existing framework of liberalism so as to accommodate us?'

In terms of our analysis, what they were actually asking for was the fulfilment of the latent liberal promise: the realisation of the multiple self. But as this example demonstrates, in the lack of proper conditions in multicultural societies, it is very likely that the state will have to temporarily suspend liberalism's very promise: free expression of the multiple self. This creates a paradox for newly arrived immigrants: instead of expanding their spheres of association and expression, these individuals are pushed into immoderate identification with one facet of their selves: the cultural. Rather than becoming *more* of themselves, they become less. And paradoxically, this occurs in a liberal society, the society that was meant to enable free and creative expression of the multiple self.

Let us summarise our argument up to this point. We have claimed that liberalism's promise is the expression of the creative multiple self. We then argued that in order to secure the expression of the multiple self, the individual requires autonomy and liberty and in addition a state that equally respects as many ideas of the good as possible. We then continued to argue that the implementation of autonomy and liberty, well established and practised in homogeneous liberal cultures, becomes problematic when applied to heterogeneous newly formed multicultural societies. We continued to demonstrate the tension between the promise of liberalism – i.e. the expression of the creative multiple self – and the undoing of that promise. In order to furnish the conditions necessary for the realisation of the promise, the state has at least temporarily to put on hold the promise. In itself, this is cause enough for the newly arrived immigrant – or for any newcomer to liberalism – to lose the psychological motivation to adopt liberalism. Now it is left to explain why there is an additional problem with regard to the state, which equally respects as many ideas of the good as possible.

Three theses of pluralism

Our analysis of the challenges facing liberalism in the contemporary world attends to the relations between the self's multiplicity and pluralism. Expression of one's inner multiplicity necessitates a form of politics that fosters and encourages pluralism. So for us to comprehend the transition from illiberal to liberal societies and the meeting of liberal societies with multiculturalism, we must focus on the ability of the state in both contexts to uphold multiplicity and at the same time to promote pluralism. It is within this context that we want to examine pluralism, and we start by distinguishing between three theses of pluralism relevant to this discussion.

One thesis is sociological: pluralism arises from the very simple fact that there are many people in this world, each holding a slightly different idea of the good. As long as liberalism does not want to be coercive or paternalistic, and since liberalism respects *people*, the liberal state respects each of these persons' idea of the good. This way of looking at pluralism is minimalist in its demand from the state. At minimum, the latter should be neutral between *persons*. Pluralism is thus a social fact – inherent in the *plurality of people* – which liberals have no other choice but to face and accept: 'Perhaps, ideally, and in due course,' says the sociological pluralist, 'society will be able to overcome these differences, say by convincing those who hold false beliefs that they are wrong in their convictions. At the moment, however, this is beyond the scope of politics. Instead we should move on and progress economically and personally.' Ideological and ethical disagreements are bracketed, and the person – not the idea – is the object of this form of pluralism.

There is a second way to look at pluralism, which we would like to call an axiological theory of pluralism.[11] According to this thesis, pluralism's presence in society reflects *pluralism in values*: the fact that there are many people holding competing ideas of the good is *not* due to these people holding false beliefs, but rather due to the nature of values, i.e. their plurality. That this plurality does not necessarily reflect many false beliefs is explained as follows: if you start to explore values embedded in 'ideas of the good', you may find yourself eliminating some ideas or values as deriving from more fundamental ones. But you will reach a point in your contemplation beyond which they cannot be reduced to a single idea or value. Therefore, all these irreducible ideas or values will seem proper: you will have plurality as plurality of values rather than plurality of persons. In other words, from the perspective of the axiological thesis of pluralism, *even if there is a single person in the world, you will have pluralism*.

The third thesis is psychological: it assumes that the source of pluralism is the plurality of selves within each person. Each of these selves may adhere to, or reflect, different values. As such, the third thesis is different from the second by virtue of its concentrating on the psychological (and therefore 'internal' to the person) roots of pluralism rather than on pluralism's sociological or axiological (and therefore 'external' to the person) manifestations.

Let us exemplify this thesis with an example. Suppose that as Dan is writing this essay, talking to Avner about the three theses of pluralism, Dan's young child enters. All of a sudden Dan changes: his terminology becomes less sophisticated, his body language expresses his vacillation between the knowledgeable academic and the adoring father, and – para-doxically – while writing about the autonomy and liberty of liberal persons, he very assertively and paternalistically sends his son off to take a nap. His son does not budge. In this moment Dan is split between his academic self, his soft and loving self, and his dominating self. While contemplating these sudden changes, and observing the parade of multiple selves, the buyer of Dan's second-hand car enters. Dan must conclude the deal now, as the bank will close in one hour. He has no choice but to respond to the challenge, and to try extracting the best possible price, without losing face in front of his colleague Avner and his wondering son. Dan reveals his bargaining self: the pragmatic and street-wise dealer.

What do we see here? At least four different aspects of his self, each one manifesting a different form of psychological identification with his 'I'. With his colleague he is open-minded and tolerant, egalitarian and co-operative; with his son, loving and caring, and – in addition – authoritative and paternalistic; with the buyer of his car he is shrewd and cunning, instrumental and possessive. These selves reflect different values, yet co-exist within the same person, fulfilling diverse functions in direct accordance with both the needs of the creative multiple self *and* the demands of the social situation. As such, they are not in conflict (as they would seem to have been had we conducted an external – sociological or axiological – study of apparently conflicting values such as egalitarianism and authoritarianism). However, even if the values implicit in one's psychological pluralism are *not* in conflict, as in this example, still they are not necessarily reducible to a single basic idea or value. An attempt to reduce irreducible values into a single basic idea or value implies a reduction of the multiple self. Such a reduction would negate the latent promise of liberalism.

Pluralism and state neutrality

We now want to consider what is often claimed to be the liberal mechanism to accommodate these three kinds of pluralism, namely the neutral state. The neutral state protects the rights of all its citizens to identify with their conceptions of the good, and every person to uphold his or her own judgements about the good life. Such neutrality does not imply indifference to what is right and just. However, a state that is neutral in this sense is not biased towards the fulfilment of any certain idea of the good, and therefore treats all it citizens equally.[12]

Without discussing neutrality in depth, we do want to distinguish between three kinds of state neutrality, responding to the three kinds of pluralism that we have postulated: neutrality between persons, neutrality between values and neutrality towards the relations between values and selves. The first is the mechanism for sociological pluralism, the second is the mechanism of axiological pluralism and the third is the mechanism that ensures psychological pluralism.

Neutrality between persons (sociological) suits external pluralism. The state treats pluralism as a phenomenon that exists between discrete entities, i.e. between persons, conceptualised as unitary individuals. Neutrality between values (axiological) can be considered either external (because it relates to an assumed sphere of values that is independent of particular human beings) or internal (because it relates to particular values that are internalised by this or that person). Neutrality towards the relations between values and selves (psychological) is most evidently related to internal pluralism. It means that the state is neutral in relation to different values, which may exist within a single person.[13] Based on these distinctions, we shall now argue that conventional conceptions of the liberal, neutral state fail to take sufficient account of the variety of pluralisms that state neutrality seeks to accommodate. Liberal justifications of state neutrality focus only on *external* (sociological) pluralism (between persons). Yet this is inadequate, because as we have claimed, the great promise of liberalism is *internal* (psychological) pluralism (the needs of the creative multiple self).

Earlier we defined sociological versus axiological and psychological pluralism, and neutrality between persons (external pluralism) and neutrality between values (internal pluralism). But remember that we started this discussion with the assumption that the multiple self requires a political environment that respects and fosters pluralism. So now we shall apply the distinctions made above to the crucial question: Can internal pluralism survive in multicultural environments? If internal pluralism is a need, can neutrality alone deliver this basic need? In terms of our categories, we are asking whether we interpret the source of plurality as persons, or do we detect the source of external conduct in the psychology of the multiple self?[14] With regard to state neutrality, what we need to ask is whether the state interprets its role as being neutral between persons or between values.

To begin with, as for external (sociological) pluralism, we see no problem in fostering pluralism through adherence to a policy of neutrality, because in both homogeneous and heterogeneous societies, the guiding principle of this neutrality is respecting people. If neutrality is based on respect for persons as such, the fact that this is done within a multicultural, rather than a culturally homogeneous society, should not make a difference. (In this sort of liberalism, politics is supposed to be indifferent to values; cf. Rawls' assertion that justice is political, not metaphysical.)

As for internal pluralism, we distinguish between homogeneous and heterogeneous liberal societies. In a more or less homogeneous liberal society, even neutrality between values (rather than between persons) should not be problematic. That is because it is reasonable to assume that in a homogeneous society the scale of values *actually* held and put forward in the public discourse is relatively limited. Thus very extreme values will not be advocated, and state neutrality will not be problematic. If, however, extreme ideas are suggested, there will be an easy way of dismissing them on neutral grounds, without invoking the terminology of the ideas of the good. Such ideas will be dismissed not as opposing a certain idea of the good, but because they do not tie in with the common culture or ethos. The values that they represent will be considered anomalous.[15]

But in heterogeneous multicultural societies, internal neutrality may be difficult to attain. This is particularly the case in liberal societies that assume a dominant homogeneous culture that is threatened by ideas imported either by newcomers or by exposure to ideas originating in other societies and cultures. Here some of the new values may be neither wholly supportive nor wholly undermining of the liberal system; they may simply originate in a different region of language,[16] from a view of the world that is incommensurable with that of liberalism, its discourse and practice. In such cases, internal neutrality is not likely to make a lot of sense: because the values are incomparable, they reflect incommensurate perceptions of what is good. Therefore liberals finding themselves in such situations have been doing one of two things: they have either retreated to external neutrality (between people),[17] or they have changed the terms of the discussion, bringing in the idea of reasonableness.[18]

What is wrong with these responses? As for retreating to external neutrality, this constitutes a withdrawal from liberalism's promise to foster internal plurality, because by detaching values from persons, the values are once again external to the person. Moreover, the retreat to external neutrality implies *indifference to*, rather than *respect for*, values. In both ways, the retreat to external neutrality is insensitive to the psychological needs of the multiple self. At heart, the multiple self does not wish to be merely acknowledged; it wants to be present in all its complexity and diversity. It wants the 'other' to relate to all its values as important and worthy of respect, rather than to be only unthreatening, avoidable and thereby subject to being bracketed.

Aware of the problems we have discussed, several liberal philosophers have advanced the idea of reasonableness as a way to hold together the notion of neutrality and the complexity of self. However, in terms of our analysis, this solution may be even more problematic than the retreat to external neutrality.

When thinking about political order, the liberal who upholds 'reasonableness' assumes that instead of discussing ideas of the good (due to the assumption that the state must be neutral), we can discuss 'reasonable' ideas. And yet, how can one discuss a 'reasonable' idea without comparing incommensurable ideas of the good? In general, how can one distinguish between values on the basis of their relative 'reasonableness', and at the same time remain neutral?

Certain liberals meet such questions by defining reasonable ideas as ideas held by reasonable persons.[19] Reasonable persons would respect other persons' ideas of the good, because in this way they would not push the other outside of the political game, hence nobody will be alienated. This will allow for stability, which will, in turn, allow these reasonable persons to do what *they* want to do, to fulfil themselves. Since these liberals do not want to distinguish between a reasonable and an unreasonable value, they instead distinguish between a reasonable and an unreasonable person. By which the liberal seemingly overcomes the problem of having to define reasonableness in the domain of values. However, from our perspective, the inadequacy of such a response is self-evident: our analysis reveals that reasonableness is defined *socially* rather than *ethically*. Consequently, internal neutrality (between values) collapses in multicultural societies into external neutrality (between people). Values are bracketed.

On top of this, the notion of a reasonable person is predicated on the assumption that creative multiple aspects of self must be restrained if one wishes to establish a 'reasonable' social order. This effect originates in the fact that reasonableness is treated socially rather than psychologically. What we get is a bracketing of the internal, creative dimension of self. This is the price deemed necessary if one seeks a stable political order. Thus, the price of stability is a diminishing of liberalism's latent promise.

We see that the two responses associated with state neutrality – retreat to external neutrality or the idea of reasonableness – either bracket values or bracket the multiple self, and thereby cannot genuinely fulfil liberalism's promise. The creative multiple self is overlooked and therefore not genuinely respected. Instead, persons – regardless of their inherent creativity and multiplicity of values – are respected. In other words, while we consider internal pluralism to be the most important aspect of pluralism (needed to fulfil the promise of the multiple self), in effect state neutrality deals with interpersonal, i.e. external, pluralism. The result is that state neutrality between ideas, the mechanism necessary to meet the promise of liberalism, is not feasible in multicultural societies.

The democratic bypass

Our analysis in this essay is a response to the nagging question: 'Why do so many people continue to promote liberalism in spite of the many quandaries/paradoxes/tensions generated in the transition from liberal theories to liberal practices?' Our answer directs attention to the creative multiple self's need to flourish in a public sphere that is characterised by sensitivity to the deep roots of pluralism. That is liberalism's latent, psychological promise. This promise, we postulate, appeals to any person who is in a position to influence its social and political setting.

One way of circumventing the tensions we have noted when the demands of multiculturalism meet the limits of liberalism, is to be sought in the meeting of liberalism and democracy. The tension between democracy and liberalism has been noted by many astute observers. This apparent 'mismarriage' may be understood if we think of democracy as providing a political framework that supports pluralism without *necessarily* supporting liberalism. This explanation ties in with our analysis of liberalism as an expression of the need to foster plurality. So our final comment directs attention to the relation between democracy and pluralism. In this view, pluralism is the binding joint of liberalism and democracy.

How is this so? One may express one's pluralism through the democratic structure, institutions and procedures. Democratic practices enable one to act in different ways and to influence reality in diverse contexts. In other words, a person's need to express internal pluralism can be met through participation in democratic procedures and thus potential tension with a polity (ordered according to the values of a homogeneous culture) is lifted. So while liberalism may not enable one's multiple self to be expressed, democracy may deliver this promise. Stated otherwise, where we see societies managing transitions from being relatively culturally homogeneous to multicultural, we may explain these transitions not in terms of the newcomers' assimilation into liberalism, but rather into democracy. This may be considered a democratic bypass of liberalism's shortcomings.

We raise this point to emphasise the importance of social and political arrangements in terms of their ability to meet the needs of the multiple self that take priority over strict adherence to particular forms of social order. In these terms, democratic politics may be seen as a way of transference of the desire for pluralism that we have associated with liberalism.[20] In this way one may develop a model of balancing between a culturally heterogeneous society and a politically homogeneous culture. However, this proposition is sketchy and in need of elaboration, for to fully understand the challenges facing liberalism in contemporary times one cannot restrict oneself to a single perspective or line of analysis. Therefore it is appropriate to continue this exploration of liberalism's quandaries, turning to the other contributors to this volume for further analysis of the tensions between liberalism's promise and its practice.

We begin with four different – yet complementary – perspectives on the challenges facing liberalism at the end of the century.

Notes

1 Perhaps the image of the individual depicted by right-wing liberals is the best example of this flat individual. (See R. Nozick, *Anarchy, State and Utopia*, (Oxford: Blackwell, 1974), and D. Gauthier, 'The Liberal Individual', in his *Morals by Agreement* (Oxford: Oxford University Press, 1986). It is also interesting to note that in the communitarian–individualistic debate, most assume that the individual is either embedded in or detached from communities. But wouldn't it be true to claim that the picture is more complicated? Sometimes we belong and sometimes we want to be distinguished. See, for an alternative view of this dynamic, Martin Buber, 'Distance and Relation', *The Knowledge of Man* (New York: Harper and Row, 1965).

2 T. M. Scanlon, ' The Significance of Choice', *The Tanner Lectures*, vol. xiii (Cambridge: Cambridge University Press, 1986), 149–217; R. Beiner, *What's the Matter With Liberalism?* (Berkeley: University of California Press, 1992), pp. 25ff.

3 For example, Charles Larmore argues that moral thinking need not be exclusively deontological or consequentialist. See his *Patterns of Moral Complexity* (Cambridge: Cambridge University Press, 1987).

4 We realise that this is a somewhat naive picture, but we believe that it reflects the still largely unexplored psychological desire that lies behind the tendency to stick to liberalism. In this ideal presentation, multiple self-expressions will always manifest some positive creative potential. One may think of this proposition as a modest revision of the 'state of nature' theory in which the person is conceived as multiple by nature, and not only in reaction to norms and to the expectations of 'others'.

5 A more formal expression of internal pluralism is put forward by Brian Barry in his *Political Argument* (Brighton: Harvester Wheatsheaf, (1965) 1990), pp. 3–8. He claims that people define equally basic moral principles, none of which, to use David Miller's reflection on his thesis, we are inclined to abandon. (See Miller's *Market, State and Community* (Oxford: Clarendon Press), p. 4.) Thus people have 'indifference curves', representing their preferences as between various combinations of values at stake. Our notion of the creative multiple self goes beyond Barry's formal analysis by directing attention to the inner dynamics that give rise to the plurality of values that Barry analyses.

6 In this volume, the essays discussing (a) are Moller Okin's and Parekh's, and the papers discussing (b) are mainly Sznajder's and Holmes's.

7 Perhaps John Stuart Mill was first to claim this, when he, rather controversially, argued that people who were not capable of 'rationality' were not fit for liberty and autonomy. Bhikhu Parekh has criticised this standpoint in his well-known article 'Superior People', *Times Literary Supplement*, 25 Feb 1994. We are not necessarily in agreement with Mill when we, much more modestly, claim that constraints external to the person limit the possibility of exercising autonomy and liberty.

8 For theoretical discussion see Holmes's essay in this volume, and for an empirical case see the essay by Sznajder.

9 See the essay by Bhikhu Parekh in this volume.

10 See the essay by Susan Moller Okin in this volume.

11 Axiology is the study of the nature of values, especially relevant in ethics and aesthetics.

12 See S. Mulhall and A. Swift, *Liberals and Communitarians* (Oxford: Blackwell, 2nd edn, 1996), 29–32, and A. Reeve, *Liberal Neutrality* (London: Routledge, 1989).

13 While being aware of the duality of neutrality between values (it can relate to both external and internal pluralism), for the sake of analytical convenience we shall refer to both neutrality between values, and neutrality towards the relations between values and selves, as 'internal'.

14 It is important to note that pluralism is often observed in its manifestation in the conduct of persons, simply because ideas cannot be discerned until words or actions express them.

15 This is not to say that this homogeneous society will limit itself to a limited variety of ideas. It *will* be open to ideas that pose challenges to certain aspects of liberalism, yet without challenging the entire package of ideas included in liberalism. For example, animal welfarism, which challenges the liberal idea of anthropocentrism, does not threaten liberalism altogether.

16 H. Pitkin, *Wittgenstein and Justice* (Berkeley: University of California Press, 1993), pp. 140–49. Pitkin discusses what appears to be an irreducible gap between the concepts of one language region and those of another.

17 E.g. Rawls's veil of ignorance, where he postulates that it is pointless to argue between different principles of justice.

18 Brian Barry, *Justice as Impartiality* (Oxford: Oxford University Press, 1995), or the 'new' Rawls, in his *Political Liberalism* (New York: Columbia University Press, 1993).

19 Rawls, ibid., lecture II.

20 See the essays by Frank Cunningham and Ronald Beiner in this volume.

Part I

Liberalism at the end of the century

Introduction

There is no one ideal type of political order that is the 'pure' expression of liberalism.[1]
*Still, one may suggest that liberalism, in its attempt to fulfil its promise, is usually a
combination that includes some or all of the following features: individual liberty and
autonomy, particular institutions such as rights, and market economy. Each of the four
papers in the first part of this volume focuses on a distinct feature of liberalism, brought
together in the context of the more general question of what current liberalism is. Ralf
Dahrendorf examines the role of liberty vis-à-vis the need to 'deliver' prosperity and social
cohesion; Stephen Holmes relates to liberalism as a set of institutions and practices;
Mario Sznajder examines what happens to liberalism if the idea of market economy is
divorced from the ideas of liberty and autonomy, and the institution of rights; comple-
menting Sznajder's discussion, Edna Ullmann-Margalit wonders how liberal is the
practice of the free market, in particular when we remember its relation to the idea of the
'invisible hand'.*

*Ralf Dahrendorf situates the moral and economic dilemmas of contemporary liberal
societies in the context of internationalised modern economies. He shows in theory and
through a series of examples, that it is difficult to achieve a perfect, ideal balance between
economic prosperity, social cohesion and political freedom. He assumes that in liberal
societies the emphasis on competitiveness – enabled by institutionalising freedom in the
economic sphere – is likely to damage social cohesion. If, on the other hand, such free
societies choose to give social cohesion higher priority, their competitiveness and thus their
prosperity are at risk. The danger for liberals is that states that would go for prosperity
first and foremost, would do this by restricting liberty. Worried by the breakdown of
civility under the strain of economic pressures, Dahrendorf calls for a return to civil
society with its emphasis on grass roots participation. We shall encounter elaboration of
this theme in the essays by David Miller, Frank Cunningham and Ronald Beiner in Part
III.*

*Dahrendorf's discussion is based on three hypothetical 'cities'. Stephen Holmes
derives his theory from a close examination of the East European experience.*

Challenging the conventional wisdom that liberalism's potential is optimised in weak states, Stephen Holmes shows that it is a strong state that enables liberalism to flourish. Analysing contemporary Russian illiberalism, he explains the failure of liberalism in Russia as stemming from a fatal combination of state ineffectiveness on the one hand and social disorganisation on the other. According to Holmes, liberalism as a set of institutions is no longer about the diffusion of power but rather about its capacity to 'unify power in relatively accountable hands and to use it relatively effectively'. The Russian example enables Holmes to re-evaluate both the principles underlying political practices in established liberal societies and the institutions needed to found liberalism in illiberal societies.

These two articles by Dahrendorf and Holmes bring to the fore the role of the market economy in creating the moral dilemmas that liberalism is currently facing. This is where Mario Sznajder's discussion of Chile's transition to a market economy comes in. Chile is a very interesting example of using and implementing a radical liberal theory (Hayek's) in a previously nonliberal society. Examining the use and implementation of Hayek's theory in Chile, Sznajder's thesis is that when liberal values are taken out of the liberal 'package', they are often misinterpreted and misused, until eventually they may become the justification for an authoritarian and anti-liberal regime.

Indeed, as suggested by Sznajder, a strongly authoritarian government in Chile was justified by the regime by the claim that through economic reforms and the opening of the market, Chile was establishing the basis for individual liberty. But in reality the price was high, and in direct contrast to rhetoric: the most scarce commodity, to put it in Hayek's terms, was personal freedom. This can be a sober reply to those who claim that the right way to introduce liberalism into a society lacking liberal political culture is to adopt a step-by-step approach, commencing with market economy and economic freedom.

The lessons of the Chilean experience complement Holmes's lessons from the attempt to introduce liberal practices into the Russia of the 1990s. In both instances, the transition to liberalism was characterised by undue emphasis on solely one aspect of liberalism's features, the market economy. In Russia, the need to create a political environment in which rights are protected by the state – a need that is enhanced by a 'strong' state – was overlooked. In Chile the emphasis on market economy reflected an authoritarian ideology in which respect for individual freedom and autonomy was limited to economic activity. In both cases, the authors claim, the institutional aspects of liberalism were shunted aside and attempts to introduce liberalism failed.

While taking into account all of liberalism's features, the essays by Dahrendorf, Holmes and Sznajder are primarily concerned with the apparently unsettling effects of the free market economy when applied immoderately into complex social and political environments. These contributions raise the following question. If, on the one hand, the free market is inseparable from liberalism, indeed a reflection in the economic sphere of the idea of liberty and economy, why is it, on the other hand, that it can be used so 'liberally' to justify conservative and/or authoritarian forces? Edna Ullmann-Margalit helps us think about this question.

Ullmann-Margalit's article focuses on the ideological 'career' of the eighteenth-century idea of the 'invisible hand'. She asks how it is that the most fundamental idea of economic liberalism – the invisible hand – which in previous centuries was used to promote ideals of secular, enlightened progress, is used in our times as a weapon against liberals and social planners. Her argument is that this occurred when only a certain aspect of the theory of the invisible hand was granted prominence (by Hayek), hence losing the idea's original complexity and meaning. This, we think, is a good example of what we have maintained throughout our discussion: liberalism is an interrelated cluster of features, each of which is important in itself, but which relies on the other aspects in order to be fulfilled in practice. Like Dahrendorf, Holmes and Sznajder, albeit through different reasoning, Ullmann-Margalit offers stimulating thoughts about immoderate and incomplete application of ideas that give rise to the market economy.

Note

1 See J. Gray, *Liberalism* (Buckingham: Open University Press, 2nd edn, 1995).

2   Squaring the circle

Prosperity, civility and liberty

Ralf Dahrendorf

My core thesis is simple. Internationalized modern economies pose a social and political dilemma. In free societies, the search for competitiveness seems to damage social cohesion. If, on the other hand, such free societies choose to give social cohesion a higher priority, their competitiveness, and with it their prosperity, are at risk. Some countries, or at least their leaders, insist on competitiveness but do not want to sacrifice social cohesion, and seem to achieve this by restricting political freedom. More and more people think that you can have two but not all three: prosperity and cohesion without freedom, prosperity and freedom without civility, civility and freedom without prosperity. What would need to be done to square the circle?

The thesis sounds abstract but is in fact very close to the experience of many. To prove this point, the rest of my essay is the tale of three cities in different parts of the world, admittedly unequal in size but each, in its way, a part of the story that needs to be told. To the three I shall then add a sketch of a fourth; not exactly a city on the hill, but one that approximates the unachievable and nearly squares the circle of prosperity, civility and liberty.

The first city is a small town in the Midwest of the United States of America. Twenty years ago, the engine manufacturer was at the heart of the lives of its 40,000 or so inhabitants. Most of them were directly or indirectly employed by the company. The local hospital thrived on company-supported health schemes. The local college benefited from direct donations and, of course, from the ability of well-paid parents to pay fees for their children's studies. Famous architects were invited by the company to design public buildings. Sports teams and amateur orchestras, school trips and retirement parties and much else, including a well-known French chef to please the palates of visitors, all owed their wherewithal to the company.

Then the winds of internationalization hit the happy township with gale force. In two waves, several thousand employees were made redundant. Many of them found other jobs – we are, one must remember, in America – but these were and are jobs at half the previous income and without any of the old perks. The hospital closed most of its specialist departments; the college lost its standing with its distinguished teachers; what is left of fun and games is no longer public and communal but has withdrawn to the virtual reality of television. The company is still competitive and successful, but the town is a sad shadow of its former self.

The example may sound a little too neat to be true; my friend, the chairman and chief executive of the company, would probably say that I have overstated the change; moreover, the example is that of a one-factory town and such towns have always been vulnerable. Also, American examples are unique in that they are set in a cultural environment unlike most others. The capacity for job creation is but one relevant difference; the strength of civil society, and the corresponding weakness of central government, is another. Yet, when all is said and done, the city tells the Anglo-American story of the last fifteen years.

Let me use the example which I know best, that of Britain, to explain what I mean. Since 1979, the emphasis of public policy was on creating conditions of competitive growth and encouraging entrepreneurs from both home and abroad to make use of this environment. The contribution of public policy to this end followed almost IMF-style recipes (or were these recipes borrowed from the American experience in the first place?): low direct taxation, low non-wage labour cost, greater labour market flexibility, low entry cost for new companies, deregulation, privatization of state enterprises; in a word, the withdrawal of the state from the economic playing field. This environment allowed companies to become leaner and perhaps fitter; it opened the door to experimentation with allegedly optimal company sizes; it encouraged inward investment. Compared with those who took another route, the performance of the British economy in these years may not have been astounding – there certainly was no economic miracle – but Britain did better than was to be expected on past performance.

All this, moreover, was achieved under the auspices of elected governments and with the support of Parliament. Whatever the constitutional issues which have become a part of public debate may be, there can be little doubt that the constitution of liberty is basically alive and well in Britain.

If there is another side to the picture, it is social, and this is serious. Its most telling expression is the fact that in the mid-1990s, GNP growth is no longer an indicator of people's well-being. While governments still triumphantly produce macro-economic statistics, voters feel that something has gone wrong, or at least not gone right. The very concept of wealth has become an issue. (It has been an issue in the United States for some time, at least since Robert Reich, President Clinton's first Labour Secretary, put it into the stark words that for the first time in American history parents have to tell their children that they may not be as well off as they, the parents, are). Indeed citizens have begun to distinguish between wealth and well-being. The latter, they found, was not a direct result of competitiveness.

The reasons for this disjunction are many. One is that the class which expected to be the harbinger of a better future, the middle class, is the main victim of the new competitiveness thrust. From (very) early retirement, if not outright redundancy, to a flagging housing market, middle-class disenchantment has many causes and facets. They even include the reduced services of the welfare state which, paradoxically – some would say, perversely – always benefited the middle classes as much as the poor. Another reason why competitiveness does not produce happiness is the weakening of stakeholder relationships in favour of the cruder cash nexus of shareholders who can buy and sell their interest all too easily. The diminishing role of local communities tells the story most dramatically.

Looking at the wider society, the most serious effect of a leaner and fitter economy is the new exclusion of large social groups. This takes a number of forms. One is lateral exclusion, or, with a more drastic word, xenophobia. Frightened citizens do not like strangers. Another form of exclusion is the new poverty. It is now widely recognized that flexibility, especially labour market flexibility, has side effects. It may well be that the most flexible economies create more jobs than the rigid ones, but a significant number of these jobs are so low paid that they leave their holders unable to sustain a decent standard of living. The figures produced by the Rowntree Trust about growing inequalities are most significant with respect to the absolute position of poverty among the lowest paid 20 per cent. In addition, there is the underclass of those who have lost all hope of being a part of the labour market, the political community, civil society. Some say that as many as 10 per cent have dropped to this status. The figure of 20 plus would tally with the 40:30:30 society described by Will Hutton in his book, *The State We're In*: 40 per cent fairly secure middle class, 30 per cent in a precarious and shifting condition, 30 per cent excluded in one way or another.[1]

The precise figures are important but they are not the main point of the argument. Nor is the threat of revolution the point: the excluded will not start a new revolutionary movement. The problem is, in the most serious sense of the word, moral. A society which claims to be civil but tolerates the exclusion of significant numbers from its opportunities, has betrayed the values on which it is based. The citizens of such a society cannot be surprised if its values are flaunted not just by the excluded themselves but by anyone who sees what is going on, and notably by the young. This is where the link between social exclusion and threats to law and order becomes apparent. It is not that the long-term unemployed, let alone the single mothers of the underclass, are the main perpetrators of crime (their main offence is, for the most part, to defraud an ineffectual social security system); the point is that the existence of such groups encourages others to ignore and then violate the civic values which are apparently no longer taken seriously.

The combination of greedy individualism and new exclusion is a high price to pay for macro-economic success in a free society. Britain's major partners in continental Europe are as yet not ready to pay the price. They cling to what is variously called *économie sociale* or *soziale Marktwirschaft*, to a social market economy. In France or Germany or Italy, as in Britain, the constitution of liberty is an accepted framework. Democracy and the rule of law may not be as firmly anchored as in the Anglo-Saxon world, and may even have another meaning for many, but they are, by and large, beyond dispute. The difference is in the relative weight given to economic and social factors of well-being.

Another city comes to mind, somewhat larger than the one-factory town which I described earlier, and in Italy. While not a one-factory town, the beautiful place is basically a one-industry town. One way or another, everyone is connected with food-processing, including the production of machines for the purpose. The town is closely linked to its surrounding countryside where much of the food for processing is produced. It is justly proud of the quality of its products. But more, its economic community is as close-knit as its social and political texture. If any one of the dozens of small and medium-sized companies is in trouble, the others will help. Enthusiasm for the local football club is general, especially since at one point it became a contender for the national championship. The local radio and television station, as well as the leading newspaper, are owned by the Industrialists' Association. The companies also sustain a theatre and a gallery. People naturally like good eating, for which the city is famous. It is, indeed, the envy of many.

And competitiveness? Global markets? Just recently, a trace of fear has crept into the European city. At first, confident producers would not believe that cheaper 'imitation' products could sweep the market; but when the first supermarket began to sell them outside the city boundaries, they began to wonder. Of course they believe that their tomato concentrate is better than tomato ketchup (of which there may soon be a synthetic variety); but young people will insist on covering everything they eat in cheap ketchup and not ever buy what our civic entrepreneurs regard as the real thing. Whatever textbooks may say, quality does not always win in the global marketplace. Moreover, contrary to their peers in the French province of Champagne, people failed to patent the name of the city as a brand name; suddenly 'their' products appear from all over the European Union and beyond. Even the largest of the many companies begins to worry. To make matters worse, the local football club now finds itself in the relegation zone. And so, this apparently healthy and happy town runs into the problems which we can now observe all over the European continent.

The profound differences in economic culture between Britain and its European partners are often underrated. (If we move beyond the boundaries of the European Union, such differences get even larger.) Despite the fact that the winds of globalization are common to all, these differences are unlikely to go away. Companies on the continent are, for the most part, not simply profit machines for shareholders; even in published statistics, turnover is regarded as more significant than profit or market capitalization. Companies are even ranked by the number of people they employ, the implication being that high employment marks a positive contribution to the social economy. As a result – or as part of the same syndrome – people see no particular problem in high taxes, high non-wage labour cost, a well-financed welfare state, low labour mobility. For many, a pay-as-you-go pension system, or, as Germans prefer to call it, a 'contract between generations', is maintained, whereby today's workers pay for yesterday's and pensions are, therefore, not funded. This may well be the key difference between economic cultures, and also the one that raises the largest number of questions at a time when the working population is shrinking and the retired population is growing apace.

For, not only is the second city of my tale beginning to worry, the entire social market economy of continental Europe is under strain. Sweden's transformation in recent years has been commented on by many. A country which used to have no unemployment and a cradle-to-grave welfare state (as well as prohibitive taxes which drove many of the most successful abroad) has undergone a dramatic transformation. In fact, this was, and is, traumatic as much as dramatic, for it touches the core of Sweden's self-image and national pride. Many think that Germany will have to go down the same road. There are certainly indications: large-scale redundancies in major companies; a serious debate about the attractiveness, or otherwise, of Germany for business; massive cuts in public expenditure; increasing individual contributions to welfare state services. The list is long, and familiar, and the issues dominate public and political debate.

However, there is little reason for *Schadenfreude* on the part of those who have been through the purgatory of competitiveness already. The main themes of socio-economic policy making are very different in Britain and in, say, Germany. (It must be noted in passing that this does not exactly help European integration.) But it would be wrong to assume that as each country tackles its own perils, we are all eventually moving to the same destination. Economic cultures run as deep as the cultures of language and literature, or of governance. There may be a certain degree of convergence but, despite exposure to the same winds of internationalization, pension systems, levels of taxation, welfare arrangements, the role of stakeholders, of local communities and even the structure of firms will remain very different in the English-speaking countries from those who speak French or German or Italian or Spanish. It may be that the new democracies of East Central Europe will find that their dream of emulating the social market economies cannot be realized for lack of resources, and that they will have to move, therefore, in the Anglo-Saxon direction. One country, the Czech Republic, has already done so. In any case, a true convergence of economic culture in Europe is very unlikely for a long time to come.

East Central Europe, of course, is not just faced with the alternative of individualistic Anglo-Saxon competitiveness and the social market economy. There is a third mode of combining economic, social and political factors, a third city, as it were. It is beyond doubt competitive; indeed it is often held up as a model for economic success in internationalizing markets. But competitiveness and increasing prosperity is not all. The third city – larger than the other two, and in Asia – also places great emphasis on social cohesion. It actually has public policies explicitly designed 'to promote social cohesiveness'. One central element of these policies is a gigantic organization which provides people with housing. More than 80 per cent of the population comes under its control. People have to buy their apartments, though they cannot sell them without permission. Moreover, the housing agency places them in estates in which the various ethnic groups of the city are represented in proportion to their strength. Once resident in their housing estate, people assume a number of obligations to look after others, and they are looked after themselves in cases of need.

The organization of housing is only a part of a comprehensive system of state-backed social control. Young people are guided through the educational system in accordance with their assessed abilities. If they make it to a university degree, they are even likely to be sent out to sea for cruises or on 'love boats' with graduates of the other sex, in the expectation that they will breed a new generation of graduates. (Echoes of the eugenics debate among Fabians and other early social engineers a century ago?) The state determines not only in general terms but often in detail how people are to behave. They must not chew gum or throw away cigarette ends, for example. Such laws are enforced rigorously. Even minor trespasses are punished by caning or prison sentences.

And, of course, this paradise without crime or unemployment, without eccentrics or dissidents, is also a place in which political life is strictly regulated. The local papers report much about the evils of the rest of the world, but only government pronouncements from home. Foreign papers are allowed in as long as they are compliant; if not, they are banned or sued. Those locals who tried to stand for opposition parties – and in two or three cases were actually elected to parliament – soon found their activities severely curtailed, if not cut short by trumped-up charges which landed them in prison.

This is the 'Asia that can say no' (to quote the prime minister of a state neighbouring on my third city). It is competitive and cohesive but certainly not free. It is, in the terms of political science, authoritarian. Authoritarian does not mean totalitarian; as long as people do their thing, abide by the laws and abstain from meddling in public affairs, they are left unmolested. The temptation of such authoritarianism is not confined to Asia. I mentioned East Central Europe. The return of former communists to political power is, at least in part, due to the nostalgia of elderly voters for the orderly world of late communism and its full employment, institutionalized child care, secure if modest housing at low rents, complete welfare services and the famous 'niches' of privacy in which people were allowed to enjoy their 'inner freedom' as long as they did not produce *samizdat* papers or support priests who refused to become poodles of the *nomenklatura*.

What is more, the temptation of authoritarianism is now widespread in the West. I have a growing file of utterances by Western businessmen and politicians, intellectuals and newspaper tycoons, which sound, for example, like this:

> Singapore is not liberal but clean and free of drug addicts. Not so long ago it was an impoverished, exploited colony with hunger, disease and other problems. Now people find themselves in three-bedroom apartments, with jobs and well-cleaned streets. Countries like Singapore take the right way forward.

Those of us with long memories will remember similar descriptions of Nazi Germany at the time of the 1936 Olympics, and, of course, Mussolini's promise to make Italian trains run on time. This is not to say that authoritarianism is bound to lead to totalitarianism. On the contrary, while totalitarianism is inherently catastrophic and, therefore, unstable, authoritarian government can last for a long time. A new authoritarianism may, indeed, be the main challenge to liberal democracy in the decades to come. If we are prosperous and secure, why worry about liberty?

The answer is that liberty is untidy and complex, it is full of disunity and conflict, it demands activity rather than allowing passive withdrawal, but it is the only condition which enables us to be our best selves and enhance the life chances of all. Karl Popper has put this well in this peroration on the open society: 'If we wish to remain human,' he said, 'we must go on into the unknown, the uncertain and insecure, using what reason we may have to plan for both security *and* freedom.'[2] Long before Popper, Immanuel Kant, in his 'Idea for a Universal History from a Cosmopolitan Point of View', had mocked man's dream of an Arcadia in which 'people, good-natured like the sheep in their pastures, would give their existence no greater value than their animal flocks have'. Fortunately (thus Kant) 'nature' has endowed humans with contradictions, and notably with that of 'unsocial sociability'. Humans want peace and quiet but nature knows better what is good for them, it wants conflict and change. This is what liberty means. How do we bring it about? By creating, says Kant, a 'civil society within the rule of law'. [3]

This is an academic essay, not a parliamentary speech. I feel free, therefore, to end with principles rather than policy prescriptions. Not that it would be difficult to present such prescriptions. They would range from incentives for long-term investment to reforms of the welfare state; from a new approach to education based on individual learning accounts to an improvement of economic reporting by a wealth audit. However, behind such specific policy proposals there is the search for an application of Kant's vision and Popper's moral imperative to the ever-expanding First World of developed countries.

The key to squaring the circle is strengthening and, in part, rebuilding civil society. This is notably the task in countries where much has been done to enhance economic competitiveness, and where democratic institutions are still strong. By civil society, I mean that texture of our lives with others which does not need governments to sustain it because it is created by grass-root initiatives. Tocqueville called it democracy, though the institutional connotation is misleading. James Madison, at the time of the foundation of democracy in America, praised civil society as a guarantee of liberty because, by being 'broken into so many parts, interests and classes of citizens', it curbs even majority rule. No word describes better the 'parts, interests and classes of citizens' which civil society is about than *association*. The creative chaos of associations coalesces, as if guided by an invisible hand, into the setting in which the greatest number find the greatest life chances. In economic terms, the market describes that setting; in political terms, it is the public. Nowadays, both are mediated in numerous ways; the days of simple markets, or indeed of the public assembling outside the town hall for debate and decision, are almost gone. But the principles of both are still valid. The market and the public are where the associations of civil society interact.

In other words, there is such a thing as society. What is more, there has to be if we do not want to end up in a state of anomie. The word 'association' also indicates the necessary element of cohesion in civil society. I like Dan Horowitz's statement: 'Social cohesion does not necessarily imply social homogeneity or harmony or absence of social tensions.'[4] It does, by contrast, have certain positive implications. Apart from the indispensable framework of the rule of law, the associations of civil society represent values of trust and cooperation, and of inclusion. A civil society is a society of citizens who have rights and accept obligations, and who behave in a civil and civilized manner towards each other. It is a society which tries to make sure that no one is excluded and which offers its members a sense of belonging, as well as a constitution of liberty.

This is no Utopia. For a century after the Civil War, the United States of America was certainly driven by the aspiration to be such a civil society. The same can be said for the United Kingdom during the larger part of the twentieth century. In Canada and Australia, but also in Sweden and Switzerland, other versions of achieving the same aspirations could be found. For a while after the Second World War, the entire First World was, in these terms, quite a good place to live. The trouble is that so many of these statements now have to be made in the past tense. Somehow or other, either prosperity or civility or liberty (if not two of these, or even all three) have taken a knock almost everywhere. That is why rebuilding civil society under new conditions is so important.

What, then, of the fourth city in my tale? First of all, it has to be a city. Whether it numbers 40,000, 180,000 or 2.5 million inhabitants, it must be an identifiable community with a strong sense of local commitment and institutions to match. The city itself is an element of civil society. In economic terms, a variety of companies of different sizes and branches of business is obviously desirable. More important, indeed essential, for economic well-being is, however, a combination of competitiveness and stakeholder involvement. If one wants to avoid fashionable language, one could say that companies need to seek arrangements which assure, as far as possible, their long-term success, and engender relations of trust and commitment with all who are involved in their fortunes. This is actually what many companies are groping for today, and the best of them provide benchmarks for the rest. Individuals have to respond to the analogous dual challenge of flexibility and security. People's lives will look different from the way they did in the days of old-style careers in an expectation of full employment. Security is no longer built into the world of work, or of education for that matter; people have to carry it with and within them, which means that their entitlements have to be transportable, and their strength lies in their skills, including the ability to go on adjusting and enhancing them. There are signs that women find it easier to cope with the new balance of flexibility and security than men; perhaps they had to do so earlier. In institutional as well as personal terms, associations in the narrow and the organized sense will play a major part. The tradition of voluntarism, of volunteering, as well as charitable giving, will see a new flowering. The result will be untidy and imperfect; it will not do away with pain and fear, or with conflict; but it may point the way to a prosperous, civil and liberal world.

Notes

1 Will Hutton, *The State We're In* (London: Jonathan Cape, 1995).
2 K. R. Popper, *The Open Society and its Enemies*, vol. 1 (London: Routledge & Kegan Paul, 5th edn, 1966), p. 201.
3 Immanuel Kant, 'Idea for a Universal History from a Cosmopolitan Point of View', in W. L. Beck (ed.), *On History* (New York: The Bobbs-Merrill Company Inc., 1963), pp. 11–26, especially pp. 15–17.
4 Dan Horowitz and Moshe Lissak, *Trouble in Utopia* (Albany, NY: State University of New York, 1989), p. 31.

3   Can weak-state liberalism survive?

Stephen Holmes

nur durch Vergleichung unterscheidet man sich und erfaehrt, was man ist,
um ganz zu werden, was man sein soll.

Thomas Mann

For half a century, the Soviet Union was not only our principal military
adversary. It was also our ideological and moral "other." Both left and
right defined their competing visions of American liberalism in reaction to
the Stalinist nightmare. In this sense, the Cold War profoundly shaped our
public philosophy. Indeed, we might say that the Cold War *was* our public
philosophy. The demanding contest with Soviet communism guided the
way we thought about the core principles underlying our basic institutions.
For liberalism was, or appeared to be, totalitarianism turned inside out.

What features of the American creed did this master contrast lead us to
stress? Freedom of speech and the press, first of all, and freedom of
conscience, for these were cruelly repressed under Moscow's sway.
Likewise emphasized was the latitude, more or less broad, to accumulate
private wealth, on the assumption that a decentralized and unplanned
economy alone could provide the material basis for political opposition.
And anti-totalitarian commentators of all political hues also laid considerable weight, for understandable reasons, on the undesirability of
policemen making warrantless nighttime arrests at private homes. In the
same spirit, they underscored the freedom of movement, the right to form
private associations and mount public demonstrations, the right to a fair
trial, the right to be free from custodial torture, and the right to criticize
the government and vote in competitive elections where incumbents might
be toppled from power. Revulsion at the gulag and the thought police,
moreover, encouraged a particular way of construing these classical liberal
freedoms. They were styled, in general, as negative liberties, as rights
against the state, as shields guarding vulnerable individuals from arbitrary

imprisonment and other forms of governmental abuse. Limitations on police power were grotesquely lacking under Soviet, especially Stalinist, rule. So where were we to locate the guiding ideal of the American system if not in safeguards against excessive authority? Their system was anti-liberal because an irresistible, relentless and overcentralized government imposed a stifling ideological conformism, cowed inhabitants into servility and penetrated pervasively into all spheres of life. Our system was anti-Stalinist because a rule-bound government was divided against itself – was unable to intrude or abridge or infringe or interfere – and therefore left plenty of room for private individuals to breathe and act freely in unregu-lated social realms. Liberal institutions preserved us from both grisly and petty indignities, and the liberal idea was a safe and sober alternative to extreme egalitarian ends that justified unspeakable means.

Not only do times change, needless to say, but some times change more spectacularly than others. Big Brother has been swept off the map, and we can no longer lend sharp contours to our basic principles and practices by contrasting them favorably to the unrealistic ideals and repressive behavior of a living totalitarian foe. Their closed society no longer teaches us, with colorful illustration, the true merit of our open society. Their concentra-tion of authority and subjugation to government no longer helps justify and explain our diffusion of authority and autonomy from government. True, the planet continues to breed illiberal political systems and move-ments. But the anti-liberal scene is now hopelessly cluttered, and we are not yet at loggerheads with any single dominant nationalism or authoritari-anism or fundamentalism in a world-historical struggle to decide the fate of mankind. As the sole surviving superpower, therefore, we no longer know who we are not.

As an exercise in self-knowledge, therefore, I propose a somewhat nostalgic thought experiment. Perhaps liberalism has as much to learn about itself from communism's aftermath as it once believed it had to learn from communism itself. If we re-survey the American system against the backdrop of Russian society today, what principles and practices, what norms and institutions, call special attention to themselves? On the surface, at least, this is a promising line of inquiry. For Russia, despite the radical loosening up it has recently undergone, remains an illiberal state in most respects. So what can the new Russian illiberalism, by way of contrast, teach us about ourselves? By answering this question, we might conceiv-ably recover some insights about liberal politics that the now out-of-date contrast to Soviet tyranny once led us, justifiably or not, to neglect.

Contemporary Russian illiberalism, I should say at the outset, is not principally a matter of nationalism.[1] The popular perception that nation-alism is a looming threat in Russia reflects our inclination to paste familiar labels on situations we poorly understand. Nationalism ordinarily becomes a bestial political force, after all, when mobilized populations vie for control over a piece of territory or over the organizational resources of a state. Where the benefits of membership in a political community are negligible, populist nationalism tends to flag. For why make the effort to deny cultural minorities the rights and privileges enjoyed by the majority when such rights and privileges are universally despised as a meaningless hoax? Cynicism about the perquisites of membership – among other causes, historical and contemporary – helps explain why nationalist thinking is marginal for Russian illiberalism today.

This is not to deny that xenophobia, as opposed to chauvinism or solidarity, can occasionally be observed. It is only to say that the root of contemporary Russian illiberalism should not be sought in any communitarian ideology, fueled by resentment and narratives of "them against us." The failure of Russian liberalism, while it no doubt has many causes, stems most immediately from state incapacity or ineffectiveness, on the one hand, and social disorganization and directionlessness on the other. The problem faced by Russian liberals is no longer censorship and the command economy, then, but something quite new: an incoherent state tenuously connected to a demoralized society. The system of central control and coordination is in shambles, and the citizenry, while bitterly resenting political elites, remains passive and inert. Incumbents are venal and incompetent, and social interests are too anemic and diffuse to coalesce into effective collective organizations or constituencies for reform. While not especially oppressive (with the important exception of Chechnya), the government is fragmented, unaccountable, and seemingly indifferent to the plight of its citizens. The life expectancy of ordinary Russians is sinking, while they struggle, expecting nothing from politics, to eke out a living on their own. Thus, what characterizes the failure of Russian liberalism is exactly a wall between state and society.

Some of the best publicized syndromes of the current crisis of governability in Russia are massive tax evasion and the murders of tax assessors,[2] draft dodging and salary arrears to the military, communication blockages and the lack of clear divisions of responsibility between various levels, branches, and agencies of government, and the eye-popping enrichment of prominent individuals who sit astride the blurred boundaries between public agencies and semi-privatized enterprises. Equally notable are prison outbreaks, railroad banditism, packs of dogs on the streets of provincial cities, unrepaired oil leaks, public hospitals unable to create sterile environments, perilously deteriorating water reservoirs, and the failure to monitor food handlers for cholera. Total tax revenues as a percentage of GDP, while hard to calculate, hover somewhere below 10 per cent (this excludes the vast and untaxable gray economy), compared to roughly 30 per cent in the US and an average of 45 per cent in Western Europe.

While the country has by no means fallen apart, and the buses still manage to run, it is safe to say that Russian society is politically disorganized. For the government, by and large, is unable to enforce its own laws. True, the debility of the Russian state has caught the West's attention less for the suffering it inflicts upon the Russian people – some of whom have reverted to subsistence agriculture – than for the dangers it apparently poses to the rest of us: shamefully maintained oil tankers, porous borders, a questionable command-and-control system, the possibility of more Chernobyl-style meltdowns, a proclaimed technical and financial inability to liquidate existing stockpiles of biological and chemical weapons, over-the-counter sales of nuclear know-how, a contagious disease crisis that may eventually threaten Europe, organized crime activity metastasizing alarmingly abroad, the inability of the central government to live up to its obligations (as in the case of NASA's space station), and a lack of coordination among the defense and foreign ministries on questions vital to neighboring states.

Even if less serious than reporters make them sound, these worrying developments represent practical challenges to American foreign policy. But they also pose a theoretical challenge to the self-understanding of American liberalism. Communism's unforeseen collapse has already unsettled our diplomatic routines. My argument, or hope, is that its unexpected aftermath also trigger a revaluation of values, a back-to-basics reassessment of the principles underlying our political practice. Although there is no need to upend our economic system, for instance, should not the celebration of "free markets" and "spontaneous exchange," with which the Chicago School has made us familiar, be somewhat muted by the increasing importance of totally unregulated markets in ground-to-air missiles and other lethal residua of the Soviet arsenal? And what about "pluralism," "decentralization," "countervailing powers," "private associations," and the "independence of society from the state"? This cluster of slogans will no doubt continue to play an important role in American self-understanding. But should not the advent of political fragmentation, where despotism once reigned, justify a more discriminatory and less celebratory approach to the diffusion of power? The pluralistic vitality of organized crime in Russia should remind Tocquevillean liberals of something Tocqueville himself knew perfectly well, that civil society, characterized by nonpredatory relations among strangers, is always a society civilized by the state. If they are not to degenerate into private fiefdoms or sewers of lawlessness, free enterprise zones must be policed. In Madison's famous formulation, constitutional restrictions on government assume that we "first enable the government to control the governed."[3] Liberal reforms have been, let us say, incompletely successful in Russia so far because, among other things, liberalism takes it for granted that public authorities will not be outgunned or bribed or made proposals they cannot safely decline by private beasts of prey. A plurality of independent nongovernmental associations and the vibrancy of the private sector can be pathological from a liberal point of view. For there is no rule of law until the Mafia needs lawyers. Russia's failure to achieve the rule of law can be measured by the autonomy of its mobsters, who cannot be compelled to engage the country's legal system on the legal system's own terms.

I am not suggesting that the increasing visibility of grave social harms engendered by unregulated markets and cut-throat bands should prompt us to dilute our liberal commitments and view iron-fisted government, able to quash criminality, with a friendlier eye. What I am saying is only that the woes of a politically disorganized society should heighten our appreciation of – or encourage us to lay more stress upon – the role of government in promoting liberal freedom. Authority was deemed necessary, in classical liberal theory, because individuals are partial to themselves and, left to their own devices, the strong and the deceitful have an irresistible proclivity to exempt themselves from generally valid laws. That old insight is amply confirmed in Russia today. When the state is so easy to despoil, why play by rules that apply equally to all? Libertarians sometimes argue that the coercive authority of the state extends only to the prevention of harm and the protection of property rights. In the Russian context, the word "only" here strikes a very false note. It turns out to be mind-bogglingly difficult to erect, in a chaotic setting, anything like a nightwatchman state capable of enforcing rules impartially and of repressing force and fraud effectively. The new sick man of Eurasia makes it excruciatingly plain that liberal values are threatened just as thoroughly by state incapacity as by despotic power. Destatization is not the solution; destatization is the problem. For without a well-functioning public power of a certain kind there will be no prevention of mutual harm, no personal security and no "standing rule to live by," to use a Lockean phrase. While the threat of "anarchy" played little role in liberal self-understanding during the Cold War, when all political evils seemed to swarm from "too much government," it was thoroughly appreciated in the eighteenth century. William Blackstone was saying nothing unusual when he declared that "anarchy" was "a worse state than tyranny itself, as any government is better than none at all."[4] But will not liberalism look somewhat different if we highlight its capacity to prevent political crackup rather than its capacity to prevent political crackdown?

A dissipating or disintegration of the political authority once engrossed by the Communist Party has prompted some commentators to draw analogies with European feudalism.[5] By contrast to such political fragmentation, liberalism no longer seems like a system aimed exclusively, or even principally, at diffusing power. What now stands out, on the contrary, is its capacity to unify power in relatively accountable hands and to use it relatively effectively. While the rights inscribed in the 1977 Brezhnev Constitution went unprotected because of a repressive state apparatus, the rights inscribed in the 1993 Yeltsin Constitution go unenforced because the state apparatus is plagued by bickering, paralysis, the lack of any clear purpose or ideology, and chronic underfunding, and because incumbents are more keen on harvesting kickbacks and insider give-aways than on solving public problems.

Russian political dissidents are no longer being jailed, it is true. With the notable exception of Sergei Kovalev, the very role of "dissident" seems to have been erased from the script. No one is punished or even threatened for violating the party line, for there is no party line. Journalists are blown to smithereens by suitcase bombs, but only when they rummage indiscreetly into corruption at the Ministry of Defense. They are certainly not being incarcerated for their heretical beliefs, for heresy is not possible in the absence of orthodoxy. Both ideological censorship and indoctrination have disappeared along with ideology itself. No one in power fears, or takes any guidance from, political ideas.

The image of the lone refusnik or "deviationist" crushed by a remorseless Behemoth reinforced a one-sided interpretation of liberal rights. It placed the accumulated weight of painful experience behind the assumption that rights are essentially "walls" erected against state power. This metaphor no doubt contains an element of truth. But its fundamental inadequacy is disclosed by the Russian situation today, where the defeat of liberal reforms is most clearly visible in the wall of indifference separating state from society. Corrupt incumbents live in a separate world from depoliticized citizens. The way in which liberal reforms have failed in Russia, in other words, suggests that liberalism, ideally understood, aims not to seal off society from the state but, on the contrary, to keep open robust channels for consultation and partnership between public officials and private citizens.

Liberal rights themselves depend essentially on the competent exercise of a certain kind of public power. This is why violating an individual's rights involves disobeying the liberal state. Statelessness is such a deplorable condition because it signals the absence of the sole institution that is capable, under rare but achievable conditions, of extending its protection to the vulnerable. Formulated differently, the largest and most reliable human rights organization is the liberal state. Outside the jurisdiction, beyond the effective reach of such a state, rights will not be consistently protected or enforced. Liberalism cannot provide a principled justification for the political control which exclusive social groups exercise over particular expanses of territory. But what liberalism cannot justify, it must nevertheless assume. The dependency of liberal rights on a prior solution to the problem of "stateness,"[6] on the successful political organization of society, is one of the principal lessons brought home by the underenforcement of rights in Russia today. It is an obvious lesson, in a way, but one that runs counter to what the anti-totalitarianism ethos induced us to assume.

Why do basic rights to decent treatment go unenforced in pre-trial detention cells across Russia? There are many reasons, but an essential one is the breakdown of the chain of command. For the right to be treated decently by the system of criminal justice (by policemen, prosecutors, judges, and prison guards) undoubtedly presupposes a system of hierarchical authority, that is, well-defined and effective relations of subordination and accountability. It presupposes the power of bureaucratic superiors to punish and deter misconduct by subordinate public officials. In the system of criminal justice, protecting rights requires us to solve the principal-agent problem, that is, to control the law enforcement apparatus. The underenforcement of basic rights in Russia's criminal justice system reminds us why liberals, whatever their attitude toward red tape, cannot be anti-bureaucratic, for custodial personnel behave more decently when monitored than when unwatched. By illustrating vividly the dependence of individual liberty on state power of a certain kind, the new Russia should help us focus more clearly, then, on the ways that authority enhances freedom in our own system. For example, the right to be protected from racial discrimination is better enforced in the United States military than in our civil society because civilian racists have a greater capacity to resist the commands of authority than do racists in uniform. Similarly, liberalism demands that people without guns tell people with guns what to do. While any credibly liberal government must be limited in important ways, it must not be so crippled or irresolute that, for example, local military or police or secret service authorities escape centralized civilian control.

In other ways, too, the blockage of liberal reform in Russia might conceivably bring American liberalism back to basics. The explosive growth there of legally unregulated social sectors should deflate overblown rhetoric about that "autonomous" sphere where American families can keep every penny they earn and from which government is scrupulously barred. Indeed, observing the effects of a genuinely hands-off regime should help us clear up some serious confusions surrounding the words "dependency" and "independence" as they are casually heaved about in our political debate. The dim idea that rights are "walls against the state," to return to that, is especially strange because it implies that a country without a judicially enforceable constitution, such as Great Britain, must be bereft of individual rights. That is to say, it implicitly denies the continuity between constitutional rights and ordinary rights in contract law, tort law, property law, and so forth. No one disputes that the latter rights are essentially liberal or that they are defined and enforced by the state. An individual who asserts his common law rights must necessarily avail himself of the public power. The creditor's right to collect from a defaulting debtor is a right of access to a taxpayer-funded system of litigation and an entitlement to relief by the coercive intervention of public authorities. The plaintiff's right to bring an action against a defendant is not a right against the state, therefore. It is neither a right to be independent of the state nor a right which protects the rights-bearer from the state, but rather a right to use state power to give legal effect to a private agreement, to enjoin trespassers from entering private property, to collect compensatory or punitive damages from tort-feasors, and so on. The liberal state must not only assert its monopoly on violence (or at least push the Mafia out of banking and raw material exports and into prostitution, drugs, gambling, and pornography) and abolish anarchy. It must also enforce the private law framework of civil society. What liberals call "independence," therefore, is simply dependence on a certain set of (liberal) institutions. I can escape the corkscrew of a local strongman – that is, be independent – only if I have the public power on my side. When I sue under contract or tort law, I am neither shifting for myself, acting on my own in a coercion-free sphere; nor am I trying to get the state to forbear, to get it off my back. Rather, I am asking the state to perform, to get it "on my case." A politically disorganized society can carpet-bomb a provincial city, but it cannot bring the public force to bear, in a pinpoint operation, to deter antisocial behavior or redress individual wrongs. A state that leaves loan collection to private thugs and can offer no remedy to victims of aggravated negligence cannot be a liberal state in the most basic sense.

The right of a creditor to have a loan repaid is obviously a product of law and a creature of state authority. That the same is true of constitutional rights is obscured by the familiar description of our Bill of Rights as a "charter of negative liberties." The simultaneous feebleness, in today's Russia, of common law rights and constitutional rights brings the analogies between the two – and the faultiness of the "wall" metaphor – sharply into focus. For constitutional rights, too, will be protected only if governmental authorities perform rather than merely forbear. The right to vote is meaningless if electoral officials fail to show up for work. The right to just compensation for confiscated property is empty if the treasury fails to disburse. The right to subpoena witnesses in one's own defense is useless if the court's solemn writs are greeted with laughter. The constitutional right to due process – like the private right to bring an action in contract or tort – presupposes that, at the taxpayers' expense, the state maintains and makes accessible complex legal institutions within which the cumbersome formalities of fair adjudication occur. For this reason, a nonperforming state cannot be a liberal state, just as a society genuinely walled-off from a liberal state cannot be a liberal society.

This is not to deny that some important constitutional rights, even in the area of criminal justice, are plausibly styled as duties of the government to forbear rather than to perform. But even "negative rights" – such as the prohibitions on double jeopardy and excessive fines – will be protected only if they find a protector, only if there exists a supervisory state body, usually a court of appeal, able to force its will upon the violators and potential violators of the rights at stake. The misleading idea that rights are obstacles to state interference, in fact, rests upon the dim fiction that the judiciary is not a branch of government at all, that judges (who command the public force) are not civil servants, that the court system is not part and parcel of the state. A look at judicial impotence in Russia should help dispel this illusion. The incapacity of Russian judges to impose their will upon Russian prosecutors is not a sign that the Russian state is too big or interferes too much. Rather, it is an indication that the Russian government is poorly organized and that proper authorities cannot intervene in the proper way. For when rights are at risk, every forbearance by public authorities presupposes performance, or the anticipation of possible performance, by another public authority. No rights are fully "negative," then. Indeed, all liberal rights are partly positive; all of them are exercised on the basis of resources provided by taxpayers and managed by government.

The reference to resources here is worth pausing over. Basic rights go unenforced in Russia not only because the state is distracted and inconsistent, but also because it is insolvent. Chronic underfunding erodes individual liberty for the same reason as it damages military preparedness. That rights depend on the efficient use of public resources, as well as on the competent exercise of public authority, becomes clear when we examine the sickening conditions in Russia's correctional facilities, where rampant tuberculosis, even among guards, and high mortality rates are due less to custodial abuse than to horrible overcrowding, inedible food, and the absence of basic medical care. Not custodial torture, in this case, but a breakdown of public finances is the principal cause of the violation of inmate rights.[7] So a bankrupt state cannot be a liberal state – whatever the "cultural level" of its citizens. What I mean by insolvency is not a lack of resources in society at large or the absence of wealthy citizens, for Russia has both. An insolvent state, in the pertinent sense, is one that, among its other disabilities, cannot extract, in a way that is widely deemed to be fair, a modest share of social wealth and then channel the resources extracted into the creation and delivery of public services, rather than into the pockets of incumbents and their cronies. The Russian state is an illiberal state not only because its courts lack authority, then, but also because it is insolvent (in this sense), and it is insolvent because it is corrupt, because its bureaucracy is in poor condition even by modest Weberian standards, because norms of public service are weak, and because potential taxpayers do not trust a government that is neither transparent nor accountable.

One of the principal lessons of Russian illiberalism, then, is that individual rights are unprotectable without the power to tax and spend. To extract resources efficiently, it needs stressing, a government must be able to mobilize cooperation, not merely command compliance. Strong-state liberalism is not iron-fisted liberalism because "state strength," in a liberal context, depends essentially on the capacity of the government to enlist voluntary support. Threats of reprisal for nonpayment of taxes, growled by nonperforming and self-enriching state officials, do not always elicit complete honesty about private assets. To raise revenue with relative efficiency, a state must not only be seen to treat citizens fairly, but it must also communicate public purposes in an understandable way and strike partnerships with important social groups and actors in an attempt to solve what are generally seen as common problems. This is yet another reason why liberalism cannot insulate society from the state.

Rights, to dwell on this centerpiece of the liberal polity for another moment, will be jeopardized whenever public finances are in decay. I am thinking here not only of pensioners' rights and the right of the indigent to state-appointed counsel, but more generally of classical liberal rights such as the right to procedural fairness before a court or administrative agency. The Russian government cannot protect such basic rights for the same reason that it cannot provide other elementary public goods – a nontoxic environment, books in elementary schools, x-ray film in public hospitals, veterans benefits, a nationwide highway system, railroad maintenance, and potable water. It cannot protect rights because it cannot target extracted resources to the provision of public goods. Even where courts are working, judicial dockets are chronically backlogged, because budgetary outlays earmarked for the courts are pitiful and often do not arrive. The dependency of basic rights on tax revenues, revealed by the fiscal crisis of the Russian state, helps us see that, in a way, rights are public goods. Far from being walls bricking out the meddlesome state, even the so-called negative rights are taxpayer-funded and government-managed social services designed to improve collective and individual well-being. Rightslessness under a financially strapped Russian government, in other words, suggests a new way of conceptualizing rights. What it implies, curiously enough, is that all rights are welfare rights. That property rights and the right to buy and sell on the free market, too, should be described in such terms is another surprising lesson of the Russian experience. Sovietism drew attention to the way laws and regulations can stifle economic activity. Post-Sovietism lends credence to the opposite truth. Without clearly defined, unambiguously assigned, and legally enforceable property rights, ownership does not encourage stewardship and privatization does not elicit an entrepreneurial response.[8] Just as you cannot have capitalism where everything is planned, so you cannot have capitalism where everything is for sale, not at least if the saleable items include employees at the public registry of titles and deeds. To the extent that markets presuppose a reliable system of recordation, protecting title from never-ending attack, they also presuppose the existence of a competent and honest bureaucracy, on whom private actors depend. My rights to enter, use, exclude from, sell, bequeath, mortgage, and abate nuisances threatening "my" property all palpably presuppose something that does not yet exist in Russia, namely, a well-organized, well-funded, authoritative, and relatively honest court system. But a liberal legal system does not merely protect and defend my property, which I have accumulated by the sweat of my brow or the beneficence of my parents. More fundamentally, it specifies and delimits the aspects and modalities of ownership which public authorities are charged to defend. It therefore makes no more sense to associate property rights with "freedom from government" than to associate the right to play chess or baseball with freedom from the rules of chess or baseball. Property rights are weak in Russia because possession and use are weakly regulated by law.

The contemplation of weak-state capitalism, in other words, should make plain why "independence" is a hopeless way to characterize economic behavior in liberal systems. The autonomous individual, celebrated by liberals, cannot create the conditions of his own autonomy autonomously, but only collectively. If the wielders of the police power are not on your side, you will not successfully "assert your right" to enter your own home and make use of its contents, as the Muslims recently evicted from West Mostar learned once more. For property is a complex set of rules – of access, exclusion, and so forth – enforced by the state. Even more dramatically, private property is a sham if the community cannot train and equip an army capable of defending its territory against foreign marauders and predators. That is the lesson of, say, Srebrenica. The implications are worth spelling out: All liberal rights presuppose or imply the

dependency of the individual on the collectivity and on the principal
instrument of the collectivity, that is, on the coercive-extractive state. In a
way, this is a truism and a banality. But it is another one of those truisms,
the consequences of which has not been fully absorbed into Cold War
dominated thought.

At the basis of a liberal economy lies the willingness of people to rely
on each others' word. That the "reliance interest" does not find a strong
supporter in Russia's virtual state does not require further emphasis.
Because contracts are not reliably enforced, for instance, payment by the
installment plan is not an especially attractive arrangement for Russian
creditors.[9] In the truly autonomous realm, beyond the reach of government, extortion is rampant, but borrowers have a hard time obtaining
long-term loans. For one function of the liberal state is to lengthen the
time horizons of private actors by predictably enforcing known and stable
rules. Property is worthless if you, and potential purchasers, do not believe
in the future.

Capitalists know this and tend not to invest in countries, such as Russia,
where – to employ a different idiom – the discount rate of economic actors
is extremely high. Long-gestation investment in productive facilities is
particularly unlikely where assets are indefensible against private and
public extortionists. Currency stabilization alone is not enough to improve
the investment climate because the instability of trade, banking, customs,
and tax regulations, too, casts a cloud over the future. While the Russian
government is no longer oppressively tyrannical, it is not yet predictable,
and therefore remains illiberal. Because the state's extractive capacities are
inadequate, authorities have taken to slapping retroactive taxes on foreign
firms, who keep relatively honest books and are in no position to refuse.
This myopic raiding of potential investors is a fair example of the effects of
political disarray on the public welfare.

Moral outrage at weak-state capitalism is not necessarily a reflection of
residual socialism or aversion to inequality, as is often assumed. In Russia,
it should be noted, the current distribution of ownership – which underlies
the market – appears illegitimate to ordinary people because most owners
did not become so by working for their wealth or by inheriting it according
to publicly known and accepted rules. Private property is a much more
troublesome and troubled institution in Russia (and in Eastern Europe as
well) than in the West because, for obvious reasons, no postcommunist
society can consistently implement the rule: "give back what is stolen."
Another problem is that profit-seekers still assume that the most appropriate means for dealing with business competitors are plastic explosives.
The unpoliced economy arouses discontent to the extent that its principal
players are seen as racketeers whose techniques for "dispute resolution"

run the gamut from intimidation to contract killings. Having failed to establish rules for settling economic conflicts without violence, public officials line their pockets and otherwise leave crime syndicates pretty much alone. State incapacity is also revealed in the way the new rich have managed to exploit the blurred boundaries between state agencies and privatized industries to prize assets apart from liabilities. They walk away with assets and dump liabilities back into the public debt.[10] They can skim so deftly only because no one with the public interest in mind has the power to stop them.

Dog-eat-dog capitalism also thrives on the absence of enforceable anti-fraud law. Russia is certainly no "procedural republic," that is to say, every man is judge in his own case. Its citizens do not share core liberal institutions, most notably the legal machinery capable of remedying misrepresentation and false dealing. The impunity of con men, although it will surely not last for ever, keeps people out of the market today who might otherwise come in. Ordinary Russians are less put off by the act of buying and selling than by the lack of any means to counteract the inevitable asymmetry of knowledge between buyer and seller. That the seller may know something the buyer needs to know is one reason why the risk-averse fear commercial exchanges as possible scams, why they cling to suppliers they know personally rather than shopping around for bargains.[11] Similarly, in the West, consumers benefit from a competitive market in restaurants because, as voters and taxpayers, they have created and funded sanitation boards that allow them to range adventurously beyond a restricted circle of personally known and trusted establishments. The enforcement of anti-fraud statutes is no less a taxpayer-funded spur to market behavior than the government inspection of food handlers.

The feebleness of markets in Russia, despite economic liberalization, suggests the importance of political organization and state performance for fostering the trust among strangers is necessary if the market is to become national and not merely local. Many people will predictably avoid mutually beneficial market transactions, to return to the point, so long as the court system (in the absence of social equivalents) is too weak to penalize and deter fraud. For a punishing percentage, thugs may selectively enforce the repayment of loans; but they are not going to enforce general rules against fraud or unfair business practices for an obvious reason. Anti-fraud law is a common good, based on a biblically simple moral principle (cheating is wrong), the benefits of which cannot be captured by a few but are diffused widely throughout society. So here again, Russian conditions draw attention to the way liberal markets depend, for their moral basis, on a liberal style of governance. For an essential aim of liberal institutions is to restrain human partiality, to put a brake on the self-dealing of incumbents and the self-exemption of any and all. A state capable of dampening human partiality, needless to say, is not a supergangster running, for its own benefit, the protection racket to end all protection rackets, but is rather a "public power," acting, because of institutional incentives, as the disciplined agent of society as a whole.

Wild capitalism could nevertheless win public approval – despite its ruthlessness, its stunning inequalities, and its fondness for fraud – if it produced general prosperity. But Russians living outside Moscow have not received a booming economy to compensate for their loss of job security. For state incapacity entails not only gangland massacres and pyramid schemes, but also a paucity of investments in infrastructure and skills, feeble enforcement of stockholders' rights, lack of securities exchange oversight, weak trademark protection, legal unclarity about the status of collateral, and inadequate regulation of the banking sector to ensure a steady flow of credit to businessmen rather than cronies. The non-enforcement of anti-trust law may also reduce the shared benefits of economic liberalization. For these reasons – and above all because property rights are not clearly defined, unambiguously assigned, and impartially and reliably protected – "privatization" in Russia does not foster innovation, encourage investment, boost worker productivity, raise production standards, or stimulate the efficient use of scarce resources. Russians are not governed by promulgated and standing laws, held steady from case to case and applied impartially to rich and poor alike. The illiberalism of the Russian situation consists in the state's incapacity to formulate and impose predictable rules, to enforce basic rights, and to create the conditions for a well-functioning market economy. These deficiencies, as I said, highlight the essential dependence, in any liberal system, of private liberty on public authority. The idea that autonomous individuals can enjoy their freedom if they are simply unpestered by the public power dissolves before the disturbing realities of the new Russia. For the Russian economy does function largely "outside the law," that is, beyond the control of any public power devoted to implementing fair rules of the game and enforcing the rudimentary duties to refrain from physical aggression, to take due care not to injure, and to keep one's promises. A barrier denying ordinary citizens reasonable support from public officials is incompatible with an impartial execution of the laws.

We can deepen and refine this lesson if we turn briefly to the Russian political system. Liberalism presumes that the "standing rule" we live by is made and revised by politically accountable representatives. Russia mounts elections and tolerates a free press; but it does not have democracy. Why not? That voting in Russia is not a means by which citizens discipline their rulers should be clear from the stunning lack of benefits voters receive from elected officials. Elections in Russia, in fact, do not create power. For the most part, they mirror the power that already exists and that controls the TV, the Election Commission, and so forth. No incumbent draws his power, in any way, from the majority of average voters, which is why the public, although bitterly resenting its rulers, has given up actively opposing the government. (Incumbents find their supporters exclusively in hidden networks.) Russian elections do not produce anything even vaguely resembling accountable or responsive government largely because of institutional weakness. For example, since the bicameral parliament has little knowledge of, and no control over, decisions made in the ministries, electing a deputy does not contribute one iota to governmental accountability. Popular cynicism about "democracy" is perfectly understandable for an even more obvious reason as well. If the state is too weak to enforce its own laws, what is the point of grasping for a share of the lawmaking power? Why dispute, in a freewheeling public debate, the government's conception of the common advantage if the government does not even pretend to have such a conception? Moreover, political parties, as organizations for channeling social grievances, demands, and aspirations to the state, hardly exist in Russia, and so on. What the electoral charade brings home is something we already knew, of course, that democratic procedures are of value only if they establish some sort of dependency of public officials on ordinary citizens. While free citizens are dependent on the government for the exercise of their rights, incumbents elected popularly and pro tempore have some reason to behave responsibly, to act as the agent of society, and produce benefits of palpable value to a majority of voters. Russian officials apparently see no reason to act this way. They live in a secretive bubble, supported by stolen assets, the IMF, and various criminal affiliations. (I exaggerate to make the point.) This lack of "dependence on the people" does not create coherence or reduce vicious rivalry among governing clans – the Russian state is anything but a unified actor – but it does mean that incumbents have little incentive to produce public goods that the average voter might find of some value. Just as society is undisciplined by "general and equal laws," so the state is unperturbed by the problems of average voters. Just as citizens will not cooperate in the enforcement of laws and decrees, so the government seems unable to profit from the centralized information and intelligence of private individuals. Contemplating this lack of any discernible partnership between honest public officials and honest private citizens should lead us to re-identify the principal function of liberal constitutionalism. Perhaps liberal constitutionalism is valuable not because it protects us from the tyranny of the minority or the majority, but because it protects us from the indifference of the few and the irrelevance of the many.

The social contract in Russia today can be described as an exchange of unaccountable power for untaxable wealth. This, needless to say, is a contract among "elites," a sleazy deal between political and economic insiders – the so-called criminal–nomenklatura symbiosis – who, in bed with each other, engage in mutually beneficial unpunishable misdeeds. The Russian government's most urgent tasks today, an observer might assume, are to decriminalize business and stimulate the development of organized rule-of-law constituencies, presumably businessmen who accumulate wealth without force or fraud. But thoroughly compromised incumbents, locked in the perverse postcommunist contract just described, cannot even begin such a process. Lenin's question "What is to be done?" may have a theoretical answer, in other words, but it has no practical answer unless there is someone to do it.

Put differently, the overriding question in Russia is not: Who governs?, but rather: Why govern? Why take the trouble to govern, if you can feed off the imperial remains and vacation frequently in European resorts? The rest of society, the great mass of citizens, is left out of the contract, left – in extreme cases – to die out in a Darwinist struggle for survival. (In Russia, at least among foreigners pampered in luxury hotels, when you scratch an optimist, you find a Darwinist.) Russia seems to be a broken hour-glass society in which the privileged do not exploit or oppress or even govern, but simply ignore the majority.[12] Labor quiescence is due to the fact that, roughly speaking, the rich are opportunistic scavengers who have gained their wealth by "cherry picking" and exporting raw materials, not by taking advantage of the working masses. Russian labor is value-subtracting. Outside of a few sectors, therefore, strikes would yield no benefits. The threat to withdraw cooperation by workers in a bankrupt state-owned enterprise, where outputs have a lower market value than the sum of inputs, is not credible: no one needs their cooperation. You cannot create a "middle class," moreover, by handing workers shares in negative-value-added firms which retain their residual welfare functions and will never be able to compete on world markets.

This leads me to my closing question. Might not communism's unexpected aftermath also encourage us to reconceptualize the nature and function of our contested social expenditures? When comparing liberal systems with Soviet-style regimes, it seemed perfectly plausible to associate entitlements with cradle-to-grave dependency. For what is a recipient of public aid if not the antithesis of an enterprising individual shifting for himself? But if we reevaluate liberalism by comparing it with Russian disorder – where independence from the state takes the form of flight into subsistence agriculture and where public officials have taken anti-paternalism to the point of child abandonment – we may be prompted to describe our own welfare spending in a slightly different way. Instead of focusing exclusively on the choice between dependency and independence, we might begin to place greater emphasis on the alternative between inclusion and exclusion.

The fiscal crisis of the Russian state is not caused principally, or even substantially, by pensioners and other entitlement holders clamoring for the hand-outs to which they have become accustomed. Blockers of budgetary responsibility (and of responsible governance in general) should be sought among "spoiler elites" who thrive on legal chaos, rather than among the disorganized and discarded poor, whose bargaining leverage, after all, is relatively slight. In any case, budgetary outlays for vulnerable groups have been plummeting for the same reason that all government expenditures have dropped. The Russian state is unable to tax and spend. A starved treasury has not produced an economic miracle, however, because fiscal incapacity to fund entitlements reflects the same general insolvency which, in turn, erodes the security of acquisitions and transactions.

Why are pensioners, veterans, and former Chernobyl clean-up workers infuriated by rumors that their welfare entitlements are soon to be reduced even further for budgetary reasons? Their problem is not (or not only) that seven decades of socialism has weakened their moral fiber, making them passively addicted to state help. Rather, they do not relish being advised to tighten their belts, to give up, say, their pension benefits on which they counted for the whole of their working lives, by unscrupulous apparatchiks who recently became windfall millionaires through insider-giveaways of assets which once ostensibly belonged to all, and who are now surreptitiously stashing Russia's investible resources in Cypriot banks. The roots of postcommunist popular discontent, that is to say, lie less in residual habits of dependency than in accurate perceptions of betrayal.

Should liberals belittle social contracts, of the sort so crudely breached in the Russian case, as illustrations of childlike dependency? Notice that the pathological disconnection between the Russian government and the Russian people is simultaneously a disturbing insulation of the rich from the poor. The separatism of the privileged, their palpable relief at not being in the same boat with their unfortunate fellow citizens, should force us to specify, by way of contrast, the kinds of rich–poor relations desirable in a liberal regime. During the Cold War, worries about poverty were sometimes, however implausibly, associated with the road to serfdom. Today, the terms of reference have changed. Should not the spectacular inequity of nomenklatura privatization lead us to ask how much and what kind of distributions are compatible with liberal principles? How unfair can a liberal society be? How does the liberal social contract – where citizens pay taxes and public officials provide public services – differ from a nomenklatura–criminal swap by which insiders simply wash their hands of the poor?

At the origins of liberalism lay the perception that private property could not be protected by police power alone, and that only a system of public assistance could moderate the desperation that would spur the poor to theft, arson, and other forms of uncooperative behavior.[13] Liberalism has never aimed at the abolition of classes, therefore, but at class compromise. In its twentieth-century form, the liberal "mixed regime" honors the property rights of the well-to-do, while guaranteeing procedural fairness, voting rights, the right to strike, entitlement to public education, and various welfare rights to the less advantaged.

Perceptions of gross unfairness, as is well known, severely damage group morale. In order to fight wars, impose law and order, and even to promote economic growth, therefore, liberal states have found it useful to take the edge off conspicuous economic inequality by relieving desperation and providing a bottom floor beneath which no one might drop. The origin of welfare in veterans' benefits, therefore, is a reflection of liberal *raison d'état*. A free economy, where great accumulations of private wealth must be protected from the appetites of foreign and domestic predators, presupposes that the less privileged feel some perceptible stake in the system. The Babylon called Moscow, characterized by the back-turning of the privileged and the tossing aside of the human remnants of an obsolete system, clarifies, by way of contrast, the liberal ideal of society as a cooperative venture. This new apartheid, which does not resemble oppression, shows that at the basis of any liberal regime, including our own, lies a powerful moral principle. This core norm is, I would say, nothing as strenuous as Rawlsian equality. It can be described most simply as inclusion. A liberal state cannot claim, with any degree of plausibility, to be the impartial agent of society as a whole, since it manifestly favors the strong over the weak, unless it emphatically identifies exclusion as a moral problem and responds to it vigorously as a political challenge. Only a state devoted to addressing this problem, which will never be definitively solved, can lay a colorable claim to being a liberal state.

Notes

1 There were few signs of Balkan-style ethnic targeting in the incineration of Grozny, for example; Russian troops, even when left unsupervised, killed ethnic Russians and ethnic Chechens in roughly equal numbers.
2 According to ITAR-TASS: "The Russian Tax Service said on 27 January that 26 of its inspectors were killed, 74 injured, [and] six kidnapped" in 1996, while

"eighteen taxation offices experienced bomb blasts and shooting incidents" (OMRI Reports, 28 Jan. 1996).

3 James Madison, *Federalist*, no. 51, p. 322.

4 William Blackstone, *Commentaries on the Laws of England* (Chicago: University of Chicago Press, 1979), vol. i, p. 123.

5 Katherine Verdery, *What Was Socialism and What Comes Next?* (Princeton, NJ: Princeton University Press, 1996), pp. 204–28.

6 See Juan J. Linz and Alfred Stepan, *Problems of Democratic Transition and Consolidation: Southern Europe, South America, and Post-Communist Europe* (Baltimore: Johns Hopkins University Press, 1996), pp. 16–37, who make a similar argument about democracy.

7 Valery Abramkin *et al.*, *In Search of a Solution: Crime, Criminal Policy and Prison Facilities in the Former Soviet Union* (Moscow: Human Rights Publishers, 1996).

8 Richard E. Ericson, "The Russian Economy since Independence," in Gail W. Lapidus (ed.), *The New Russia: Trouble Transformation* (Boulder, CO: Westview, 1995), pp. 62–3; Gordon B. Smith, *Reforming the Russian Legal System* (Cambridge: Cambridge University Press, 1996), p. 188.

9 The social trust, mutual reliance, and habits of promise keeping upon which market relations depend may be (perhaps must be) created by other means than the judicial enforcement of contract, by primary socialization and dense family networks, for instance; but such extra-legal guarantors of the reliance interest seem to be weak in Russia as well. That personal styles of behavior, such as thrift, industriousness, and eagerness to get out of bed at 6 am, cannot be easily imposed by courts of law, goes without saying.

10 David Stark, "Networks of Assets, Chains of Debt: Recombinant Property in Hungary," in Roman Frydman *et al.*, *Corporate Governance in Central Europe and Russia*, vol. ii, *Insiders and the State* (Budapest: Central European University Press, 1996), pp. 109–50.

11 George Akerloff, "The Market for Lemons," in *An Economic Theorist's Book of Tales* (Cambridge: Cambridge University Press, 1984), pp. 7–22.

12 Stephen Handleman, *Comrade Criminal* (New Haven: Yale University Press, 1995), p. 330.

13 Blackstone argued that property rights could be "absolute" only because "by our laws … sufficient provision is made for the poor by the power of the civil magistrate" (*Commentaries*, II, 32).

4   Hayek in Chile

Mario Sznajder

In August 1991, immediately after the attempted coup, I went to Moscow, to participate in a conference on democracy and authoritarianism in the Third World, in which I was about to present a paper on the transition to democracy in Chile. I was surprised by the interest shown by our Soviet colleagues in Pinochet and the case of Chile. They posed many questions and were specially interested in the way Pinochet's government had successfully transformed Chile into a free market economy, according to the guidelines of Friedrich von Hayek, one of the staunchest intellectual enemies of the Soviet system. In the transition to democratic rule, led by Pinochet, they saw an additional benefit. But their main interest was focused on the Chilean model of development as one of sustained economic stability, growth and governability, possessing all the elements that were lacking in the disintegrating Soviet Union. Through the democratisation process controlled by Pinochet and his followers, Chile was – at least in ex-Soviet eyes – on its way to becoming Lord Dahrendorf's *fourth city*, acquiring a balance between prosperity, civility and liberty.[1] In Chile, civil associations had become the leading forces of both a free market and an open public sphere, and their interaction not only served for the elaboration of tensions and contradictory interests but also generated the energies needed for economic growth and social development. The governments of redemocratised Chile, while preserving the free market model and its advantages, in terms of economic efficiency, had clearly identified social and economic exclusion as a moral problem to be addressed, but the question here was whether limited democracy allowed the state the possibility to enforce the policies needed to curb the increasing socio-economic gap.[2] The Chilean state had become smaller but stronger in its governance capabilities. Society, politically demobilised through repression during the years of military rule, made a democratic choice in 1988, rejecting Pinochet's plebiscitarian bid to be elected for a further eight-year period. But after democracy was installed, the levels of political participation and interest descended rapidly. The neo-liberal model seems to have been internalised and the feelings of social cohesion that characterised Chile in early decades have become marginal.

In my answers I tried to point out the fact that redemocratised Chile has been constructed as a limited democracy, in which the defence of Hayek's neo-liberal economic model, as implanted in Chile, and of the interests of the stronger parts of society – including the military – were enshrined in a rigid constitution of almost impossible reform, in current terms. Moreover, if, in Dahrendorf's terms, military rule in Chile resembled a polity preoccupied mainly with obtaining economic prosperity, disregarding both civility and liberty, redemocratised Chile had a long way to travel in order to restore pre-dictatorial levels of social cohesion and achieve a totally open political model. According to my explanation, the main problem was that the adoption and implementation of Hayek's model under military rule had stressed the dualistic character of Chilean society. The stronger sectors of society, favoured by the workings of the model, had all the characteristics of the civil societies found in developed Western liberal democracies. Under military rule, their associated strength was focused into the economic market, producing high levels of growth for the whole country but mainly sectorial profits that further enhanced their own status and influence in the public sphere. With redemocratisation, the strength of the associations characteristic of the upper income quintiles of Chile's society was directed also into the political arena. The other side of Chile's dualistic society enjoyed general economic growth in a different way. Still beleaguered by the problems of misery and poverty, with no real political options, especially after the tragic end of Allende's experiment in democratic socialism, and having lost social cohesion as a traditional term of reference, it bounced between protest and adherence to the margins of the neo-liberal model. Again, limited democracy did not offer Chile's lower strata a political chance of changing the rules of the game in order to curb exclusion through governmental intervention and welfare policies. Furthermore, I stressed the cost, in terms of military and political repression, human rights violations, unemployment and deepening poverty, that large sectors of Chilean society had unwillingly suffered through the authoritarian implementation of the neo-liberal model inspired by Hayek thought.

This work deals with the impact of the application of a neo-liberal economic model based on Hayek's thought, in Chile under military rule. It claims that in order to prevent the dismantling of the economic model, as part of the process of democratisation, Pinochet and his supporters constructed a limited democracy. Hayek was well aware of these processes. His strong liberal stands bring us to ask some questions. How could an

economist and philosopher of the calibre of Friedrich A. von Hayek will-
ingly become a source of intellectual inspiration to the main group of
supporters and technocrats who, under General Pinochet, carried out the
process of modernisation in Chile in the 1970s and 1980s? How was it
possible to reconcile Hayek's image as 'a doctrinaire defender of liberty,
whose general outlook is little different from that of Nozick, or a partisan
of *laissez-faire* such as Milton Friedman',[3] with his support for the policies
of Chile's military authoritarian government? And how could Hayek's
philosophy be transformed into policies designed to overcome problems of
poverty, underdevelopment, the discrimination of minority groups and
extreme political polarisation?

The Process

The answer to these questions is to be found in political developments in
Chile, as well as in intellectual debates on economic policies, theories of
development and on the political systems deemed most appropriate for
their implementation. Here, philosophical views interact with political
ideologies and with attendant questions of legitimacy. Intellectual sources
of public policy are also of importance, not only because their acceptance
provides the kind of legitimacy that allows for the formation of alliances to
support and implement political control and policies (which in Pinochet's
case were necessary to carry out the project of demobilising the masses
that had supported Allende), but also because they provide international
links and contacts with foreign powers with similar ideological sources, a
scenario vital to Chile due to the dependent nature of its economy .

The political crisis that affected Chile under the Allende government
generated much debate and discussion within the ranks of the Christian
Democratic and Liberal-Conservative opposition. However, while the
former were divided between those that favoured a political compromise
that would help to preserve formal democracy and moderate the reforms
proposed and enacted by the Popular Unity government, the latter were
staunch in their opposition and demanded a forceful solution that was
finally carried out by the armed forces in the military coup of 11
September 1973.

The political-intellectual debate was older than the crisis generated
under Allende and included the development of elaborate anti-Keynesian
discourse in the circles of the right. From the 1950s, and especially during
the 1960s, the Catholic University of Chile in Santiago was home to the
two main intellectual groups that would support Pinochet's government in
the 1970s and 1980s. The first was of Catholic Integralist origin and had
developed a particular brand of social corporativism – *gremialismo*; it was

led by Jaime Guzmán, student leader, future lawyer and professor of constitutional law, staunch polemicist, opposition spokesperson to Allende and the main political adviser of Pinochet. The other, of neoliberal character, was led by Sergio De Castro, an economist trained at the Catholic University and later in the department of economics of Chicago University. De Castro was the first disciple of Arnold Harberger, Professor of Economics at Chicago, and had come to teach at the Catholic University in the framework of the academic co-operation agreement signed between the universities in 1956.

De Castro became a professor of economics at the Catholic University of Chile and the first of a *pleyade* of nearly one hundred Chilean economists trained in Chicago that would introduce the economic philosophy developed by Hayek and Milton Friedman into Chilean intellectual, political and entrepreneurial circles, and later also the social and political ideas associated with the economic thought and practice of neoliberalism.[4]

In the framework of their anti-Keynesian views, a group of Chilean 'Chicago Boys' supported and provided economic advice to the 1970 candidacy of Jorge Alessandri against Allende. During Allende's rule, and especially in the months prior to military intervention, they drew up an economic plan to redress the effect of Allende's reforms. The summary of this plan was submitted to the armed forces command through a contact in the navy in the months prior to September 1973, under the name of *El ladrillo* (the Brick).

After the military takeover, De Castro and some of his colleagues were designated advisers to the generals, and would later act as ministers in the economic sphere.[5] *El ladrillo* was a very detailed analysis of the Chilean economy and included proposals for specific policies in all areas of economic activity, drawn up according to the basic neoliberal principles of free markets, freedom of economic initiative, the preservation of private property rights, the elimination of state intervention in the economy through regulation and subsidies, massive privatisation, the reduction of state bureaucracy and the adoption of market criteria of efficiency.

De Castro and his followers, participating merely as advisers to a military government, found themselves trapped between a deepening economic crisis which required austerity and macroeconomic adjustment, and the governmental need for political legitimacy, which made neoliberal reform formulae unpopular. This dilemma continued until 1975, when the worsening economic crisis catapulted the neoliberal advisers into the ministries that controlled economic planning and policies.

Until 1975, the military government had looked for legitimacy, support and political inspiration mainly from the *gremialistas* – of Catholic social-corporatist inspiration – who led the right-wing coalition behind the

September 1973 coup. Their leader, Jaime Guzmán, had drawn up the first political documents of the military Junta, but he, his supporters and the military lacked a viable economic strategy to combat the deep crisis the country suffered.[6]

It was De Castro and his followers who provided a solution when, in 1975, the Chilean GDP fell by nearly 15 per cent and unemployment and inflation were out of control. Their solution was the strict application of *El ladrillo*, without restrictions deriving from problems of political legitimacy and government popularity. Pinochet himself decided to follow the radical neoliberal measures proposed by the Chilean Chicago Boys whilst at the same time bringing in the *gremialistas* and other conservative supporters of his government to draw up a future political framework of limited democracy for Chile, which would become the 1980 Constitution and its controlled referendarial acceptance.

This division of labour was not without its shortcomings. Military authoritarianism was stepped up to deal with those adversely affected by the economic reform, i.e. the industrial and lower income sectors of society after the removal of protective custom duties, as well as to deal with those affected by the political reform, i.e. proscribed political parties, especially those of Marxist orientation, that were meant to be constitutionally excluded from existence even after Chile's return to democracy. A further characteristic of the political process at the time was the Caesarean-like centralisation of power in the figure of Pinochet, who overcame internal opposition within the ranks of the armed forces, which tended to favour a more rapid and softer model of democratisation and economic policies.

Chile had become a kind of socio-economic laboratory in which a neoliberal experiment was being carried out with scant political hindrance. In the second half of the 1970s, the military government gave priority to the economic experiment, relying on its success to legitimise the future political framework of limited democracy, which in turn would provide the required guarantee for the survival and defence of the neoliberal model.

After the enactment of the 1980 Constitution, a double ideological-political process took place within the ranks of the neoliberals and the *gremialistas*. The latter began to adapt their social-corporatist views, where an autonomous civil society composed of intermediate bodies acting according to the rules of subsidiarity takes over all the state functions it feels better equipped to run, to a version that relied more on a radical kind of individualism, akin to neoliberalism. In this development, the principle of subsidiarity was applied in favour of individual initiative, leaving to the intermediate bodies only those functions that individuals could not carry out more efficiently, and to the state a minimal social and economic role.[7]

Any obstacle to individual freedom, whether anchored in the state or in the intermediate bodies of civil society, would, therefore, be removed.

The spirit of social corporatism was relegated by the *gremialistas* to the realm of the past, when the existence of an omnipotent state placed a society imbued with Catholic values in a defensive position in which the intermediate bodies of civil society had to defend the individual against the arbitrary nature of majority rule. The neoliberals on their part 'globalized' their project, bringing it out of the economic realm into the social one by presenting a seven-point modernisation plan that would change Chile into a country not only able to develop, but also to compete in highly sophisticated international markets.

The seven-point modernisation plan involved transforming the labour market, pension funds, the areas of justice, health, education and agriculture into highly efficient units, and the regionalisation of the country.[8] This would allow Chile to become a Latin American Jaguar, i.e. the equivalent of an East Asian Tiger, meaning a country possessing a sustainable model of development whilst simultaneously living through a process of democratisation.[9]

After the debt crisis of 1982 and the serious economic crisis which affected the country at that time, Chile's neoliberal experiment was moderated, whilst still adhering to its basic principles. After 1985 a second economic boom that continues to the present day began, producing high rates of growth, economic stability and generating positive economic expectations for the future of the country. The political model was left unchanged and led to a process of democratisation controlled by the military. This process produced a limited version of democracy – according to which the country is ruled today – which includes authoritarian enclaves, i.e. a binominal regional electoral system clearly favouring the right-wing coalition of parties that supported Pinochet, nominated senators that obstruct any possibility of constitutional reform, a National Security Council dominated by the military, budgetary and rank-appointment autonomy for the armed forces, an insoluble legacy of human rights violations etc., that guarantee the survival of the socio-economic model inspired by Hayek's ideas.

The background

The cultural character of Chilean intellectual and academic elites has historically produced serious debate about prevalent intellectual trends in the more developed European and North American countries. Whether these trends have then been adopted (and adapted to meet Chilean needs) has been determined by economic dependency, political and social

constraints and polarisation, and by the special ties between local intellectual circles and the state.

Hayek's ideas had already gained a foothold in Chile in the 1950s.
Andrónico Luksic, currently owner of a Chilean mining, transportation
and financial multinational, wrote his law degree thesis on the issue of
neoliberalism, focusing on Hayek's economic philosophy. The main newspaper in the country, *El Mercurio*, was always 'a persistent and untiring
defender of liberal economic thought', and its owner, Agustín Edwards,
led a group that studied and proposed to apply in Chile the thought of von
Mises and von Hayek.[10] Other prominent figures at the time were conver-
sant in Hayek theories, especially Jorge Errázuriz, a prominent lawyer and
businessman, and Pedro Ibáñez, later senator and founder of the business
school in Valparaiso.

It can be argued that the attempts to renew the spirit of Chilean liberalism, which was facing the challenge of an electorally increasingly strong
socialism, were behind these efforts. The main idea was to present a valid
alternative to Marxism which would respond to the economic, social and
political problems facing the country, especially when it became clear in
the second half of the 1960s that the Christian Democratic alternative of
'Revolution in Freedom' was failing and polarisation increasing.

This background and the political developments described earlier
combined to bring Hayek to Chile – in person, not only in spirit. The
Chicago professor and winner of a Nobel Prize (1974) visited Chile several
times in the 1970s and 1980s, and accepted honorary presidency of the
Centro de Estudios Públicos, the liberal think-tank established in 1980
which published articles and organised seminars to debate its economic,
social and political ideas. He did this despite the fact that Chile was
perceived as a pariah country for its grim record of human rights violation
and massive political repression which, ironically, made the application of
the neoliberal economic model possible. Hayek and Friedman publicly
supported the Pinochet government's economic experiment although they
refrained from addressing the problem of its authoritarian practices.

The theories

The main supporters of Hayek's ideas always stressed that their model
went far beyond the issue of the ideal economic system and that it touched
upon a basic epistemological question. For them, the main issue that
Hayek had clarified was the relationship between the economic process
and the creation and transmission of practical knowledge. They claimed
that Hayek presented market economics as a 'method of discovery' which
required decentralisation, competition and initiative in order to create

progress. The free market entrepreneurial model becomes, in this view, a paradigm for the acquisition of knowledge which in itself is a central factor for development.[11]

This kind of analysis found particular resonance with Chilean liberal interests and views at the time because it led to the conclusion that concentrating economic decision-making in the hands of the few (the kind of central economic planning and state intervention that Allende's reform tried to enforce in Chile) was not only detrimental for the functioning of the economy, but also precluded the possibility of wider knowledge and progress. For Hayek's supporters in Chile, the rejection of central planning – as equivalent to totalitarianism – and the elimination of individual freedoms and the penetration of civil society by the state bureaucracy, was a very attractive idea, which again served internal political purposes.[12] The supporters also applauded Hayek's anti-constructivist approach, stressing that the latter generated coercion, whilst accepting the defence of individual liberties and the acquisition of knowledge as part of the natural order.[13]

Hayek preferred spontaneity, based on the natural order, to rational constructivism, on the premise that in the most extreme case rational constructivism could lead to the imposition of one will over a whole society. Another side of the argument was that individual rationality was unable to absorb and deal with the whole of accumulated human knowledge. Constructivism, according to Hayek, produced artificial models, untested by experience and liable to impose serious limitations on individual freedom, which was for him the basis of civilised life.[14]

Individual freedom is the axis of Hayek's argument. For him, freedom is achieved through the absence of coercion, as in classic liberalism, and closely related to the existence of a sphere of privacy in which the individual is free to act according to his wishes. Political freedom is defined by Hayek as the right of individuals to participate in public affairs, meaning to elect a government, or be elected, to legislate and to control the administrative performance of the authorities. But for Hayek, a free people was not necessarily a people of free individuals because the mechanisms that insure political freedom do not, automatically, insure the existence of a private sphere of action in which the individual enjoys a maximum of possible action.

Hayek estimated that political freedom could serve a majority to decide and curb individual liberties. Thus for him, the basic tenets of freedom were related to the individual. From the other side, political freedom was a *sine qua non* for individual freedom. This reasoning led Hayek to propose the term *demarchy* 'as a system of government in which *demos* (people) has no brute power (*kratos*) but is confined to ruling (*archein*) by established

standing laws promulgated and known to the people, and not by extempo-
rary decrees'.[15] In this model, the right balance between the public and the
private spheres depends on the existence of an authority strong enough to
preclude coercion over the individual, acting according to an agreed set of
pre-established rules enforced by the state, that sanctify individual freedom
and its main economic outcome – the existence and preservation of
private property. This is related to the main economic freedom, that of
unrestricted contracting between individuals, which means the existence of
an unhampered free market.[16]

Related to this issue is Hayek's total rejection of the term 'social justice',
which in his opinion is a synonym for distributive justice. For Hayek,
economic distribution is a process carried out by free markets. Since he
defines justice as related to rules of human conduct that do not apply to
the functioning of economic markets, the results of this cannot, in his
opinion, be seen as just or unjust.[17]

Hayek strongly recommended the use of free markets in underdevel-
oped societies like Chile, explaining that it would foster 'the discovery of
yet unknown opportunities of a society in which competition has previously not been active', adding that 'it is simply fantastic to believe that we
can determine in advance the social structure in a country where the chief
problem is still to discover what material and human resources are available, or to think that we can predict the particular consequences of any
measure we may take in such a country'.[18]

The practice

All this created a series of dilemmas for the supporters of Hayek in Chile.
Under military rule, the enforcement of basic economic freedoms and the
installation of free market mechanisms was being carried out repressively
and against the strong opposition of many sectors of the population. Chile
lived in a state of siege for many years, a situation in which the scarcest
commodity for most of the population, to put it in Hayek's terms, was
personal freedom.

To make matters worse, the enforced application of the above-
mentioned economic formulae had by 1982 produced an unprecedented
economic depression, and massive state intervention was necessary to
salvage the banking system and economy. Serious recession generated high
unemployment, which in turn produced a wave of political protest against
Pinochet and his government. This triggered a new wave of politico-mili-
tary repression. The socio-economic roots of the problem were directly
linked to the structure of the country and its political development *vis-à-vis*

the economic and political model that the military were trying to install in Chile.

The first basic contradiction came from the fact that economic freedom was being imposed by means of the liquidation of all other freedoms. The opening of the markets did not produce a comprehensive strengthening of the private sphere of every individual, but only of those that through their support of military rule and privileged socio-economic position were able to enjoy it. And even amongst these sectors there was a problem of guarantees for their basic freedoms. Changes in the political situation could place individuals in unfavorable positions and further limit their freedoms.

The second contradiction concerned the wide socio-economic gap, which grew even wider with the application of neoliberal policies. In a country where a large part of the population lived below the poverty line, additional sectors became poorer as a direct result of the economic recession and unemployment it generated. In the periods of economic growth, 1978–82 and 1985–98, poverty was somewhat alleviated, largely due to decreasing unemployment and, under democracy, by focused social policies. Still, the gap between the rich and the poor continued to grow. Access to the markets in conditions of poverty or growing socio-economic gaps neither strengthened individual freedom for most of the population, nor created better mechanisms for the acquisition and dissemination of knowledge. A large part of the formerly strong middle class in Chile, considered by experts to be one of the mainstays of democracy in that country, suffered a process of pauperisation with consequences for the development of its members' skills and their capacity to contribute to the future development of the country.

A third point was the impact of the open markets on the country's ecology. The opening of formerly protected sectors to international and internal competition – fisheries, forestry, public transportation deregulation – had a strong impact on the ecological balance of the country. Unregulated over-exploitation led to the indiscriminate cutting down of forests, depletion of shell and fish banks and a notorious worsening of the smog situation in Santiago.

A fourth point related to the Indian minorities whose communal landholding system was destroyed by deregulation of land tenure. This again produced protests and violence, leading to further repression.

The counter arguments of Hayek's supporters in Chile were that a sustainable model of development and true democracy was being installed in the country. The existence of a strongly authoritarian government was justified by the fact that, through economic reform and the opening of the markets, the Pinochet government was establishing the basis for liberty in

Chile. Former democracy, controlled by political parties and corporatist groups, was depicted as a 'pseudo-democracy'.

This analysis provided the common ground for a meeting between the *gremialistas* and Chilean Chicago Boys. They agreed with the military that the reforms introduced would not allow Chile to return to its previous status quo. A new kind of democracy would be established according to the terms of the 1980 Constitution. In this democracy the free market model and property rights would be beyond the scope of legislation. In order to ensure that no reform of these principles would take place in the near future, authoritarian enclaves were established and the armed forces, enjoying unprecedented degrees of autonomy, were formally placed as guarantors of 'national security and the institutional order', leaving to their better judgement the precise definition of these terms, and of the right to intervene.[19]

In Chile, some of the policies initiated in the authoritarian period were voluntarily or quasi-voluntarily carried over by the democratically elected authorities, such as the neoliberal economic model initiated during Pinochet's period and slightly modified during Aylwin's government, and the modernisation measures that accompanied the process of privatisation and streamlining (the paring down and reorganisation) of the state. Nevertheless, it is clear that those in Chile who introduced the neoliberal economic model did not neglect the political aspect, as is shown by the adoption of the 1980 Constitution which imposed, in Whitehead's words, 'a stunted version of liberal democracy that works'.[20]

Three democratic national elections and an eighth year of democratic practice, even if within the limits imposed by the authoritarian enclaves inherited from the period of military government, have passed without major threat. The economic performance of the Jaguar, even if slightly less successful than that of the Tigers, has demonstrated that the Chilean development model works with no less success under a democratic government than it did under authoritarian rule. 1992, with an 11 per cent growth in GDP, was the best year for Chile's economy in three decades.[21]

Conclusions

The economic model has become consolidated and the question that is now central to the issue is whether limited democracy is a *sine qua non* for its survival. The question is important because while the Chilean economy, modernised during the period of military rule, continues to flourish, society, politics and culture have not experienced parallel processes. The social and political aspects of Pinochet's modernisation – rigid social structures in which change is effected through market mechanism regulations and through authoritarian enclaves in politics – are incompatible with modern democracy and a modern economy. Improvements in education, health, food, housing and the environment are the results of development, but also the impetus for further development. A better distribution of income, by strengthening Chile's internal markets, may make the economy less vulnerable to the fluctuations of raw material prices on the international market, especially copper, which still constitutes almost a third of Chile's total exports, as well as to recession in its main markets: Japan, USA, Brazil, Germany and the UK.

The reduced state still has important roles to play in the above-mentioned areas because the market is unable to take care of them adequately. Poverty is associated with social marginalisation, a widespread phenomenon throughout Latin America that increases social tension, not through revolutionary menace, but through a constant threat to individual security. The internal security forces have been strengthened to cope with the phenomenon, but Chile's complex legacy of human rights violations makes forceful solutions to the problems of social marginalisation and rising crime problematic. A modification of the state's role in these areas would constitute a fundamental step towards the political modernisation of the country.[22]

Coping with the ecological impact of the application of neoliberal policies is an ongoing and urgent need in Chile. It is difficult to imagine how the situation can be improved without regulation, social awareness and state intervention. The same is true for labour relations. The state basically has the dual task of ensuring the efficient performance of markets, but at the same time of curbing the social Darwinist dimension characteristic of neoliberal experiments of the Chilean type.

Chile's bid to become a full member of NAFTA and of MERCOSUR – the latter almost accomplished – adds further pressure on the need to redefine relations between state and society. Economic integration and increased competitiveness require a better educated, healthier, well-housed and ecologically aware population, able to articulate, as an autonomous civil society, its needs and capabilities. Chile's democracy is ruled by a relatively strong and coherent state. Levels of corruption are probably the lowest in the region. Although some of the characteristics of advanced democracies are becoming again part of Chile's political and social life, the problems of duality, as shown before, impair the process of democratisation. The lack of resolution of most of the legacy of human rights violations extends the problem of duality to the rule of law. Impunity for those that carried out most of the human rights violations during military rule is not only a matter of redressing grievances of the past but of the essence of democratic rule in the present and in the future. The obstacles to reforming and liberalising Chile's political model reside not only in the authoritarian institutional enclaves but also on the political apathy accompanying socio-economic neoliberal practices. In order to reach Dahrendorf's ideal model Chile still has to ensure that prosperity is not the realm of the few, civility is expanded to the whole society and liberty is achieved through further opening of the political model.

Notes

1 See Lord Dahrendorf's essay in this volume.
2 Here I am addressing Stephen Holmes's point on the impact of perceptions of gross unfairness in a group's morale and his affirmation that a liberal state can not claim to be an impartial agent in society, since this kind of stand clearly favours the stronger sectors of society. Undoubtedly, in Chile, democratic rule identifies exclusion as a moral problem but the constitutional limits and authoritarian enclaves set by the former military rulers restrict the state capacity to enforce effective anti-exclusion policies, impairing the capacity to reach higher levels of social cohesion and civility. See Stephen Holmes's essay in this volume.
3 John Gray, *Post-Liberalism: Studies in Political Thought* (New York and London: Routledge, 1993), p. 32.
4 Manuel Delano y Hugo Traslaviña, *La herencia de los Chicago Boys* (Santiago: Ornitorrinco, 1989), pp. 14–16.
5 Sergio de Castro, 'Prólogo', *El Ladrillo: Bases de la política económica del gobierno militar chileno* (Santiago: Centro de Estudios Públicos, 1992), pp. 7–12.
6 Patricio Silva, 'Intelectuales, tecnócratas y cambio social en Chile', *Revista Mexicana de Sociología*, 1 (1992), p. 151.
7 Pilar Vergara, *Auge y caída del neoliberalismo en Chile* (Santiago: FLACSO, 1985), pp. 168–73.
8 Delano and Traslaviña, op. cit., n. 4, pp. 73–90.
9 Mario Sznajder, 'Dilemmas of Economic and Political Development in Chile: The Jaguar that Wants to Be a Puma', *Third World Quarterly*, 17, 4 (1996), pp. 730–33. On the military approach to modernisation and modernity, see Francisco Javier Pinedo, 'Chile a fines del siglo XX: entre la modernidad, la modernización y la identidad', *Universum*, 12 (1997), pp. 141–54.
10 Juan Gabriel Valdés, *Pinochet's Economists: The Chicago School in Chile* (Cambridge, New York and Melbourne: Cambridge University Press, 1988), pp. 106 and 299.
11 Friedrich A. Hayek, 'The Pretence of Knowledge', in *New Studies in Philosophy, Politics, Economics and the History of Ideas* (Chicago: University of Chicago Press, 1978), p. 34. See also his 'Competition as a Discovery Procedure', in ibid., pp. 188–90.
12 Arturo Fontaine Talavera, 'Friedrich A. von Hayek', *Estudios Públicos* (Autumn 1993), pp. 19–21. For a basic bibliography related to Hayek's presence in Chile's intellectual circles and an analysis of his main political ideas, see Ricardo Israel Zipper, *Democracia y liberalismo* (Santiago: Instituto de Ciencia Política, Universidad de Chile, 1984), pp. 11–35.

13 Oscar Godoy Araya, 'Hayek: libertad y naturaleza', *Estudios Públicos* (Autumn 1993), pp. 25–33, and Friedrich A. von Hayek, 'La libertad como proceso de descubrimiento', ibid., pp. 15–17.

14 Friedrich A. Hayek. 'The Errors of Constructivism', in op. cit., n. 11, p. 6.

15 Friedrich A. Hayek, 'The Constitution of a Liberal State', in op. cit., n. 11, p. 104.

16 Friedrich A. Hayek, 'The Principles of a Liberal Social Order', in *Studies in Philosophy, Politics and Economics* (London: Routledge & Kegan Paul, 1967), p. 175.

17 Friedrich A. Hayek, 'The Atavism of Social Justice,' in ibid., pp. 57–8 and 67–8.

18 Friedrich A. Hayek, 'Competition as a Discovery Procedure', in ibid., p. 188.

19 'Fuerzas armadas, de orden y seguridad pública', Articulo 90, *Constitución política de la República de Chile 1980* (Santiago: Editorial Jurídica Publiley, n.d.), p. 63.

20 Laurence Whitehead, 'Alternatives to "Liberal Democracy": A Latin American Perspective', *Political Studies*, Special Issue (1992), p. 154.

21 Economist Intelligence Unit, *Country Report: 1st Quarter 1996: Chile* (London: EIU, 1996), p.3.

22 Manuel Antonio Garretón, *Hacia una nueva era política: estudio sobre las democratizaciones* (Santiago: Fondo de Cultura Económica, 1995), pp. 151–2, and Patricio Silva, 'Modernization, Consumerism and Politics in Chile', in David E. Hojman (ed.), *Neoliberalism with a Human Face: The Politics and Economics of the Chilean Model* (Liverpool: University of Liverpool, Institute of Latin American Studies, 1995), p. 69.

5   The invisible hand and the cunning of reason*

Edna Ullmann-Margalit

> There is a legend of the olden times
> That all our foolish plans and vain conceits
> Are overruled to work the public good.
> Aristophanes, 'Ecclesiazusae'

The notion of the invisible hand is commonly taken to be intertwined with the free market principle which, in turn, underlies the liberal outlook. It is noteworthy that nowadays it is mostly conservative economists (like those mentioned in Mario Sznajder's discussion of Hayek's reception in Chile; see Chapter 4) who cherish the notion of the invisible hand. Among liberal thinkers there seems to be a retreat from policies and practices traditionally justified in terms of the invisible hand. This retreat has to do, *inter alia*, with the cruel excesses, as described in Stephen Holmes's essay (Chapter 3), of anti-paternalist and non-interventionist policies put into practice in post-communist Russia.

In trying to make sense of liberalism in thought and practice at the end of the twentieth century, the centrepiece notion of the invisible hand needs to be looked at anew. In this essay I chart its curious ideological career, from a progressive to a conservative idea. I argue that upon its inception in the eighteenth century it was used to promote ideals of secular, enlightened progress, while at present it is used inversely, to promote conservative reverence toward tradition. I argue, further, that this shift can in part be accounted for when it is realized that there are in fact two different models of invisible-hand explanations: one progressively oriented, the other conservatively oriented. The current, inverse ideological use of the idea of the invisible hand by conservative circles against liberals and social planners is shown to spring from a failure to distinguish between these two models.

While looking anew at the notion of the invisible hand, Hegel's idea of

---

* An earlier version of this paper appeared in *Social Research*, 64 (1997), pp. 181–98.

the cunning of reason is revisited too. I argue that the two notions are historically related, and that the idea of the cunning of reason, like that of the invisible hand, is also invoked in contemporary political argumentation. However, it is my contention that the affinity between these two ideas is superficial, and that they serve profoundly different political doctrines.

F. A. Hayek talks about the 'shock caused by the discovery that [not only the *kosmos* of nature but] the moral and political *kosmos* was also the result of a process of evolution and not of design'.[1] What he alludes to here is the natural human response to the phenomenon of order. Upon encountering orderliness and patterned structures, people tend naturally to interpret these as the products of someone's intentional design. If complex order is exhibited by an artifact – say, a clock – the postulated designer would be a human agent, an artist or an engineer. If complex order is exhibited by the physical world – say, the lunar period – the postulated designer would be a superhuman agent, God. The 'argument from design' (or the cosmological argument, as it is sometimes called) is indeed a most powerful argument, psychologically, for the existence of God. At the very core of religious sensibility is the conviction that the world is not just the product of divine creation, but that it is the manifestation of divine, cosmic design.

It is against this background that the idea that the *kosmos* can be seen as the result of a process of evolution rather than design is described by Hayek as 'shocking'. To this shock, moreover, he goes on to attribute a significant contribution in the production 'of what we call the modern mind'.[2] And since the nineteenth-century notion of evolution, or spontaneous order, is itself rooted in the eighteenth-century notion of the invisible hand, there is a sense in which we may take the notion of the invisible hand as expressing a major anti-religious intuition. This notion was meant to replace that of the 'finger of God', or 'divine providence'. It was to play a central role in forging modern, secular, sensibility.

In tracing the history of the notion of the invisible hand, it is commonly attributed to the great Scottish Enlightenment figures of David Hume, Adam Smith and Adam Ferguson. It is Adam Smith who is credited with coining the expression 'invisible hand';[3] it is Adam Ferguson who formulated the splendid, formative phrase about people 'stumbling upon establishments, which are indeed the result of human action, but not the execution of any human design';[4] and it is David Hume who is generally acknowledged to have laid the philosophical foundations for these ideas. It is intellectually pleasing, however, to go still further back and to claim, with Hayek (and others), that it was Bernard Mandeville, the Dutch-turned-English doctor, who 'made Hume possible'.[5] In his famous *Fable of the Bees*, subtitled *Private Vices Public Benefits* (1714, 2nd edn 1723), the idea is articulated that complex social order forms itself without design. Orderly social structures and institutions – law, morals and language, the market and money and many more – spontaneously grow up without men having deliberately planned them or even anticipated them, and it is these institutions which bring it about that men's divergent interests are reconciled. In discussing the growth of law, Mandeville says: 'We often ascribe to the excellency of man's genius, and the depth of his penetration, what is in reality owing to the length of time, and the experience of many generations.'[6]

However, even though the idea *that* order may form itself without design was expounded by Mandeville, the question *how* remained unaddressed. The initial breakthroughs in suggesting some sort of mechanisms for the workings of the invisible hand were not to be provided before the appearance upon the stage of the Scottish social and moral thinkers. Their work made it possible to delineate a mechanism that can show in specific detail how the actions of numerous individuals who pursue their own divergent interests may actually aggregate so as to bring about a well-structured yet undesigned social institution. And it is this sort of aggregative mechanism which is the heart of an invisible-hand explanation worthy of its name. Only when an invisible-hand mechanism can be pointed to, can the spell of an explanation which postulates a creator, a designer or a conspiracy be effectively broken.

It is in this sense, and in this context, that we may allude to Wittgenstein's notion of being 'in the grip of a picture': the picture is the theological picture, within which one is held in the grip of the 'argument from design'. The liberating role from the grip of this picture is assumed by an invisible-hand explanation which succeeds in showing, through spelling out the workings of an appropriate mechanism (or process), how the social institution in question could have come about 'as a result of human action but not of human design'. This liberating role firmly establishes the notion of the invisible hand as a cornerstone in the secular, rationalist worldview which we associate with the Enlightenment.

The role of the notion of the invisible hand does not end here, however. It continues to exert influence on the intellectual climate (or on the 'modern mind') down to our own time. Interestingly, though, its spheres of influence shift. The original framework in which it began playing its eighteenth-century role *vis-à-vis* the theological outlook was that of economic models, with Adam Smith's discussion of the working of the free market as the paradigmatic example. Later, in the nineteenth century, the locus of its influence was to be found primarily in biology, bound up with the notion of evolution and the origin of species – but also in history and historiography, bound up with Hegel's notion of the cunning of reason. In its latest, present-day manifestation the invisible hand looms within ecology, where it relates to the equilibrium of ecosystems, and also, if we are willing to go along with Hayek, within general discussions about culture and morals.

While in the early phase of its career the invisible hand made it possible for economics, and social theory in general, to serve as a model for biology, what Hayek does in fact is the reverse. For him it is the workings of the invisible hand in biology, or in what he understands as the biological evolution of spontaneous order, which is – which should be – the model for social structures and institutions. Now something funny happens to the notion of the invisible hand on this reverse way. When first introduced, this notion played a liberating role – in the name of light, reason and progress – as against the religious outlook. However, within the secular outlook which came to prevail, the invisible hand is predominantly an instrument in the service of darker ideologies, conservative and counter-Enlightenment ones.

There is no other theme that Hayek, whom I shall take to be the latterday spokesman of these gloomier ideologies, emphasizes more than the need for human reason to recognize the limitations of human reason. In the more distant past, to preach for recognizing the limitations of human reason was tantamount to preaching for recognizing the supremacy of external, super-human, i.e. divine authority. The project of the Enlightenment, which consisted in the rejection of this authority, came to be identified not only with the supremacy of human reason but with the deification of human reason. This, to Hayek, is man's ultimate, 'supercilious',[7] fatal conceit.

For Hayek the recognition of the limitations of human reason, instead of leading us to accept divine authority, should rather force us to concede superiority

> to a moral order to which we owe our existence … to a tradition which we must revere and care for … to a system which we must accept as given…to a gradually evolved set of abstract rules of which human reason can avail itself to build better than it knows … to structures based on more information than any human agency can use.[8]

Hayek follows Hume in taking seriously the limitations of human understanding, or, more specifically, the upper bounds on the human capacity to possess, process and compute information. He thus wages a war against the rationalist confidence in the human ability to plan and to design ('it is indeed quite difficult', he says, 'to find a positivist who is not a socialist'[9]). The most we can do – the most Hayek believes we should be allowed to do

– is to 'humbly tinker' with a system which serves us well ('a moral order which keeps us alive') but which we can never hope to understand more than imperfectly.

The 'moral order' Hayek talks about comprises in effect the entire cultural realm – the social, economic, political and legal institutions,[10] as well as the moral tradition. For him the moral order is the product of spontaneous growth, that is, of a generation-long process of cultural evolution. As already mentioned, for Hayek the cultural evolution of traditions and habits is modelled on the biological evolution of 'the particular kinds of spontaneous orders which we call organisms'.[11] And, furthermore, when Hayek says of certain social institutions that they are the product of an evolutionary process, for him this seems the only adequate explication of the older, Scottish Enlightenment idea of explaining social institutions through the workings of an invisible hand.

Now, it is one thing to say that the idea of the invisible hand paved the way for the idea of evolution, and it is quite another to conflate the two ideas. My challenge to Hayek at this point is this: while evolutionary explanations are indeed one type, or species, of invisible-hand explanations, they are not the only species of invisible-hand explanations; they do not exhaust the genus. Moreover, while there is a strong sense in which evolutionary explanations can be said to be value laden, or, if you will, ideology laden, invisible-hand explanations as such are ideology free. This last point is of crucial significance with respect to Hayek's ideological use of the notion of the invisible hand.

Some clarification is in order.[12] I shall begin by spelling out, in brief, the nature of evolutionary explanations. First, let me recall the invisible-hand aspect of evolutionary explanations – whether biological or social. It consists, of course, in the fact that when an item, be it a social institution or an organism, is claimed to be the product of an evolutionary process, its existence is thereby taken to be explained without any reference to a designing agent. Evolutionary explanations qualify as invisible-hand explanations insofar as they are liberated from the grip of the formative – yet in a way primitive – picture according to which to account for the existence of something is to point to its creator.

The expression 'to account for something's existence', however, can be taken in more than one way. And it is the two different ways in which this expression is construed that distinguish the evolutionary explanations from the other, non-evolutionary, invisible-hand explanations. One way to account for something's existence is as an answer to the question of origin: how did it come into being, how did it begin to exist? The other is as an answer to the question of endurance: why does it persist (regardless of how it came about in the first place), why does it continue to exist? The distinction, then, is between an explanation of emergence and an explanation of endurance.

Evolutionary explanations are clearly of the second kind. Their central conceptual tool of 'natural selection', and its concomitant notion of 'survival of the fittest', are supposed to account for continued existence, not for origins. At this point, however, an important difference between evolutionary explanations within biology, and evolutionary explanations in the domain of society and culture, has to be noted. In the biological case some sort of an account (or a place-holder for an account) of origins is part and parcel of the explanatory apparatus. It is, namely, spontaneous and random mutations which are supposed to account for the emergence of the items (organisms, organs) whose continued existence is evolutionarily explained. No analogue to the notion of mutation exists in the socio-cultural case: an evolutionary explanation of a social institution involves no commitment, and tells no causal story, as to its historical origins.

There is yet another difference between the biological and the social evolutionary explanations, a difference which will play a significant role in what follows. It involves the notion of function. In the biological case, where the item to be explained (say an organ, like a kidney) is known to have withstood the generations-long evolutionary test, it may safely be assumed – or, at least, rebuttably presumed – that the item in question has some survival value to the organism containing it, that it fulfil a positive function contributing to its overall fitness. Matters are notably different in the social domain. When a social item is to be explained (a practice, a norm, an institution), it cannot in general be assumed that it has withstood the generations-long evolutionary test – it may be too recent for that. Nor can it in general be assumed that it fulfil a positive function which contributes to the survival and well-being of the society incorporating it – it may, for example, promote sectarian interests, or it may lack a function (in the relevant sense) altogether. The attributes of lastingness and of overall positive functionality have to be *ascertained*, case by case, rather than presupposed.

So, what an evolutionary explanation in the social domain does is the following: first of all, it ascertains that the institution in question fulfil a useful social function and identifies it (say, the continuous creation of money within the banking system); that is, it establishes its contribution to the equilibrial well-being and survival of the society incorporating it. Once this is ascertained, the explanatory schema can flow on. It assumes that by performing its useful function, even the faint beginnings of the social institution in question – whatever their origins – are with time reinforced and selected for. Consequently, this institution is seen as contributing to the evolutionary 'success' of the society incorporating it, and this success, in turn, accounts for the perpetuated existence of the institution in that society. What we have here, then, is a non-man-made process of selection: a large-scale evolutionary mechanism scans, as it were, the inventory of societies and of their social structures at any given period of time, and screens through to the next phase those societies whose structures and institutions serve them best. But for all that this explanation tells us, the social institution thus explained could have come about in any one of a number of ways. It could have originated, somehow, through people 'stumbling upon establishments, which are indeed the result of human action, but not the execution of any human design'.[13] However, it could also, for that matter, have come about as a result of intentional design and careful execution by some enlightened ruler or clever committee – and yet the explanation of its continued existence would still count as an invisible-hand explanation of the evolutionary kind.

In order for an evolutionary explanation in the social domain to get off the ground, the social institution to be explained has, as we saw, to fulfil some useful function, whether manifest or latent. Only institutions which perform a beneficial function for the society incorporating them can be candidates for an evolutionary explanation. Put somewhat differently, only institutions which promote the well-being and the survival of their society better than any alternative arrangements which happened to have been historically tried, can have their continued existence explained through the evolutionary explanatory apparatus. It is through this door that conservative ideology enters the stage. The way ideology enters the stage is by blurring the delicate distinction between *requiring* that the institution which is the explanandum phenomenon have a socially beneficial function, and *presupposing* that it has such a function.

All socio-cultural evolutionary explanations align themselves with the so-called functionalist school in sociology and anthropology.[14] And within the outlook of this school it is indeed taken for granted that any social pattern, structure or institution which has been around for some time fulfils a certain society-wide positive function – or else it would have been eliminated in due course. This outlook is further committed to more far-reaching presuppositions: that any existing social pattern, besides being 'functional', is also 'optimal' (as a 'solution') in some sense, and that human societies are self-regulating, goal-directed organic systems. All of these highly controversial assumptions are heavily substantive, value-laden assumptions. Somewhat crudely put, their gist is this: while it may be the case that we do not inhabit the best of all possible worlds, we do nonetheless inhabit an optimal social world which is the fittest and best adapted of all actually-tried alternative worlds.

So much for evolutionary explanations *qua* invisible-hand explanations. Let me return now to the claim made earlier, that evolutionary explanations are but one kind of invisible-hand explanations, that they do not exhaust the field. Indeed, the way I see it, they are not the ones which constitute the hard-core, paradigmatic cases of the invisible-hand explanations envisioned by the Scottish Enlightenment thinkers. When Adam Smith talks about an invisible hand leading to the equilibrial pricing system within a perfectly competitive market,[15] what he is referring to is an altogether different model of explanation.

The model in question envisages an invisible-hand process which is largely synchronic, not diachronic like the evolutionary selection processes. This process is an aggregate mechanism which takes as 'input' the diverse and dispersed actions of numerous individuals, and produces as 'output' an overall, structured, social pattern – subject to the assumption that the individuals concerned need neither foresee this pattern nor intend to bring it about. It is this process which, when spelled out, bears the brunt of the invisible-hand explanation. Such classical invisible-hand explanations, as those explaining the pricing system, or the continuous creation of money within the banking system,[16] or the development of media of exchange,[17] or the rise of the so-called ultraminimal state,[18] are all instances of the aggregate model. The aggregate model, then, supplies a chronicle of emergence and initial existence of some social pattern, while the evolutionary model is concerned with establishing reasons for the prolonged and continued existence of a social pattern.

The point to be stressed at this stage is this: for an invisible-hand explanation of the aggregate variety to be successful, nothing in particular need be assumed about the social pattern which is a candidate for this sort of explanation – except, perhaps, that it be *structured* in some interesting sense. Matters, as we saw, are different in the case of an invisible-hand explanation of the evolutionary variety. There it is a prerequisite – if not, indeed, a presupposition – that the social pattern to be explained have a *function*, that it perform a useful service to the society incorporating it. This, as we saw, was where conservative ideology entered the picture in the evolutionary case. And we are now in a position to see why it is that no ideology enters the picture in the aggregate case. When the existence of a social institution is accounted for by means of an aggregative invisible-hand explanation, there is no assumption, explicit or implicit, that it is a good institution, a valuable one, one which ought to be preserved or revered.

To be sure, it is entirely possible that an institution whose emergence is accounted for in this way turns out, as a matter of empirical fact, to fulfil a function which contributes to the survival or well-being of the society incorporating it. If it does, then its endurance, or continued existence, may be subjected to the other, i.e. to the evolutionary model of invisible-hand explanations. Indeed, it may even be the case that many, or most, of the social institutions whose emergence can be explained by the aggregative invisible-hand explanation, are relevantly 'functional' and hence also amenable to an evolutionary invisible-hand explanation. But this is an empirical, not an analytical, connection. And as a matter of ideological hygiene, it seems to me important to keep these two models conceptually apart.

Let me return, finally, to Hayek. Put somewhat bluntly, it is my belief that for Hayek the following sweeping generalizations were true: that all the institutions constituting our social fabric can – and should – be explained invisible-handedly, that invisible-hand explanations are evolutionary explanations, and that evolutionary explanations presuppose a functionalist outlook. As I hope to have shown, none of these generalizations is strictly true. His having subscribed to them, however, made Hayek unaware that the explanations he was championing for all of our social institutions were not explanations of emergence at all. These generalizations also helped blind him to the need to subject each existing social institution to a critical examination, free of presuppositions, in order to ascertain whether it was indeed of such positive social function and of such pedigree as to make it worthy of respect and preservation. For Hayek the cited generalizations confirmed that the socio-cultural sphere is 'a system which we must accept as given', that it represents a 'tradition which we must revere and care for',[19] and, ultimately, that we obey reason when we submit to traditional rules which we cannot rationally justify.[20] It is in this way, then, that the notion of the invisible hand is nowadays being put to an ideological use by conservative circles; it is in this way that this notion serves as a weapon against liberals and social planners. And this way, I have argued, is faulty and misguided.[21]

The idea that human society produces its moral and economic institutions in an autonomous and spontaneous way had a profound impact on historical thinking as well. From Vico to Marx, the notion of the invisible hand, in one version or another, served to replace the older ideas of 'the finger of God', or divine providence. The outlook according to which the meaning of history was to be extracted from some transcendent premise or promise, gradually gave way to the view that the meaning of history was immanent. A notion of particular interest in this context is Hegel's notion of the cunning of reason ('List der Vernunft').

Hegel transformed Kant's comments on 'the hidden plan of nature' into his doctrine: 'This is to be called the cunning of reason, that it lets the passions do its work.'[22] The higher purposes of reason – the *telos* of history

– are realized, obliquely, through the exercise of the passions, self-interests and motives of individuals. The historical agent, by acting out his own will, inadvertently acts as an instrument of reason; his 'passions, ambition, jealousy, greed and the like are thus viewed as the handmaids of reason working in history'.[23] The subjective freedom of the individual may appear independent of, or even in conflict with, the objective necessity of reason. But in truth, in each historical period, they coincide – their mediation being effected by the cunning of reason.

This doctrine is problematic on many counts; it is much discussed and variously interpreted by commentators. These accounts often draw attention to an affinity between the doctrine of the cunning of reason and the notion of the invisible hand. It is to this purported affinity that I should like to turn now.

The point of contact is what is sometimes referred to as the 'dialectical tension' between intent and outcome. Both the doctrine of the invisible hand and the doctrine of the cunning of reason focus on the fact that the result of human action need not be the outcome of any human design. Moreover, both doctrines spring from the recognition that some unintended and unexpected consequences of human action may fulfil a purpose, may serve a valuable function, may lead to progress or to perfection. This, indeed, is why these unintended consequences appear (misleadingly) to be the result of some superb (if not super-) human planning. And it is precisely this which the two doctrines attempt to address in terms other than super-human planning.

This point of contact, however, while striking, does not take us very far.[24] It is important to note, by way of contrasting the two doctrines, that the notion of the cunning of reason is meant to apply to the actions of a few great men only – to the actions of the historical heroes, or the 'world-historical individuals', as Hegel calls them. It is the Pericleses, Alexanders, Caesars and Napoleons who, unbeknownst to them, are the instruments of the 'deed of the world mind'[25] which leads to the 'progress of the universal spirit':[26] it is they 'whose own particular purposes comprehend the substantial content which is the will of the world-spirit'.[27] Hegel's best-known example, perhaps, is the case of Caesar, who is assassinated as soon as he has done the work of the Spirit in bringing the Republic to an end: 'This', as Charles Taylor puts it, 'is an example of reason using expendable instruments.'[28] This feature of the doctrine of the cunning of reason stands, of course, in marked contrast to its parallel feature in the doctrine of the invisible hand. Namely, for an invisible-hand explanation to be successful, a multitude of (non-heroic) individuals have to be postulated as privately pursuing their own particular purposes.

History in Hegel's view is the drama of emancipation of human consciousness, the drama of humanity's attainment of ever-growing self-understanding. The Idea of history as the realization of conceptual development unfolds through the concrete actions of individuals. The world-historical individuals, as Karl Loewith puts it, 'act historically by being acted upon by the power and cunning of reason, which is to Hegel a rational expression for divine providence'.[29] The historical heroes contribute to this drama by their actions, while they themselves are only dimly, or 'instinctively' – if at all[30] – aware of the conceptual unfolding to which they contribute. Their contribution consists not so much in a dramatic act – like a military victory – as such, nor necessarily in the founding of new orders. It consists, rather, in the undermining of existing orders, in pointing to new alternatives, in creating a critical situation, thereby preparing history for its next stage. The gap about which Hegel talks in terms of the cunning of reason is this gap between the lack of understanding on the part of the historical hero on the one hand, and his contribution to the growing self-understanding of humanity – or of the 'Spirit' – on the other. And when Hegel says that reason is 'the sovereign of the world', and that history has a final purpose, or 'ultimate design', he is not postulating agency or intentionality of some hidden mind. The design he talks about is better understood in the sense of a pattern (as in the design of an elaborate carpet) than in the sense of a plan or a plot. It is the design of the logical-ideational necessity, of the rational causality, which the historical development embodies and unfolds.

Both Hegel's cunning reason and Smith's and Ferguson's invisible hand are conceptual tools devised for the explanation of phenomena which are 'the result of human action but not the execution of any human design'. Interestingly, both of these tools are being put to political uses these days. While the invisible hand serves as a conservative weapon against social reform, the cunning of reason is taken to account for the spectacle of leaders who carry out a policy which is antithetical to their true desires and declared intentions.

An impressive number of big political decisions in recent times can be described as having been made by leaders who betrayed their constituencies as well as their own past. Thus: de Gaulle who quitted Algiers, Nixon who went to China, de Klerk who terminated apartheid, Begin who withdrew from the Sinai, and more. These leaders underwent formative processes which made them come to terms with the inescapable constraints and exigencies of reality. In Hegelian terms such leaders, by acting counter-intentionally, were being used by Reason as an instrument for carrying out their counter-policy. A desire/ability dialectics is at work here, whereby the leader who wants to bring about a certain dramatic state of affairs is often politically unable to do so, while the opposing leader who intends to – and is elected in order to – prevent it, will end up bringing it about, if forced to by reality. It is thus not the intentions, desires and wishes of political leaders that count, but rather their capability and power. And the irony is that the leader who strongly and credibly opposes a certain move often has the larger manoeuvrability for making it, once reality brings him or her around to its imperativeness: the support of those who are anyway in favour of this move is guaranteed, while the trust of this leader's own followers – if he or she has sufficient stature – will bring many of them around as well. Indeed, in political argumentation today it is this understanding of the notion of the cunning of reason which is sometimes cynically cited by people as a justification for supporting a political candidate who in their judgement will be *capable* of carrying out the policy they favour, rather than the candidate who declares his or her intention to carry it out.

In sum: tying the various threads together, we note that the original doctrines which the notions of the cunning of reason and of the invisible hand were devised to serve, differ on several fundamental counts. They differ as to the domain within which the explanation applies, as to what it is that is being explained, and as to the nature of the explanatory mechanism. In the case of Hegel the domain is spiritual history, the phenomenon to be explained is humanity's ever growing self-understanding, and the explanation consists in showing how history uses as its vehicles the results of the actions of a few heroic humans so as to unfold the execution of Reason's design. In the case of Smith and Ferguson the domain is the social order, the phenomena to be explained are social structures, practices and institutions, and the explanation consists in showing how they come about as the result of the actions of numerous ordinary humans and of no design whatever.

Notes

1 F. A. Hayek, 'Dr Bernard Mandeville' (1978), in C. Nishiyama and K. R. Leube (eds), *The Essence of Hayek* (Stanford: Hoover Institute Press, 1984), p. 190.

2 Ibid.

3 The well-known passage occurs in Adam Smith, *The Wealth of Nations* (London, 1776), IV.ii.9. A less well-known, and earlier, occurrence of the notion is in *The Theory of Moral Sentiments* (London, 1759), IV.i.10. Smith's very first use of 'invisible hand' is in his *History of Astronomy*, III.2, but there it seems to have ironic theological connotations. Emma Rothschild, however, suggests – in 'Adam Smith and the Invisible Hand', *American Economic Review* (May 1994), pp. 319–22 – that Smith's attitude to the invisible hand was ironic throughout.

4 Adam Ferguson, *An Essay on the History of Civil Society* (London, 1767), p. 187.

5 F. A. Hayek, op. cit., n. 1, p. 188.

6   *Fable of the Bees*, ii, 142, ed. F. B. Kaye (Oxford: Oxford University Press, 1924).
7   F. A. Hayek, 'The Origins and Effects of Our Morals' (1983), in *The Essence of Hayek* (op. cit., n. 1), p. 330.
8   Ibid., pp. 330, 326.
9   Ibid., p. 326.
10 As far as the law is concerned, Hayek's position is not entirely clear. On the one hand, he often lumps legal norms and institutions together with all other social, political and economic norms and institutions, and makes the sweeping claim that they are all products of 'spontaneous order'. On the other hand, however, he acknowledges that effectively competitive markets depend on state-created legal preconditions (such as rules of property and contract law).
11 F. A. Hayek, 'The Results of Human Action but not of Human Design', in *Studies in Philosophy, Politics and Economics* (London: Routledge and Kegan Paul, 1967), p. 101.
12 In the following I draw on my 'Invisible-Hand Explanations', *Synthese*, 39 (1978): pp. 263–91.
13 Adam Ferguson, op. cit., n. 4.
14 The prominent figures of this school are B. Malinowski and A. R. Radcliffe-Brown.
15 *The Wealth of Nations*, IV.ii.9. He also talks about the invisible hand leading to the optimal distribution by the rich to the poor of 'the necessaries of life': *The Theory of Moral Sentiments*, IV.i.10.
16 See, for example, P. A. Samuelson, *Economics* (New York: McGraw-Hill, 4th edn, 1958), ch. 15.
17 See, for example, R. A. Jones, 'The Origin and Development of Media of Exchange', *Journal of Political Economy*, 84 (1976), pp. 757–75.
18 See Robert Nozick, *Anarchy, State, and Utopia* (New York: Basic Books, 1974), Part I.
19 Hayek, op. cit., n. 7, p. 330.
20 Ibid., p. 325.
21 A personal note: it so happened that some years ago Friedrich A. von Hayek read my article about invisible-hand explanations (see n. 12 above). After some correspondence, he invited me to pay him a visit in Freiburg. Overwhelmed as I was by this pilgrimage, it took me a while to realize that for Hayek the mere fact that one is interested in the invisible hand meant that they are surely ideo-logical allies of his. He seemed genuinely puzzled to find out that I was not, and I became subsequently intrigued by the question why he should have been so convinced that I must have been. The present paper represents my attempt to figure this out.
22 *Philosophie der Weltgeschichte*, ed. Georg Lasson (Leipzig: Felix Meiner, 1930 [1917]), vol. 1, p. 83.
23 Shlomo Avineri, *Hegel's Theory of the Modern State* (Cambridge: Cambridge University Press, 1972), p. 232.
24 Consider, for example, this formulation: 'In general the Cunning of Reason makes a great deal of mischief at times, and the same may be said of the Unseen Hand, another name which has been given to the summing of conse-quences', Martin Hollis, *The Cunning of Reason* (Cambridge: Cambridge University Press, 1987), p. 48.
25 *Philosophy of Right* (London: Oxford University Press, 1952), p. 348.
26 *Reason in History* (Indianapolis: Bobbs-Merril, 1953), p. 105.

27 Ibid.
28 Charles Taylor, *Hegel and Modern Society* (Cambridge: Cambridge University Press, 1979), p. 99.
29 Karl Loewith, *Meaning in History* (Chicago: University of Chicago Press, 1949), p. 56.
30 On this point, see Taylor's argument with Avineri: Charles Taylor, *Hegel* (Cambridge: Cambridge University Press, 1975), p. 393 n.

Part II

Liberalism in multicultural societies

Introduction

The experience of Eastern Europe and of Chile, discussed in the first part of this book, focused on societies lacking both a strong tradition and institutions of liberalism. However, what about societies that do have established liberal political culture and practices? We have already learned – from the articles by Dahrendorf and Ullmann-Margalit – that changes in economic theories and practices challenge features of liberalism that have been taken for granted in such societies. However, not all tensions within liberalism and liberal societies originate in changes in the world economic structure or in skewed implementations of the free market idea. Liberalism implies individual freedom, including free flow of labour and of capital. However, the 'flow' of persons between boundaries of nation-states has created the problem of including in liberal societies persons and citizens whose personal and communal background do not include the liberal experience. That is why the most salient challenge to liberal theory and practice in contemporary established liberal societies is that of cultural and ethnic diversity.

The second part of the book discusses this challenge. Susan Moller Okin addresses two of liberalism's features: individual liberty and autonomy, and the institution of rights. However, she claims that in multicultural societies (with a strong liberal tradition) they clash with rather than complement one another. She defends a universal, individualistic and feminist standpoint against both the challenge of 'ethnicity' (multiculturalism) and a liberal theory of group rights (e.g. Kymlicka's theory). She claims that a feminist outlook points to the discrimination that is built into any such defence of toleration towards non-liberal and chauvinistic practices. To an extent, she comes back to liberalism, supporting a strict universal commitment to equal respect for the sexes, emphasising that the individual, not the group, is the overriding concern of a truly liberal philosophy and practice.

Bhikhu Parekh holds a different view with respect to the general question of tolerating minority, non-liberal cultures in societies that consider themselves liberal. Unlike Moller Okin's defence of the individual per se, Parekh draws attention to the individual as one *whose identity includes a strong cultural affiliation. Echoing Ralf Dahrendorf's concern for social cohesion, Parekh postulates that unity in liberal settings has become equated with homogeneity, equality with uniformity. In such settings, claims Parekh, diversity causes moral and emotional disorientation. He presents five models for overcoming the conflict between social cohesion and cultural diversity in liberal states. In conclusion, Parekh supports what may be regarded as the more liberal, though radically pluralist, model. And yet, he claims that it cannot be held up as a model for all contemporary, empirical, societies. Rather, it is an ideal model to be sought after. One way of doing this is to sustain a spirit of responsibility and common citizenship through educational institutions in an impartial state.*

6 Feminism and multiculturalism

Some tensions

Susan Moller Okin[1]

This essay addresses a conflict between two political aims that are not commonly recognized as in tension with each other. Since both of the terms in my title are complex and contested concepts, they require definition before I can address how and why I perceive tensions between them. There are a multitude of feminisms, feminist theories, feminist methodologies; the term as used here means the beliefs that women should not be disadvantaged by their sex, that they should be recognized as having human dignity equally with men, and that they should have the opportunity to live as fulfilling and as freely chosen lives as men can.

"Multiculturalism" is more difficult to define, since people tend currently to use it (and the term "culture") in quite varying ways, and sometimes in more than one way at the same time. There are two contexts in which it is most commonly found, at least within current political theory: the first is the context of education, in which the problem confronted is that what is taught as "culture" – including history, literature, philosophy, and so on – has largely left out groups such as women, people of races other than Caucasian, gays and lesbians, formerly colonized peoples, minority ethnic or religious groups, and indigenous populations. In this context, multiculturalists have claimed, with varying degrees of success, that these omissions must be rectified – both by the inclusion of works by these excluded groups and by the consideration of these groups' points of view in the interpretation of works, especially the "great books," whose authors were almost all white males. This, sometimes referred to as "the politics of recognition" or "identity politics," is not the kind of multiculturalism I am concerned with here.

The context of the multiculturalism I am concerned with is the wider social, economic, and political context, though still within the nation state. Here, many have argued in recent years, groups with cultures distinct from the majority culture are not sufficiently protected by the individual rights of their members, and therefore need special group rights, in order to protect their distinct cultures, meaning "ways of life," in such settings. Some examples of group rights so claimed are rights to guaranteed political representation, rights to public subsidies for cultural activities or education, and rights to be exempt from certain generally applicable laws.[2] In the context of this multiculturalism (which I shall from now on simply call "multiculturalism"), language, history, or religion – any combination of which are sometimes referred to as "ethnicity" – are frequent markers of distinct cultures. Some of the groups that seek such rights – indigenous native populations, minority ethnic or religious groups, and formerly colonized peoples (at least, when the latter immigrate to the former colonial state) – are the same groups that claim recognition in the first version of multiculturalism. However, those who have been discriminated against on grounds of sex or sexual orientation, though they seek such recognition, do not normally seek cultural group rights.

Sometimes, these two meanings of "multiculturalism" are confused and conflated, so that quests for recognition of the first kind, by groups including straight women, gays, and lesbians, are mixed up with the latter demands for group rights.[3] I think this tends to confuse matters, for several reasons. Women, gays, and lesbians do not generally perceive themselves as having, and are not perceived by others as having, their own culture, at least in the sense of "ways of life," though this might well be contested by some members of each of these groups. Certainly, such groups want their points of view taken seriously and their interests represented; but this is different from a group's claiming protection for its distinct way of life. Second, as George Kateb has aptly put it, another difference between the two types of multicultural claims is that the claims of women, gays, and lesbians – and, I would add, members of minority racial groups – "grow out of something more real than [the other groups] and they struggle against, not in behalf of, fictions."[4] I understand him to mean that they struggle against millennia of discrimination based in part on the fictions that women, or members of non-Caucasian racial groups, are naturally inferior, that homosexuality is a crime against nature, and so on. Of course, Kateb's implication that many cultural groups base their claims at least largely on fictions is controversial, but as will become apparent, I am generally in agreement with him on the issue.

In the multiculturalism I focus on here, then, what is at stake is the survival and flourishing of ways of life. As Will Kymlicka, the foremost contemporary defender of cultural group rights, says, while a shared language and history is usually prerequisite to a group's having a distinct culture, what he calls a "societal culture"[5] (and is concerned to protect) involves more than this; it "provides its members with meaningful ways of life across the full range of human activities, including social, educational, religious, recreational, and economic life, encompassing *both public and private spheres.*"[6]

Different kinds of justifications are made for group rights for such cultures, when their minority status renders them in one way or another vulnerable. My discussion here is confined to arguments for group rights that are based on *liberal* grounds. Such arguments rest, first and foremost, on concern for individuals, seeing collectives such as communities and cultures as of significance only because they are essential, or at least very important, in the lives of individuals. Of course, it is much easier to make arguments for collective rights if one starts with communitarian rather than liberal premises.[7] But there are many problems with communitarianism, not the least of which are that it has failed to enunciate a clear, positive, political theory, and that it is often vague or inconsistent both about what a "community" is, and about what should happen when the claims of one level of community conflict with those of another.[8] Liberal arguments for group rights are, therefore, more cogent; they are also more challenging and more interesting. Being based on the well-being and interests of individuals, they seem also less likely to come into conflict with feminist claims that individual women as well as individual men be accorded equal concern and respect. So if, as I shall argue, there are conflicts between feminism and the liberal claims for group rights that I focus on, it is even more likely that communitarian claims for group rights will conflict with the aims of feminism.

Having said this, I turn to the interface between feminism and multiculturalism. Specifically, I shall argue that there are tensions between the two which have, so far, been insufficiently attended to by either feminists or defenders of group rights. I do not mean to suggest that all aspects of multiculturalism are, or should be, a problem for all feminist positions and projects. But I do question what is sometimes, even often, taken for granted, especially by those who consider themselves politically progressive and opposed to oppressions, wherever they occur: that feminism and multiculturalism are not only both good things, which we should support, but that there is little reason to think they might be in conflict. I want to argue, instead, that there is considerable likelihood of conflict between feminism and group rights for minority cultures, and that this conflict persists even when the latter are claimed on liberal grounds, and are limited to some extent by being so grounded.

First, though, I offer a few thoughts about why this conflict is not being much addressed by either multiculturalists or feminists. Two reasons why the conflict is usually not evident or addressed by multiculturalists defending group rights are the same reasons why so many problems feminists have exposed are hidden. The first is that those arguing for group rights insufficiently differentiate amongst those within a group or culture – specifically, they fail to recognize that minority cultural groups are, in this respect, like the societies in which they exist, though to a greater or lesser extent, gendered. Some of the best liberal defenses of group rights are constituted by claims that the individual needs "a culture of his or her own," in order to develop a sense of self-esteem or self-respect, or the capacity for autonomy, meaning the capacity to decide or choose what kind of life is good for one. But, as I aim to show, any such argument needs to pay special attention to the different positions or roles that various cultures require of their various members. Thus, it cannot avoid paying attention to certain aspects of the content of the cultures – specifically, to their beliefs and practices concerning gender. A second reason why multi-culturalists have not confronted the tension between the group rights they argue for and feminist beliefs is that they pay no or insufficient attention to the private sphere. But this sphere is, as I shall explain, of particular importance to discussions of cultural rights. Thus just as group rights advocates cannot reasonably ignore gender, nor can they avoid examining the context in which persons' senses of themselves and their capacities are first formed and in which culture is first strongly transmitted – the realm of domestic or family life. As it is, unfortunately, few participants in the group rights debate pay any attention at all to either gender roles within cultures or the private sphere. Most liberal defenders of group rights, such as Kymlicka, are less prepared to defend the rights of groups that are them-selves internally illiberal, in that they impose internal restrictions on their members or discriminate against some of them. However, as I shall argue, looking out for formal and public restrictions or discrimination is insuffi-cient, since a great deal of culture-based gender construction and inequality occurs informally and in the most private sphere of life, that of the household. As for those who attempt to defend on liberal grounds the group rights of cultural groups that are internally illiberal, in their case the neglect of the private sphere, of the fact of childhood, and of the process of socialization create even more problems – from both feminist and liberal points of view.

These are at least some of the reasons why defenders of group rights have neglected tensions between feminism and such rights. What, then, might be reasons feminists have neglected them? Here, I think the problem arises from what I have come to view as an excessive amount of deference to differences among women, on the part of some feminist scholars, coupled with what sometimes becomes a hyper-concern to avoid cultural imperialism that leads, at worst, to a paralysing degree of cultural rela-tivism. Neither of these tendencies is confined to feminists who confront the issue of cultural differences, of course. However, they are particularly crippling to feminism, because so many of the world's cultures are highly patriarchal. That this is so is confirmed by the fact that "But this is our culture" is a response so often given by male elites around the world to justify the continued infringement of women's rights.[9]

Let me make it quite clear that I am not advocating any wholesale denial or neglect by feminists of differences among women – including cultural and religious as well as racial and class differences. Clearly, some of early second wave feminism, not to speak of earlier feminism, was highly insensitive to class, racial, religious, and other pertinent differences among women, and this neglect needed to be redressed. At times, though, the corrective action has been excessive, with the result that any generalization about women or gender inequalities is rejected as "essentialist." At worst, the attempt is sometimes made to drive feminist scholars into a position where only subjective, autobiographical narrative (if even that) is considered valid work. Thus, whatever the quality of the evidence presented or the strength of the argument made, the mere suggestion, if made by a First World feminist, that women and girls in cultures other than our own are disadvantaged or oppressed by elements of their own cultures is regarded as offensive cultural imperialism.[10]

It has become evident in recent years that these attitudes are not widely shared by Third World feminists, especially Third World activist feminists. For during the very decade and a half in which a number of Western and Third World academic feminists have been charging others with falsely generalizing about women and gender, and have been refraining from the critique of cultural practices that oppress women in many parts of the world, Third World feminists who were working both at the grass-roots level and within a multitude of nongovernmental organizations were coming to conclusions quite similar to those that have been so assaulted when put forward by First World feminists. Consider, for example, the Program for Action that issued from the Fourth World Conference on Women, held in Beijing, September 1995. In this document appear both general statements about the patriarchal structures, in both public and private spheres, that are "integral to the problems facing women" around the world, and an unprecedentedly strong statement against "cultural" justifications for violating women's rights. It reads as follows: "While the significance of national and regional particularities and various historical, cultural and religious backgrounds must be borne in mind, it is the duty of States, regardless of their political, economic and cultural systems, to promote and protect all human rights and fundamental freedoms."[11] Further on, the document specifies: "Any harmful aspect of certain traditional, customary or modern practices that violates the rights of women should be prohibited and eliminated."[12] Clearly, thousands of Third

World activists for women's rights are saying: "We want to be rid of these cultural excuses for women's oppression that have plagued us so long." If it was not clear earlier, surely it is now clear that both focussing only on differences among women and bending over backwards out of respect for cultural diversity does great disservice to many women and girls around the world.

Culture and gender are interrelated in complex ways, in ways that make gender inequality more than just one amongst the many forms of culturally mandated inequality that might conflict with liberal multiculturalism. Two connections between them are especially important, since they make gender inequality a particularly insidious feature of most existing cultures. These connections seem obvious but, since they get little attention in the literature about multiculturalism, I have to assume that they are still controversial. One of the most crucial focuses of most cultures, and therefore one of the things cultural practices and rules are most concerned with, is the whole sphere of personal, sexual, and reproductive life. In many cases the realm of law that religious or cultural minorities are most concerned to control is "personal law" – the laws of marriage, divorce, child custody, division and control of family property, and inheritance.[13] This means that, in most existing contexts, the defense of "cultural practices" is likely to have much more impact on the lives of women and girls than on those of men and boys. I have yet to see – though I am much looking forward to seeing – the culture in which as much of men's time and energy as women's goes into preserving and maintaining the personal, familial, and reproductive side of life. In turn, how responsibilities and tasks are assigned within homes has a major impact on who can participate in and influence the more public parts of the cultural life, the sphere in which the decisions that regulate both public and private life are made. Obviously the way life at home is lived is not all of what "culture" is about, but it is certainly a major focus of most cultures, majority and minority, in the world today. One very important reason for this, of course, is that home is where much of culture is practiced, preserved, and transmitted to the young.

A second reason for the great significance for cultures of the regulation of domestic life leads us into the second important interrelation between gender and culture that I want to attend to: that most cultures have as one of their principal aims the control of women by men. I cannot discuss at any length, here, why men are so preoccupied with controlling women. Suffice it to say that the uncertainty of paternity has surely contributed to it, and that I think (following Dorothy Dinnerstein, Nancy Chodorow, Walter Ong, and Jessica Benjamin) it also has a lot to do with female primary parenting.[14] If these suggestions are right, then men's need to control women is surely far from being an inevitable fact of human life. Rather, especially in our day and age, in which biological paternity can be determined with virtual certainty and parenting could easily be equally shared, it should be regarded as a contingent factor, and one that feminists have a considerable interest in changing.

What evidence is there that much of most cultures is about controlling women and maintaining gender roles? First, looking at cultures more familiar to most readers, the founding myths of Greek and Roman antiquity, and of all three major Western religions, Judaism, Christianity, and Islam, are rife with attempts to control women and to justify controlling them. These consist of a combination of denials of women's role in reproduction, the appropriation by men of the power to reproduce themselves, characterizations of women as overly emotional, untrustworthy, evil, or sexually dangerous, and refusals to acknowledge mothers' rights over the disposition of their children.[15] Think of the Zeus/Athena myth, and of Romulus, reared without a human mother. Think of Adam, made by a male God, who then (at least according to one of the two versions of the story) made Eve out of part of Adam. Consider Eve, whose weakness led Adam astray. Think of all those endless "begats" in the Book of Genesis, where women's primary role in reproduction is completely ignored. Think of the textual justifications for polygyny, once practiced in Judaism, still practiced in many parts of the Islamic world. Consider the story of Abraham, a pivotal turning point in the development of monotheism.[16] Here God commands Abraham to sacrifice his greatly loved son. Abraham prepares to do exactly what God asks of him, without arguing with him, as he does about some other matters, and without even telling, much less asking, Isaac's mother, Sarah. Abraham's absolute obedience to God makes him, for all three religions, the fundamental model of faith; it is a story that has been told and retold for millennia.

As anthropologist Carol Delaney asks, in her recent analysis of the story and its influence: Why should a man's willingness to sacrifice his son be the pivotal model of faith in God? Why not, instead, a parent's courageous or "passionate protection of the child"? And what, as Delaney asks, "allowed the biblical writers to portray the story as if Abraham had [the] unquestioned right [to sacrifice the child whom Sarah had given birth to and raised], and what has so blinded subsequent interpreters that no one has yet questioned it?"[17] While the powerful drive to control women and also to blame and punish them for men's difficulty in controlling their own sexual impulses has been softened considerably in the more progressive, reformed versions of Judaism, Christianity, and Islam, it is still very much present in the more orthodox or fundamentalist versions of all three religions. Nor, of course, is the aim of controlling women confined to the

West, or to monotheistic cultures. Many of the world's traditions and cultures, including those practiced within conquered or former colonial nation states – certainly including most of the peoples of Africa, the Middle East, and most of Asia – are quite distinctly patriarchal. They too have elaborate rituals, matrimonial practices, and other cultural practices (as well as systems of property ownership and control of resources) aimed at bringing women's sexuality and reproductive capabilities under the control of men.[18]

It is hardly surprising, then, that the importance to many cultures of maintaining control of women shouts out to us in the examples given in the literature on cultural differences and group rights. Yet though it "shouts out," in a way, it is hardly ever really acknowledged or discussed. As far back as the late eighteenth century, when Jeremy Bentham wrote about cultural differences that might affect legislation, among the examples he cites within a few pages are polygyny, the different degrees of subordination of wives, the castration of eunuchs to preserve the conjugal fidelity of wives, dress codes to preserve women's modesty, "crimes against nature" (that is to say, homosexuality), the confinement or seclusion of wives, paternal infanticide, the sale of daughters, forced abortion, and sati or widow immolation.[19] Two hundred years later, we find much the same phenomenon, though now in a different context – the current literature on culturally based group rights. Let me cite a couple of examples: First, a paper by Sebastian Poulter about the legal rights and culture-based claims of various immigrant groups, as well as gypsies, in contemporary Britain, mentions the roles and status of women as "one very clear example" of the "clash of cultures."[20] Poulter discusses claims put forward by members of such groups for special legal treatment on account of their cultural differences. A few are non-gender-related claims: about Sikh men being exempted from motorcycle helmet laws on account of their culturally sanctioned long, turbaned hair; about a Muslim schoolteacher being allowed to be absent part of Friday afternoons in order to pray; about gypsies not having to send their children to school as much as other familes, on account of their itinerant lifestyle. But the vast majority of examples in the paper – and there are many – are about gender inequalities, such as child marriages, forced marriages, divorce systems biased against women, polygyny, and female genital mutilation. Almost all of the legal cases discussed stemmed from women's or girls' claims that their individual rights were being truncated or violated by the practices of their cultural groups. Again, in a recent paper by Amy Gutmann, fully half the examples discussed have do with gender issues – issues such as polygyny, abortion, sexual harassment, purdah, and clitoridectomy.[21] This is quite typical in the literature on subnational multicultural issues. Moreover, the same phenomenon occurs in practice in the international arena, where women's human rights are often rejected by the leaders of countries or groups of countries as incompatible with their various cultures.[22]

Despite all this, however, none of the prominent defenders of multicultural group rights has adequately or directly addressed the connections between gender and culture, or the conflicts that arise so commonly between feminism and multiculturalism. I shall now take three examples of defenses of group rights, all of which claim to defend these rights on liberal grounds, and indicate some of the problems they encounter when women and gender are taken into account.

The first is an argument by Moshe Halbertal and Avishai Margalit.[23] It consists of a claim on liberal grounds for the rights of illiberal cultures. The authors argue that "[h]uman beings have the right to culture – not just to any culture, but their own," and that this right may justify "an obligation to support cultures that flout the rights of [their individual members] in a liberal society." The second is an argument made by Chandran Kukathas.[24] Kukathas does not argue, as in the preceding example, that minority cultural groups *per se* should have any special support or privileges, since he thinks the rights of their individual members suffice to protect them from the power of the larger society. But he does argue that such groups – even illiberal ones – within a liberal society have the right to be "let alone." Thus, they have the right to treat their own members illiberally in certain respects – for example, requiring them to conform to the religious or other practices of the group. The third argument – and the best known of the three – is the case for cultural group rights that has been made by Will Kymlicka, in two books, *Liberalism, Community, and Culture* and, more recently, *Multicultural Citizenship*.[25] Kymlicka confines his defense of group rights to groups that are internally liberal, with certain exceptions which I shall not address here. All three of these claims for group rights – or, in the case of the second, non-interference with groups – run into significant problems when approached from a feminist perspective.

First, then, let us look at the argument of Margalit and Halbertal. Defining "culture" as "a comprehensive way of life" that is lived in the context of an "encompassing group," they argue that persons have the right to "their own" cultures, even if these cultures "flout the rights of the individual in a liberal society."[26] They argue that governments must honor this right, by privileging and supporting cultures that might otherwise be endangered by their minority status. Their primary example, and the one I will focus on in disagreeing with their position, is the culture of Ultra-Orthodox Jews in Israel.

First, a few facts: Israel's Ultra-Orthodox community receives substantial financial assistance from the state. Its religious day schools, which all Ultra-Orthodox children attend, segregated by sex, are heavily subsidized by the government, to the point where they are able to offer far more services than the regular public schools, such as hot lunches, transportation to and from school, and after-school programs. The community's religious institutions are also supported by the state. And the young Ultra-Orthodox men and women are exempt from the military service that is required of all other young Jewish Israelis, on the grounds that, if male, their role is to study the Torah and, if female, military service would violate their religiously sanctioned traditional women's role. All in all, "the culture of Ultra-Orthodoxy is…able to flourish, as it is given massive financial support by the government."[27]

Margalit and Halbertal argue that these subsidies and privileges are justified by the group's need to ensure its survival in the midst of a majority secular culture. They claim, specifically, that such group rights are essential in order for each member of the Ultra-Orthodox community to preserve "his personality identity," something in which they claim every person has an "overriding interest." By a person's "personality identity," they mean "preserving his way of life and the traits that are central identity components for him and the other members of his cultural group."[28] They do not make it clear whether they think that all persons have "personality identities," or only those who grow up in cultures similarly encompassing to that of Ultra-Orthodox Jews.[29] However, if they claim the latter, it seems incumbent upon them to show what is the advantage to persons of having such personality identities, rather than some kind of identity that can be acquired in a less encompassing and less restrictive setting. If they claim the former, they need to show that the type of personality identity one develops in a restrictive and encompassing community such as that of the Ultra-Orthodox is at least as good for persons as, if not superior to, the type they would be likely to develop in a more open and liberal community. For if the former type of community were to dwindle away in the absence of special public support, those who would have been its future members, being raised instead in the more liberal society, would presumably develop the latter type of personality identities instead. In order to be convinced of the justification of special rights for the religious minority, we need to be convinced that this alternative would constitute harm to them.

However, Margalit and Halbertal do not make either of the types of argument I spell out above. Since I shall argue, to the contrary, that Ultra-Orthodox culture is more likely than a more open and liberal culture to harm the individual interests of both its male and its female children, I conclude that its public support is unacceptable for both liberal and specifically feminist reasons.

First, the more general liberal objection. As Margalit and Halbertal make clear, what is central to the personality identity of men in Ultra-Orthodox culture is the attribute of being a Torah scholar. Religious study is what is most highly prized, so that the education of males is very largely devoted to it, and severely truncated in other respects: "Except for some elementary arithmetic, boys are taught almost no secular subjects."[30] How can a liberal justify the public support of such an educational system? A liberal must, by definition, be concerned with the well-being of the individuals within a culture, including, as Margalit and Halbertal concede, their right to exit from the group, if they so choose. But how can individual well-being be promoted by an education so restricted that it ill prepares boys for any other kind of life but religious study? What of a boy born into an Ultra-Orthodox family who had neither any aptitude for nor interest in religious study? What if he were, instead, a naturally gifted musician, or intensely passionate about nature, or commerce, or agriculture? What if he were dyslexic, yet a mathematical genius? Margalit and Halbertal seem to be saying that the mere accident of birth into the culture of Ultra-Orthodoxy gives such a boy the "right" to be coerced into doing what he is unsuited for, and into abdicating the development of his talents or passions, in the name of achieving "his personality identity." I can see no justification, on liberal grounds, for this at all.

From a feminist point of view, the problems are even greater. For Torah study, the central focus of Ultra-Orthodoxy, is the men's and boys' preserve. The women's role is to facilitate this, by both financially and domestically supporting the men, and by bearing and rearing many children to carry on the tradition. So girls' education is oriented towards these ends, and it is broader and fuller than that of the boys. This means, however, that the personality identities cultivated in the girls are much less central to the culture, which raises an immediate question about how they are to develop a sense of equal worth or self-respect. Also, what of a girl born into this culture who is drawn toward religious study as strongly as the boy mentioned above is repelled by it? What if she dislikes children, and has no desire to bear or rear any? What personality identity can she hope to develop, destined as she is to her adjunct female status within the culture she happened into, by accident of birth?

Worse still, as in many other orthodox or fundamentalist religions, girls and women in Ultra-Orthodox Judaism are held responsible for male sexual self-control. As Margalit has written in another article, "[o]n the whole the Ultra-Orthodox are obsessed with sexual morality" and "little girls are taught from an early age that they are dangerous sexual objects."[31] Not only are they required to dress "modestly" from very early childhood, and to shave or clip short their hair and cover it from the time of puberty. Even their voices are (in Margalit's words) "considered sexual organs," such that little girls are forbidden to sing in the presence of anyone outside their immediate family.[32] Oddly, Margalit and Halbertal do not even raise the incompatability of all this blatant sex discrimination with any kind of liberal approach to group rights, in arguing for their public support for Ultra-Orthodox culture. But how could one argue, especially on liberal grounds, that girls who happen to be born into such families have the "right" to be burdened throughout their lives with the blame for their puritanically sex-obsessed culture? How could one claim that their "personality identities" are enhanced by the lifelong repression of their freedom to dress, play, move, and even sing, because of their status within the culture as "dangerous sexual objects"?

Thus it seems that Margalit and Halbertal's claim that group rights for illiberal cultures can be based on liberal arguments is unfounded, at least in the case of Israel's Ultra-Orthodox Jews. Next, I shall take up and critique an intermediate position in defense of the rights of minority cultures – that taken by Chandran Kukathas. Kukathas is clearly a liberal, in that he considers cultural communities important morally only because they are essential for the well-being of individuals, saying, for example: "[W]hat counts, ultimately, is how the lives of actual individuals are affected."[33] As I mentioned briefly, Kukathas, unlike Margalit and Halbertal, does not think that groups that act illiberally towards their own members should have special protections, subsidies, or privileges. The members' individual rights should suffice. On the other hand, he does argue that such groups should be "left alone" by the larger liberal society, with the result that their cultural practices will at least sometimes trump the individual rights that their members could otherwise claim as citizens of liberal states. Unlike many liberals, Kukathas does not think it necessary to human flourishing that persons be capable of autonomy or choice. He asks: "[W]hy make 'meaningful individual choice' the basis for supporting cultural membership – particularly when this value is not recognized as such by the culture in question?" Instead, his version of liberalism is content to assess the legitimacy of a culture or way of life by asking "whether the individuals taking part in it are prepared to acquiesce in it."[34]

The problem with this standard, however, is that it is susceptible to the very same objections that Kukathas himself raises in arguing against special supports and privileges for illiberal groups. There, he points out that groups are not homogeneous. They may, for example, be composed of elites and masses, and the interests of the elites and of the masses may differ considerably. There, he says, noting that the masses might rightly suspect those who claim to represent the interests of the group: "it is not always the case that the entire cultural community is eager, or even willing, to preserve cultural integrity at any price."[35] But this very reasonable objection applies just as well to Kukathas's conclusion that liberal societies should "leave alone" illiberal groups in dealing with their own members. Why should differences of interests and power differentials not worry us here, too? What if elites, or men, have interests different from those of masses, or women? What if the "acquiescence" by some in cultural practices stems from lack of power, or socialization into inferior roles, resulting in lack of self-esteem or a sense of entitlement? Such is often the case, I submit, within cultures or religions whose female members are devalued, and imbibe their sense of inferiority virtually from birth.[36] By neglecting this, Kukathas shows insensitivity to power differentials, and specifically to feminist concerns.

This is borne out when Kukathas gives, as one of his examples of tolerance of illiberal practices, coerced marriages within immigrant cultures in liberal societies. He concludes that, when and if appeal is made to the state, such marriages should be annulled, because entered into under duress. He says, though: "the immigrant community, though entitled to try to live by their ways, have no right here to expect the wider society to enforce those norms against the individual."[37] The message is that parents may coerce their daughters into marriages if they can get away with it. In this sense, the liberal state would "leave them alone" in their cultural practices. But if the young woman, with or without the help of others, is able to resist and to claim the state's protection, then the liberal state should protect her rights as a citizen. This is, of course, certainly better than taking the position that the state should not protect her rights and annul the marriage. However, in specifying that the community is "entitled" to try to live by its ways, it pays too little attention to the enormous scope for coercion that exists within the private sphere of family life. There are many ways in which a family can make it extremely difficult for a daughter to invoke her individual rights against the family's insistence on cultural practices by appealing to the state and therefore, in practice, resisting a coerced marriage.[38] We are left wondering why, on liberal premises and within a liberal society, should a cultural group be "entitled to try to live by their ways" if these ways violate the individual rights of their members? Why shouldn't the liberal state, instead, make it clear to members of such groups, preferably by education but where necessary by punishment, that such practices are not to be tolerated?

The concern with power within the sphere of family life leads right into my critique of the third version of group rights for minority cultures – the version, voiced by Will Kymlicka, that (by and large) confines such privileges and protection to cultural groups that are internally liberal. Kymlicka is the best and best-known contemporary defender of the rights of minority cultures. He bases his arguments for such rights on the rights of individuals, drawing from the works of John Rawls and Ronald Dworkin.[39] While neither claims to do so, Kymlicka argues that both can be read as providing some basis of support for minority group rights. In the case of Rawls, the key to this is that one of his "primary goods" – things we want, whatever else we want and whatever our fuller conception of the good – is the social basis of self-esteem or self-respect. Kymlicka argues that membership in a "rich and secure cultural structure,"[40] with its language and history, is essential both for the development of self-respect and for giving persons a context in which they can develop the capacity to make choices about how to lead their lives. And Dworkin, as Kymlicka points out, explicitly discusses the importance of one's cultural structure for enabling one to make informed decisions about how to lead one's life. Thus certain minorities need special rights, not to give them advantages, but to restore them to a position of equality with those in the dominant culture. For without such rights, their culture, unlike that of the majority, would be in danger of extinction. In his more recent defense of minority group rights, *Multicultural Citizenship*, Kymlicka stresses more exclusively the importance of culture as an essential basis for one's freedom, in the sense of the availability of "meaningful options" about how to live one's life. He explains: "Put simply, freedom involves making choices amongst various options, and our societal culture not only provides these options, but also makes them meaningful to us."[41]

On what conditions, then, are group rights justified? In *Liberalism, Community and Culture*, Kymlicka scatters such conditions throughout his argument. The one that is relevant in the context of this paper is that, except in rare circumstances of cultural vulnerability, the group must govern itself by recognizably liberal principles, neither infringing on the basic liberties of its own members nor discriminating among them on grounds of sex, race, or sexual preference.[42] This is of great importance to Kymlicka's justification of group rights, since a "closed" or discriminatory culture cannot provide the context for individual development that liberalism requires and because, without the condition, collective rights could result in subcultures of oppression within and aided by liberal societies. Kymlicka argues that those who deny that this requirement should hold fail to recognize the capacity of cultures to change, and confuse the preservation of the character of a cultural community at a given moment with its existence as a culture.[43] This conflation, and the consequently justified denial of some individuals' rights, is legitimate, Kymlicka suggests, only in certain rare circumstances, such as "too rapid change in the character of the culture," in which its very survival may depend on some restriction on its individual members – and then only temporarily.[44] He says, "this possibility…has no application to most cultures, and anyway does nothing to challenge the view that the long-term goal – the ideally just cultural community – is one in which every individual has the full range of civil and political liberties to pursue the life she sees fit."[45]

In *Multicultural Citizenship*, Kymlicka restates his position in the earlier book, that "the demands of some groups exceed what liberalism can accept," since "[l]iberalism is committed to (perhaps even defined by) the view that individuals should have the freedom and capacity to question and possibly revise the traditional practices of their community, should they come to see them as no longer worthy of their allegiance."[46] Here, as before, he denies group rights to cultures with "internal restrictions" on their members. They may not restrict their basic civil or political liberties. Moreover, he says, distinguishing his position from communitarian views about groups:

> The liberal view I am defending insists that people can stand back and assess moral values and traditional ways of life, and should be given not only the right to do so, but also the social conditions which enhance this capacity (e.g. a liberal education)…. To inhibit people from questioning their inherited social roles can condemn them to unsatisfying, even oppressive lives.[47]

Kymlicka points out that his requirement of internal liberalism rules out the justification of group rights for the "many fundamentalists of all political and religious stripes who think that the best community is one in which all but their preferred religious, sexual, or aesthetic practices are outlawed." For the promotion and support of these cultures "undermines the very reason we had for being concerned with cultural membership – that it allows for meaningful individual choice."[48] However, as I shall argue, his insisting on "the social conditions which enhance [the capacity for choice about the good life]" means that far fewer minority cultures than Kymlicka seems to think will be able to claim group rights under his liberal justification. There are many cultures that, though they may not impose their beliefs or practices on others, and though they may appear to respect the basic civil and political liberties of women and girls, do not in practice, especially in the private sphere, treat them with anything like the same concern and respect as men and boys, or allow them to enjoy the same freedoms. As I have suggested, discrimination against and control of the freedom of females, to a greater or lesser extent, is practiced by virtually all cultures, past and present, but especially by strictly religious ones and those in the present that look to the past – to ancient texts or revered traditions – for guidelines or rules about how to live in the contemporary world. Sometimes more patriarchal minority cultures exist in the context of less patriarchal majority cultures; sometimes the reverse is true. But, as I shall argue, the degree to which each culture is patriarchal and its willingness to change, in this respect, must be seen as relevant factors in the consideration of the justification of group rights from a liberal standpoint.

Clearly, Kymlicka regards cultures that discriminate overtly and formally against women, by denying them education, or the right to vote or to hold office, as not deserving special rights.[49] The problem is that, more often than not, sex discrimination is far less overt. In many cultures, strict control of women is enforced in the private sphere by the authority of either actual or symbolic fathers, often acting through, or with the complicity of, the older women of the culture. In many cultures in which women's basic civil rights and liberties are formally assured, discrimination practiced against women and girls within the household not only severely constrains their choices about the kinds of lives they want to lead, but can cause such decline in their basic well-being as to cause their deaths.[50] Sex discrimination in its milder forms is surely familiar in all cultures; it can assume such forms as women and girls being expected to take on all or by far the larger portion of the unpaid work of the family, being given the message that they are generally inferior to men and expected to defer to them, being encouraged on the one hand to conform to higher standards of beauty and grooming than boys, while on the other hand to conform to lower standards of academic achievement. And, as we all know, sex discrimination – whether severe or more mild – often has very powerful cultural roots.

Thus, although Kymlicka rightly objects to the granting of group rights to minority cultures on the grounds of overt sex discrimination, he does not register in his arguments for multiculturalism what he shows his awareness of in his chapter on feminism in *Contemporary Political Philosophy*: that the subordination of women is often far less formal and public than it is informal and private, and that virtually no culture in the world today, whether minority or majority, could pass his "no sex discrimination" test if it were applied in the private sphere.[51] Perhaps Kymlicka might respond to this by saying that I am expecting too much, or that to enforce the requirement that males and females be treated equally within the sphere of family life would be intolerably intrusive and quintessentially illiberal. I contend, however, that the very grounds of his liberal defense of group rights requires him to take these very private, culturally reinforced kinds of discrimination into account. For surely it is not enough, for one to develop self-respect and self-esteem, that one belong to a viable culture. Surely it is not enough, for one to be able to "question one's inherited social roles" and to have the capacity to make choices about the life one wants to lead, that one's culture be protected. At least as important to the development of self-respect and self-esteem as one's culture, is one's place within that culture. And at least as important to one's capacity to question one's social roles, is whether one's culture instills in and enforces on one particular social roles. To the extent that their culture is patriarchal, in both these respects the healthy development of girls is endangered.

As a result of this, it is by no means clear, from a feminist point of view, that minority rights are part of the solution; they may exacerbate the problem. In the case of a more patriarchal minority culture in the context of a less patriarchal majority culture, no argument can be made, on the basis of the enhancement of self-respect or the greater capacity for choice, that the female members of the culture have any clear interest in its preservation. While a number of factors would have to be taken into account in assessing the situation, they may be much better off, from a liberal point of view, if the culture into which they were born were either gradually to become extinct (as its members became integrated into the surrounding culture) or, preferably, to be encouraged and supported to substantially alter itself so as to reinforce the equality, rather than the inequality, of women – at least to the degree to which this is upheld in the majority culture. Other factors that would need to be taken into account include whether the minority group speaks a different language that requires protection, and whether the group suffers from prejudices such as racial discrimination. But it would take significant factors weighing in the other direction to counterbalance evidence that a group's culture severely constrained women's life choices or otherwise undermined their well-being.

I could name dozens of examples to illustrate this point, but will confine myself to referring to three cases or series of cases that have occurred within the last few years, mostly in the United States, and to a more general pattern of which the cases seem to be rather extreme examples.[52] It should be noted that all are examples from the cultures of recent immigrants – thus, groups that would qualify for fewer special group privileges under Kymlicka's guidelines than would those he calls "national minorities." They are, however, cultural groups that constitute nonimmigrant ethnic or religious minorities in some other parts of the world. The main reason I raise the examples is to show that culturally endorsed practices that are oppressive to women can often remain hidden in the private or domestic sphere, being perceived as private family concerns, and that it can take more or less extraordinary circumstances for them to become public or for the state to have the opportunity to intervene protectively.

The first case I shall mention happened in December of 1996, when a recent immigrant from rural Iraq went to the local police in a midwestern town, to report that his daughter was missing, and to seek their help in finding her. He explained that he had arranged for a Muslim cleric to marry his two daughters, aged thirteen and fourteen, to two male friends of his in their late twenties, and that subsequent to the marriages and their consummation, one of the girls had run away with her boyfriend, aged twenty. The girl was found and, to their enormous surprise, the father, the two husbands, and the boyfriend were all arrested on charges of statutory rape.[53] But in all likelihood, if the father had not himself involved agents of the state in the affairs of his family, what happened to these girls would never have become public. A second series of cases, mostly in California, involve the Hmong, whose culture endorses a practice called "marriage by capture," in which, after due consultation with her male relatives, the intended bridegroom kidnaps and rapes his chosen "bride." These cases come into public view as rape cases, in instances where young women who strongly resist such treatment and are perhaps helped by sympathetic relatives or friends, have the strength and knowledge to bring such charges.[54] A third type of case: recently, after years of attempts by Congresswoman Patricia Shroeder, the Congress finally outlawed the practice of clitoridectomy in the United States. Just a few months earlier, a court had granted asylum to the first refugee from such abuse in her native country, Togo. When the law was passed, a number of US doctors were quoted in the media (newspapers and public radio) saying they considered the legislation unjustified, since clitoridectomy was a "private" matter, to be decided by the child and her family, in consultation with the doctor.[55]

The more general pattern in many cultures that lies behind such examples is one of unequal treatment and control of young women that can have lifelong repercussions, and that originates in and is largely carried out in the domestic sphere. In a recent study of immigrants' experiences in schools in the United States, Laurie Olsen relates how young first-generation immigrant women in an urban California high school must negotiate between two cultures, often finding themselves contending with both the racism and exclusion they experience from the majority culture and the patriarchalism of their own cultures. Of the latter constraints, she writes:

> Religion and culture are key factors. Thus, the Vietnamese or Chinese girls handle the dilemmas differently from Mexican Catholic girls, and the young Hindu and Muslim women still differently. Meanwhile, each hears the clock ticking in terms of cultural expectations about marriage, having children, and assuming female roles. The young women are unsure if or when their parents will expect, allow, or

arrange their marriages, require help in assuming responsibility for siblings or arrange to send [them] back to their homeland to help with family responsibilities there or to begin a process of traditional marriage.[56]

Olsen found that while the young immigrant men tended to feel that they could choose between the two cultures of their bicultural setting, the young women felt they had to navigate between them, at considerable expense to themselves. It was the girls who, though living in the midst of a different majority culture, were expected to maintain and to reproduce in their marriages and their children their original cultural identity. As she concludes, "the immigrants in this study felt the greatest pulls back to the home culture with regards to gender identity, more than they did with any other aspects of finding their footing in a new land."[57]

In many of the cultural groups that now form significant minorities in the United States, Canada, and Europe, families place girls under significantly greater constraints than their brothers. They restrict their dress, participation in extracurricular and social activities, unchaperoned dating, further education, choice of employment, choice of spouse, and time of marriage. They expect them to take on significant domestic responsibilities, from which their brothers are exempt and which often interfere with the girls' progress at school. They not infrequently take them out of high school to marry, despite the girls' attachment to school as offering them not only some degree of temporary independence but also the education and earning power that could affect their negotiating power and their ability to avoid the abuse many of them fear within marriage. Frequently, the girls feel they must choose between "respecting their parents," which may include marrying the older cousins or family friends chosen for them – whom they may not know or like – and furthering their educations and developing work skills so as to retain more control over their own lives. And they know that their families may send them back to their countries of origin, disown them, or worse, if they try to make their own choices.[58]

It is, therefore, difficult to understand how these young women's cultures could be viewed as providing for them the background enabling them "to make informed decisions about how to lead their lives," "to make choices amongst various meaningful options," or "to freely pursue the life they see fit" – functions that liberal defenders of multiculturalism ascribe to cultures.[59] Serious constraints, rather than personal freedom or the capacity to make meaningful choices about their lives, make up a major part of their cultural heritage. While most of the immigrant girls value highly their attachment to their cultural roots, which they perceive their American peers as lacking, they are deeply distressed by the limitations on their present personal freedom and on their future choices in life that their families justify in the name of culture.[60] Even in the absence of cultural group rights, their families exert a tremendous pull on these young women and appear to have abundant power over them. It is difficult to imagine that the young women, if consulted, would endorse such rights, unless accompanied by the requirement that their cultural groups modify their attitudes toward their female members and loosen the controls they exert on them.

Thus it is clear that many instances of private sphere discrimination against, and control of, women on cultural grounds are never likely to emerge in public, where courts can enforce women's rights and political theorists like Kymlicka can label them as illiberal and therefore unjustified violations of women's physical or mental integrity. This reinforces the idea that, as I suggested above, one's place within one's culture is likely to be at least as important as the viability of one's culture, in influencing the development of one's self-respect and capacities to make choices about life. Establishing group rights to enable some minority cultures to preserve themselves may not necessarily be in the best interest of the girls and women of the culture, even when it is in the men's. Not surprisingly, as I have shown, this problem with Kymlicka's defense of the rights of groups that are, at least apparently, liberal is even more of a problem for defenses of group rights, or arguments that groups should be "left alone," that also apply to illiberal groups.

Several recommendations follow from the above argument that, in cases where more patriarchal cultures claim group rights within less patriarchal societies, women do not necessarily benefit from the granting of such rights. The conclusions reached here suggest that when liberal arguments are being made for the rights of groups, special care must be taken to look at intra-group inequalities. It is especially important to look at inequalities between the sexes, since they are likely to be in many respects less public, and therefore less immediately apparent and harder to discern than others. It is therefore of considerable importance that policies that aim to respond to the needs and claims of cultural minority groups take seriously the need for adequate representation of the less powerful members of such groups. Unless women – and, more specifically, young women, since older women often become co-opted into reinforcing gender inequality[61] – are fully represented in negotiations about group rights, their interests may be harmed rather than promoted by the granting of such rights.

Notes

1 I would like to acknowledge helpful comments on an earlier version of this paper from Brooke Ackerly, Dan Avnon, Lawrence Becker, Avner de-Shalit, Robert Reich, Elisabeth Hansot, Will Kymlicka, and two anonymous editors of *Ethics*.

2 Jacob Levy has recently provided an excellent classification of the types of rights commonly claimed by cultural minorities within nation states. "Classifying Cultural Rights," in Ian Shapiro and Will Kymlicka (eds), *Ethnicity and Group Rights, Nomos*, vol. xxxix (New York and London: New York University Press, 1997), pp. 22–66.

3 Charles Taylor, Amy Gutmann, and most of the other contributors to Gutmann (ed.), *Multiculturalism* (Princeton: Princeton University Press, 1994) use "multiculturalism" in both the ways I distinguish here, interchangeably. The same usage occurs in Yael Tamir, "Two Concepts of Multiculturalism," *Journal of Philosophy of Education*, 29, 2 (1995), pp. 161–72. I think this usage tends to cause confusion in these arguments, both because the relevant groups are not the same, though they overlap, and because situations that call for the recognition of previously neglected perspectives in educational curricula would seem to be distinct from (though, again, they may overlap with) situations in which the legal enforcement of group rights is justified, even when such rights conflict with or override certain individual rights.

4 George Kateb, "Notes on Pluralism," *Social Research*, Special Issue on Liberalism, 61, 3 (Fall, 1994), p. 512.

5 Will Kymlicka, *Multicultural Citizenship: A Liberal Theory of Minority Rights* (Oxford: Oxford University Press, 1995), p. 89. Kymlicka points out that this is what Margalit and Raz call a "pervasive culture" (Avishai Margalit and Joseph Raz, "National Self-determination," *Journal of Philosophy*, 87, 9 (1990), pp. 439–61).

6 Kymlicka, op. cit., n. 5, p. 76 (emphasis added).

7 For examples of such defenses, see Vernon Van Dyke, "The Individual, the State, and Ethnic Communities in Political Theory," *World Politics*, 29 (1977), pp. 343–69; "Collective Entities and Moral Rights: Problems in Liberal-Democratic Thought," *Journal of Politics*, 44 (1982), pp. 21–40.

8 All three problems are still apparent in Michael Sandel's recent *Democracy's Discontent* (Cambridge, MA: Harvard University Press, 1996). See review by Susan Moller Okin, *American Political Science Review*, 91, 2 (June 1997), pp. 440–42.

9 See Susan Moller Okin, "Feminism, Women's Human Rights, and Cultural Differences," forthcoming in *Hypatia*, Special Issue, 1998.

10 See for example Jane Flax, "Race/Gender and the Ethics of Difference: A Reply to Okin's 'Gender Inequality and Cultural Differences'," *Political Theory* 23, 3 (August 1995), pp. 500–10; Norma Claire Moruzzi, "A Problem with Headscarves: Contemporary Complexities of Political and Social Identity," *Political Theory* 22, 4 (November 1994), pp. 653–73; also the four references to clitoridectomy in Chandra Mohanty *et al.*, *Third World Women and the Politics of Feminism* (Bloomington: Indiana University Press, 1991), all of which consist of critiques of Western feminists for opposing the practice. I address this issue at greater length in "Feminism, Women's Human Rights, and Cultural Differences", op. cit., n. 9.

11 *Covenant for the New Millenium: The Beijing Declaration and Platform for Action* (Santa Rosa, CA: Free Hand Books, 1996), pp. 9–10.

12 Ibid., p.112.

13 See for example Kirti Singh, "Obstacles to Womens' Rights in India," in Rebecca J. Cook (ed.), *Human Rights of Women: National and International Perspectives* (Philadephia: University of Pennsylvania Press, 1994), pp. 375–96, esp. pp. 378–89.

14 Dorothy Dinnerstein, *The Mermaid and the Minotaur: Sexual Arrangements and Human Malaise* (New York: Harper and Row, 1976); Nancy Chodorow, *The Reproduction of Mothering: Psychoanalysis and the Sociology of Gender* (Berkeley: University of California Press, 1978); Walter J. Ong, *Fighting for Life* (Ithaca, NY: Cornell Univerity Press, 1981); Jessica Benjamin, *The Bonds of Love: Psychoanalysis, Feminism, and the Problem of Domination* (New York: Pantheon, 1988).

15 Arvind Sharma (ed.), *Women in World Religions* (Albany, NY: State University of New York Press, 1987); John Stratton Hawley (ed.), *Fundamentalism and Gender* (Oxford: Oxford University Press, 1994).

16 See Carol Delaney, *Abraham on Trial: Paternal Power and the Sacrifice of Children* (Princeton: Princeton University Press, 1997).

17 Ibid.

18 As Gita Sen and Karen Grown say, "Traditions have always been a double edged sword for women. Subordinate economic and social status, and restrictions on women's activity and mobility, are embedded in most traditional cultures, as our research over the last fifteen years has shown. The call to cultural purity is often a thinly veiled attempt to continue women's subjugation in a rapidly changing society," *Development, Crises, and Alternative Visions: Third World Women's Perspectives* (New York: Monthly Review Press, 1987), p. 76. See also Michelle Zimbalist Rosaldo and Louise Lamphere (eds), *Woman, Culture, and Society* (Stanford, CA: Stanford University Press, 1974), especially the Introduction and chapters by Rosaldo and Sherry Ortner; also Rosaldo, "The Use and Abuse of Anthropology: Reflections on Feminism and Cross-Cultural Understanding," *SIGNS: Journal of Women in Culture and Society*, 5, 3 (1980), pp. 389–417.

19 Jeremy Bentham, "Of the Influence of Time and Place in Matters of Legislation," in *Works*, ed. John Bowring (Edinburgh: William Tait, 1838), Part 1 (pp. 173–81, passim). Bentham, like many people writing about other cultures, is far more aware of the beam in the other culture's eye than the beam in his own (mistake intended). After all, contemporary English women lost their legal personhood upon marriage, and Bentham himself defended the exclusion of women from even observing Parliamentary debates on the grounds that their presence was too distracting to men engaged in such serious business as legislation. But he persists in thinking English women are far freer than those of the other cultures he describes.

20 Sebastian Poulter, "Ethnic Minority Customs, English Law, and Human Rights," *International and Comparative Law Quarterly* 36, 3 (July 1987), pp. 589–615.

21 Amy Gutmann, "The Challenge of Multiculturalism in Political Ethics," *Philosophy and Public Affairs*, 22, 3 (Summer 1993), pp. 171–204. Both Poulter and Gutmann use the generic, gender-neutral term "polygamy," but the practice they refer to is polygyny, marriage between a man and more than one

woman, and not polyandry, the reverse institution. There are far more examples of the former than the latter in the world today. To my knowledge, the
latter is not legally recognized or widely practiced anywhere at all.

22 For numerous examples of this, see Mahnaz Afghami (ed.), *Faith and Freedom:
Women's Human Rights in the Muslim World* (Syracuse: Syracuse University Press,
1995) and Valentine M. Moghadam (ed.), *Identity Politics and Women: Cultural
Reassertions and Feminisms in International Perspective* (Boulder, CO: Westview Press,
1994).

23 Avishai Margalit and Moshe Halbertal, "Liberalism and the Right to Culture,"
Social Research, 61, 3 (Fall 1994), pp. 491–510.

24 Chandran Kukathas, "Are There any Cultural Rights?," *Political Theory*, 20, 1
(February 1992), pp. 105–39.

25 Kymlicka, *Liberalism, Community, and Culture*, (Oxford: Clarendon Press, 1989);
Multicultural Citizenship, op. cit., n. 5.

26 Margalit and Halbertal, op. cit., n. 23, p. 491.

27 Ibid., quotation from p. 499. See also Frances Raday, "Religion,
Multiculturalism and Equality: The Israeli Case," *Israel Yearbook on Human
Rights*, 25 (1996), pp. 193–241. Raday's arguments and conclusions about the
justification for government support for the Ultra-Orthodox differ radically
from those of Margalit and Halbertal.

28 Margalit and Halbertal, op. cit., n. 23, p. 505; see also p. 502.

29 However, in private conversation, Moshe Halbertal indicated to me that he
and Margalit think everyone has a personality identity, of some sort or other
(Jerusalem, December 1996).

30 Margalit and Halbertal, op. cit., n. 23, pp. 493–4.

31 Avishai Margalit: "Israel: The Rise of the Ultra-Orthodox," *New York Review of
Books* (November 9, 1989), pp. 38–44.

32 This is also the reasoning behind the prohibition on women praying publicly in
a voice above a whisper. The danger is that the sound of women's voices will
sexually arouse men, which is strictly incompatible with the latter's praying.
This same attitude about women and sexuality is clearly apparent in a statement made by Mahammed Moujaher, spokesperson for the Association
Islamique en France, during the recent "affaire du foulard" in France.
Defending the girl's right to wear her headscarf to school, he said that it is
necessary "so that she be considered from the viewpoint of her intellectual or
spiritual capacities and not from that of her body, which is (it's a simple observation) an object of desire" ("Moujaher: Le voile, une obligation morale!," *Le
Figaro*, October 26, 1989). This male-centric notion – that a woman's body is
"an object of desire" – is what is behind virtually all religious restrictions on
the ways women may dress, as well, in many cases, as where they can and
cannot go, and in whose company, what kind of work they can and cannot do,
whether they can participate in important decision-making fora, and when and
where they can speak or sing, and so on. For a woman or girl, to be treated as a
sexual object rather than as a person whose body is her body, not someone
else's "object of desire," is an unacceptable breach of her basic rights.

33 Kukathas, op. cit., n. 24, p. 123.

34 Ibid., pp. 121 and 124.

35 Ibid., p. 114.

36 For an account of a people with a similar outlook on their status as slaves, see
Elinor Burkett, "God Created Me To Be a Slave," *The New York Times Magazine*

(October 12, 1997), pp. 56–60. But the situation of women in highly patriarchal cultures has added dimensions. I have recently outlined three explanations
for the lesser likelihood that the older women of such cultures will seek change
than the young: "[I]t is not easy to question cultural constraints that have had a
major impact on one's whole life;…the experience of such constraints may
produce a psychological need to enforce the constraints on the younger generation [of women];…[and] an older woman's relatively high status within the
group…results in part from her leading a virtuous life, which includes
successful enculturation of her children and grandchildren into their
prescribed gender roles," "Susan Okin Responds," *Boston Review*, 22, 5
(October/November 1997), p. 40. For an excellent lengthier consideration of
this issue, see Hanna Papanek, "To Each Less Than She Needs, From Each
More Than She Can Do: Allocations, Entitlements, and Value," in Irene
Tinker (ed.), *Persistent Inequalitites: Women and World Development* (New York:
Oxford University Press, 1990), pp. 162–81, esp. pp. 176–81.

37 Kukathas, op. cit., n. 24, p. 133.
38 For some extreme examples, see reference cited at n. 58 below.
39 Kymlicka relies less on these other theorists, especially Rawls, in *Multicultural
    Citizenship* than in *Liberalism, Community, and Culture*, partly because of changes
    he discerns in Rawls's relevant arguments.
40 Kymlicka, *Liberalism, Community, and Culture*, op. cit., n. 25, p. 165.
41 Kymlicka, op. cit., n. 5, p. 83.
42 Kymlicka, *Liberalism, Community, and Culture*, op. cit., n. 25, pp.168–72, 195–8.
43 His examples include Lord Devlin and Islamic fundmentalists; Margalit and
    Halbertal appear to me to make the same error.
44 Kymlicka, *Liberalism, Community, and Culture*, op. cit., n. 25, pp.170–71. His
    examples of when this has justifiably been evoked are cases in which the
    Indian community in Canada, "weakened (and denigrated) by the white
    majority," needs time for its cultural structure to recover "its normal healthy
    strength and flexibility" (p. 171).
45 Ibid., p.171.
46 Kymlicka, op. cit., n. 5, p. 152. There is one major change here from
    Kymlicka's position in his earlier book: now he argues that minority cultures
    that qualify as "national minorities" should not be required to be internally
    liberal. Thus, indigenous peoples and other groups whose lands were
    conquered should not be forced to practice internal tolerance and to forgo
    discrimination. I think his grounds for making this exception are unconvincing,
    but will set aside this aspect of his argument for now.
47 Kymlicka, op. cit., n. 5, p. 92.
48 Kymlicka, *Liberalism, Community, and Culture*, op. cit., n. 25, pp. 171–2.
49 See for example Kymlicka, op. cit., n. 5, pp. 153, 165.
50 See Amartya Sen, "More than One Hundred Million Women are Missing,"
    New York Review of Books (December 20, 1990).
51 Will Kymlicka, *Contemporary Political Philosophy: An Introduction* (Oxford:
    Clarendon Press, 1990), esp. pp. 239–62.
52 For more examples, see Okin, "Is Multiculturalism Bad for Women?," *Boston
    Review*, xxii, 5 (October/November 1997), pp. 25–8.
53 *New York Times* (December 2, 1996), p.A6.
54 For discussion of some such cases, see Deirdre Evans-Pritchard and Alison
    Dundes Renteln, "The Interpretation and Distortion of Culture: A Hmong

'Marriage by Capture' Case in Fresno, California," *California Interdisciplinary Law Journal*, 4, 1 (Fall 1995), and Catherine Trevison, "Changing Sexual Assault Law and the Hmong," *Indiana Law Review*, 27, 393 (1993).

55 *New York Times* (October 12, 1996), pp. A1 and A6. As the author, Celia Dugger, notes (p. A1): "Experts say there is no way of knowing how many girls are being genitally cut in the United States since the rite is usually performed privately."

56 Laurie Olsen, *Made in America: Immigrant Students in our Public Schools* (New York: The New Press, 1997), esp. Chapter 6: "Love and Marriage: How Immigrant Women Negotiate the Terrain Between Two Cultures." Quotation is from p. 124.

57 Ibid., p. 148.

58 Ibid., Chapter 6, passim. For the extreme case of immigrant families in Britain from rural Pakistan who kill or try to kill daughters who resist arranged marriages, see "Marked for Death, by their Families," *New York Times* (October 18, 1997), p. A4.

59 Quotations are paraphrased from Dworkin and Kymlicka, op. cit.

60 Olsen, op. cit., n. 56, Chapter 6, passim.

61 For some of the reasons for this, see n. 36 above.

7 Balancing unity and diversity in multicultural societies

Bhikhu Parekh[1]

I

Although the term culture is defined differently by different writers, I shall in this essay take it to refer to a way of understanding and organising human life. It involves a body of interrelated ideas concerning man's place in the world, the meaning and significance of human activities and relations and the nature of the good life, and a set of social practices based on them. A group of people sharing a common culture constitutes a cultural community. Most societies today are multicultural in the sense that they consist of several cultural communities.

It is sometimes argued that since cultural communities overlap, interact and influence each other, and cannot be neatly individuated and demarcated in a way that chairs and tables can be, it is misleading to talk of a plurality of cultures or a multicultural society. The argument is mistaken. The fact that cultural communities cannot be neatly demarcated does not mean that they lack individuality and cannot be distinguished, and this is all that is presupposed in calling a society multicultural. After all, languages, religions and forms of art too cannot be neatly demarcated, but that does not prevent us from saying that a society consists of different linguistic and religious groups or contains different artistic traditions.

Multicultural societies are not new to our age, for they existed in premodern times as well. Four factors, however, distinguish contemporary multicultural societies.

First, contemporary multiculturality is both wider and deeper than its premodern counterpart. Modern societies are internally differentiated and articulated into autonomous areas, each governed by distinct norms. Since people disagree about these norms, disagreements today extend to a much larger area of personal and social life than ever before. Furthermore, whatever their differences, almost all premodern societies were religious and broadly agreed on their important moral beliefs and practices. Thanks to the absence of a moral consensus and the unprecedented importance given to personal autonomy and choice, we today disagree far more deeply than ever before about such things as the best way to lead individual and collective lives and the meaning and significance of human activities and relations.

Secondly, contemporary multiculturality is more defiant. In premodern societies minority communities generally accepted their subordinate status, and remained confined to the social and even the geographical spaces assigned them by the dominant groups. Thanks to the spread of democratic ideas, they today demand not only equality of status, rights and power but also the equal opportunity to participate in and shape the collective life of the wider society. Although Turkey under the Ottoman empire had fairly large Christian and Jewish communities, and although it granted them far greater autonomy than is the case in any contemporary society, it was not and never saw itself as a multicultural society. It was basically a Muslim society which happened to have non-Muslim minorities. It followed Islamic ideals and was run by Muslims who alone enjoyed full rights of citizenship. Non-Muslims were *dhimmis* or protected minorities, enjoying extensive cultural autonomy but few political rights. Contemporary multicultural societies are different. Minorities demand and sometimes enjoy full equality of citizenship, including the right to shape the collective life. Refusing to be ghettoised and not content with cultural autonomy, they expect the wider society to accept them as equals and to recognise and reflect their presence in its major institutions and self-understanding.

Thirdly, contemporary multiculturality occurs in the context of increasing economic and cultural globalisation. Globalisation is a paradoxical phenomenon. On the one hand, it leads to homogenisation of ideas, institutions, ideals, moral and social practices, and forms of life. On the other hand it also encourages heterogeneity. It leads to migrations of individuals and even whole communities, and diversifies society. It also provokes fears about the loss of a society's identity, and stimulates resistance to external influences and rediscovery or invention of native traditions. Since a society is more likely to succeed in global competition if it has something distinctive to offer, globalisation also encourages cultural and other forms of diversity. Contemporary multiculturality is thus embedded in an immensely complex and apparently inexorable dialectical process, is heavily bound up with global economic and political forces, and is a more or less permanent feature of modern life.

Finally, modern multiculturality has developed against the background of nearly three centuries of the culturally homogenising nation state. In almost all premodern societies the individual's culture was deemed to be an integral part of his identity, in just the same way as his body was.

Cultural communities were therefore widely regarded as the bearers of rights, and were generally left free to follow their customs and practices. This was as true of the Roman as of the Ottoman and Habsburg empires.

The modern state represented a very different view of social unity. Born twins with and suffused by the spirit of individualism, it was a distinctly liberal institution. Accordingly, it set about dismantling long-established communities, and reuniting the 'emancipated' individuals on the basis of a collectively accepted and centralised structure of authority. It recognised only the individuals as the bearers of rights, and represented a homogeneous legal space made up of uniform political units subject to the same body of laws and institutions. As a territorially constituted entity, the modern state accommodated territorial but not cultural decentralisation. If any of its constituent units had different needs and required different kinds of rights, the demand was deemed to violate the principle of equality, and was either rejected or conceded with the greatest reluctance. Since the state required cultural and social homogenisation as its necessary basis, it has for nearly three centuries sought to mould the wider society in that direction. Thanks to this, we have become so accustomed to equating unity with homogeneity, and equality with uniformity, that we feel morally and emotionally disorientated by a deep and defiant diversity.

Although the mode of securing social unity represented by the modern state has much to be said for it, it is culturally specific, entails considerable moral and physical violence, and only makes sense in a society that is already or willing to become culturally and socially homogeneous. In a highly diverse society, it runs into all kinds of problems. Some groups of people might refuse to see themselves as individuals or as individuals only, and might press for communal or what are clumsily called collective rights. Again, different communities might have different needs, and demand different rights and powers. To rule these out in the name of a narrow definition of equality is not only to provoke resistance but also to deny them justice. Again, different communities might have different customs and practices, and might find it difficult to agree on a common body of laws concerning such culturally significant areas of life as marriage, divorce, adoption of children and inheritance of property. Karl Marx argued, no doubt with some exaggeration, that in a class-divided society the state cannot be economically impartial, and represents a subtle way of institutionalising and legitimising the rule of the dominant class. A similar danger exists in a culturally plural society, in which the allegedly neutral state can easily become a vehicle of enshrining the domination of a particular cultural community.

In the light of our discussion, contemporary multicultural societies are historically unique and raise problems not faced, at least in their acute form, by their premodern counterparts. Minorities today cherish and wish to preserve their ways of life and are particularly sensitive to cultural domination. However, no society can last long without some degree of cohesion and a sense of common belonging. Contemporary multicultural societies therefore need to find ways of reconciling the conflicting demands of diversity and unity. If they were to privilege unity, they would alienate minorities, provoke resistance and endanger the very unity they seek. If, on the other hand, they were to make a fetish of diversity and lack the power to regulate it, they would not be able to adjudicate the conflicting demands of their constituent communities and pursue common goals, and would risk disintegration.

How to reconcile the demands of cultural diversity and political unity – that is, how to create a political community that is both cohesive and stable and satisfies the legitimate aspirations of cultural minorities – has been a subject of considerable discussion ever since the rise of the modern state, and particularly during the past few decades. Broadly speaking, five models of integration have been canvassed. Although they naturally overlap, their organising principles and overall aims are quite different. For convenience I will call them proceduralist, assimilationist, bifurcationist, pluralist and the millet models.

II

According to the advocates of the proceduralist model, the best way to organise a multiculturalist society is to rest it on a foundation on which all its diverse communities can minimally agree. The state should become a purely formal institution requiring no more than that all its citizens agree upon and accept a common structure of authority. If the state were to pursue substantive goals of its own, it would end up preferring and enforcing a specific culture, thereby treating other cultures unequally and subjecting them to an unacceptable degree of moral coercion. Only a purely informal and culturally neutral state can both ensure political unity and give its citizens, including the minorities, the maximum possible freedom to live the way they like. The minorities remain free to embrace the majority way of life, or to do so only partially, or to evolve a synthetic way of life, or to lead totally isolated and self-contained lives, provided that they discharge their basic legal obligations to the state. This view was first articulated by Hobbes, and recently restated by Michael Oakeshott and in a different form by Robert Nozick.

For the advocates of the assimilationist model, no polity can be stable and cohesive unless all its members share a common national culture, including common values, ideals of excellence, moral beliefs and social practices. By sharing a common culture, they develop mutual attachments, affections and loyalties, and build up the necessary bonds of solidarity and a common sense of belonging. The state is a custodian of the society's ways of life, and has both a right and a duty to ensure that its cultural minorities assimilate or merge into the prevailing national culture. The choice before the minorities is simple. If they wish to become part of and be treated like the rest of the community, they should think and live like the latter; if instead they insist on retaining their separate cultures, they should not complain if they are treated differently. Rousseau, Herder and nationalist writers championed the assimilationist model, and its recent advocates include the new right in Britain, the United States and elsewhere.

Assimilation takes several forms. Some argue that minorities should adopt the majority way of life and live, think, speak and behave like the rest. Some go further and demand that they should also intermarry with and become socially and biologically assimilated into the majority community. Others go yet further and insist that they should 'love' and show unconditional 'loyalty' to the community, accept its history as 'their' history, 'identify' with its people, and so forth. This last form of assimilation, which claims the soul of the minorities and seeks their total identification, goes far beyond the ordinary forms of cultural and even biological assimilation and is best called nationalist assimilation.

The bifurcationist model adopts a half-way position between proceduralism and assimilationism, and advocates partial assimilation. Its advocates argue that proceduralism is too formal and empty to hold a society together, and that assimilationism is unnecessary, undesirable or both. All that is necessary for the unity of a polity is that its citizens should share a common *political* culture, including a common body of political values, practices and institutions. In the absence of a shared political culture the community lacks the ability to formulate and resolve differences, conduct political discourse and pursue common goals. As long as the minorities accept and become assimilated into the political culture of the community, they should remain free to live the way they like. The private–public distinction plays a crucial role in the bifurcationist model. The unity of the society is sought and located in the public realm, whereas diversity is left free to flourish in the private realm, which includes not just the family but also the civil society. In much of the British, the American and even the French literature, this model is called integration and distinguished from assimilation as sketched earlier. However this is linguistically arbitrary and obscures the fact that it involves at least partial assimilation and differs from the latter only in degree. In one form or another the model finds support in the writings of most liberals including John Locke, the founding fathers of the American republic and John Rawls, especially his *Political Liberalism*. Habermas's 'constitutional patriotism' is another modern version of it.

Although the pluralist mode of integration shares several features in common with the bifurcationist, it is quite different. According to its advocates the bifurcationist model has two basic disadvantages. It places the community's political culture beyond negotiation and revision, and expects minorities to become assimilated into it. Since the political culture does not reflect the presence and values of the minorities, they would not be able to identify with it and offer it their whole-hearted support. Furthermore, in a society dominated by a specific culture, minority cultures suffer from obvious structural disadvantages and need more than mere tolerance to flourish or even survive in the private realm.

Advocates of the pluralist approach therefore argue that rather than take the political culture of the community as given, it should be pluralised to acknowledge the presence and to embody the values and aspirations of minorities. The prevailing political values, practices, symbols, myths, ceremonies, collective self-understanding and view of national identity are all necessarily shaped by the community's history, and should be suitably revised to reflect its changing character. 'We' cannot obviously integrate 'them' so long as 'we' remain 'we'; 'we' must be loosened up to create a new common space in which 'they' can become part of a newly constituted 'we'. So far as the private realm is concerned, advocates of the pluralist model argue that the state should not follow a policy of cultural indifference or *laissez-faire* as that would work in favour of the dominant culture. If the otherwise disadvantaged cultural minorities are to survive and flourish, they need public recognition, encouragement and material support not in order to insulate them from change but rather to create conditions in which they can enjoy the security, self-confidence and broad equality necessary to make uncoerced choices. Such encouragement and support legitimise them in the eyes of the wider community, make them feel welcome and create a climate conducive to the flourishing of diversity. It is difficult to think of any classical writer who offers a coherent philosophical defence of the pluralist view. Among our contemporaries Charles Taylor, Will Kymlicka and Rainer Bauböck have proposed various versions of it.[2]

Finally, for the advocates of the millet model, individuals are above all cultural beings and embedded in specific communities, the ultimate source of what gives meaning to people's lives. All that deeply matters to them – their customs, practices, values, sense of identity, historical continuity, norms of behaviour and patterns of family life – are derived from their cultures. As an exclusively legal and administrative institution, the state has no moral status, and its sole *raison d'être* is to uphold and nurture its constituent cultural communities. It is not a community of communities, for that implies that it has an independent moral basis and its own distinct goals, but rather a union of communities, a bare framework within which they should be free to pursue their traditional ways of life and engage in necessary social, political and economic interactions.

Although this model of integration resembles the proceduralist view mentioned earlier in viewing the state as a largely formal institution with no substantive purposes of its own, it differs from it in requiring the state to maintain the existing communities. The state is expected not only to refrain from interfering with their internal affairs but also to recognise and institutionalise their autonomy. It should respect their internal structure of government, enforce their diverse customs and practices, fund their educational and cultural institutions, and so on. It is not directly related to its citizens but related through the mediating agency of its constituent cultural communities. Individuals owe their primary loyalty to their respective communities and derivatively and secondarily to the state.

Four general points need to be made about the five models of minority integration mentioned above. First, I have sketched only their basic outlines, assumptions and guiding principles, and ignored the diverse forms that each of them can take. As we saw, the assimilationist model can take cultural, biological and nationalist forms, and this is equally true of the others. Second, the five models are neither mutually exclusive, for they overlap in several respects, nor collectively exhaustive for, although they represent major ways of thinking about integration, others are not inconceivable.

Third, the five models are logically distinct in the sense that they conceptualise political unity, diversity and their relationship in very different ways. The first three privilege unity, and treat diversity as a largely residual, contingent and parasitic category confined to areas in which unity is not a central concern. The fourth model seeks to assign them equal status, while the fifth give pre-eminence to diversity and assigns unity only an instrumental and derivative value. Again, in the proceduralist model the state transcends society and takes no notice of its cultural composition. In the assimilationist model it is deeply embedded in the culture of the community and acts as its protector. In the bifurcationist model it is partly embedded in society and partly transcends it, actively assimilating the minorities in the political life but otherwise leaving them alone. In the pluralist model the state is dialectically related to society and both shapes and is shaped by the prevailing cultural diversity. In the millet view it is neither embedded in nor transcends its constituent cultural communities, but exists *outside* of them and lacks the independence required to shape them or to follow substantive purposes of its own.

The five models also entail different conceptions of citizenship. In the proceduralist model citizenship is purely formal in nature and consists in the enjoyment of a specific body of rights and obligations. In the assimilationist model it is grounded in the national culture and requires the citizen to share it as a necessary precondition of full membership of the political community. In the bifurcationist model the citizen is committed to sharing the political culture of the community. In the pluralist model citizenship has a plural cultural basis, and its citizens bring their diverse cultures to the public realm and enjoy a culturally mediated membership of the political community. The millet model privileges communal membership and has no or only a highly attenuated notion of citizenship.

Finally, the five models of integration are not just logical types but have all been tried out in history in one form or another, and simply or in combination with others. We can therefore form some idea of how they are likely to work in practice. The proceduralist model characterised the absolute monarchies and some early medieval kingdoms in Europe. The assimilationist model has dominated France since 1789, and the bifurcationist model is favoured in Britain and the United States, though the latter also has some features of the pluralist model. Pluralism has found favour in India, Canada, Australia and other self-consciously multicultural societies. Different forms of the millet model are to be found in the Ottoman empire, British administration of many of its colonies, traditional Muslim kingdoms and post-independence Lebanon.[3] Some elements of it are to be found in such countries as India and Israel as well.

III

In the previous section I sketched five different ways of constituting multicultural societies and reconciling the demands of political unity and cultural diversity. Some of them are clearly more coherent and realistic than others.

The proceduralist model is logically incoherent. Every political community has at least two basic features: it has a specific structure of authority which lays down who is entitled to take what decisions in the name of the community as a whole, and it makes and enforces collectively binding laws. Neither of these can be culturally neutral. The structure of authority refers to the community's mode of governance and can be devised in several different ways. It might be secular, theocratic or a mixture of the two. If secular, it might be based on universal franchise or on one limited by race, class or gender. The universal franchise might be equal or weighted in favour of the intellectual elite, as J. S. Mill had argued and as was the case in Britain until 1948. The system of elections might be direct or indirect, and represent the individuals, as liberals advocate, or corporate

groups, as Hegel, some pluralists and others have urged. The authority of
the state might be absolute or limited by a constitutionally prescribed
system of rights. The choice between these and other alternatives is based
on such factors as the society's views on how human beings should be
treated, the rights they should enjoy, the ways in which they generally tend
to behave, the nature and limits of political power and the proper functions of the law – in short, on its conception of the good life. Since every
structure of authority is thus embedded in and shaped by the wider
society's moral and cultural beliefs, it is biased towards a specific way of
life and cannot be morally or culturally neutral.

The laws and the policies of the state cannot be neutral either. Should it
allow slavery, polygamy, polyandry, incest, public hanging, euthanasia,
suicide, capital punishment, abortion, violent sports involving animals,
coerced marriages, divorce on demand, gay and lesbian marriages, uncon-
ventional sexual practices, rights of illegitimate children to inherit
'parental' property, inequalities of wealth, acute poverty, racial discrimination and so on? If it does not legislate on these matters, it indicates that it
does not consider them sufficiently important to the moral well-being of
the community to require a collective, uniform and compulsory mode of
behaviour. If it legislates, it takes a specific stand. In either case it presupposes a particular view of the good life. A morally and culturally neutral
state, making no moral demands on its citizens and equally hospitable to
all cultures, is logically impossible. And since every law coerces those not
sharing its underlying values, a morally and culturally non-coercive state is
a fantasy. Some states might, of course, be less partisan and hence less
coercive than others, but no state can be wholly free of moral and cultural
bias and of the concomitant coercion. Even the most liberal state which
institutionalises such values as liberty, free speech and the equality of the
sexes and races coerces those who are opposed to them.

Since the structure and exercise of political authority are informed by a
specific conception of the good life, the unity of a political community
cannot rest on procedural foundations alone. A political community
requires much more than an agreement on procedures, and the latter are
never morally or culturally neutral either. To ask minorities to accept the
prevailing structure of authority is therefore to require them to accept the
underlying conception of the good life, however thin and minimal it might
be. To suggest otherwise, as the proceduralist does, is to be disingenuous.

IV

The assimilationist model suffers from the opposite defects of the proceduralist. First, it is not clear *what* the minorities are to be assimilated into.

Although the moral and cultural structure of a society has some internal coherence, it is never a homogeneous and unified whole. It is made up of diverse and conflicting strands; consists of several different values and practices which can in turn be interpreted and related in several different ways, and so on. The assimilationist has to ignore all this in order to arrive at a homogenised and highly abridged and distorted version of the national culture, and then the minorities are assimilated not into the collective culture in all its richness and complexity but into an ideologue's crude and sanitised version of it.

Secondly, assimilation does not always work in practice. If people are left free to negotiate their relations with each other and have an incentive to do so, they might over time come closer and even perhaps assimilate into the dominant culture, as happened with the Anglo-Saxons, the Normans and the Danes in Britain. However, this is not always the case, and assimilation is unlikely to occur when it is rushed, imposed or both. The Jews have survived two millennia of Christian oppression; the ethnic and cultural minorities in the Soviet Union outlived the most brutal repression; and not all the assimilationist economic and cultural pressures of the United States have succeeded in creating a melting pot. Assimilation does not always work for a variety of reasons. Cultures are too deeply woven into the lives of their members for the latter to be fully conscious of their influence, let alone jettison them in favour of some other. Besides, most cultures are deeply embedded in or at least intertwined with religions, and outsiders cannot assimilate into them without changing their religion, which they are often most reluctant to do. Cultures are also extremely complex structures of beliefs and practices, and their nuances, unspoken assumptions and deepest sensibilities cannot be acquired unless one is born into them. Total cultural assimilation therefore requires biological assimilation, and that is not a price most outsiders are willing to pay. Again, assimilation is rarely able to redeem its promise of full and unqualified acceptance. Although one might after a strenuous effort assimilate into the dominant culture, there is always the danger that one's slightest difference or past background might be held against one by the whole or a section of the dominant cultural community. The demand for total assimilation springs from intolerance of differences, and for the intolerant every difference is one too many. Even the thoroughly assimilated German Jews fared no better than the unassimilated ones at the hands of the Nazis.

Thirdly, even if assimilation had a chance of success, it would not be an option available to liberal societies. The liberal society is committed to equal respect for persons. Since human beings are culturally embedded and derive their sense of identity and meaning from their cultures, respect for them implies respect for their cultures. To claim to respect them but not

their cultures is to abstract away much of what constitutes them as particular kinds of persons and matters most to them, and thus to respect them
not as unique human beings but as uniform atoms, not in their concrete
and historically articulated but abstract humanity. Respecting cultures does
not mean that they may not be criticised any more than respect for persons
places them above criticism, but rather that they should be understood and
appreciated in their own terms, that they should not be resented or
suppressed simply for being different, and that our criticisms of them
should be based on criteria they can comprehend and in principle share.
As we saw, assimilation requires direct or indirect and subtle or crude
forms of coercion and cultural engineering, and these too sit ill at ease
with such basic liberal values as choice and personal autonomy.

Finally, while the assimilationist rightly highlights the dangers of
cultural fragmentation and overstretching a society's capacity for tolerance,
he or she is blind to the importance of cultural diversity. Cultural diversity
increases the available range of options and extends the parameters of
freedom. It provides new sources of psychological and moral energy and
vitalises the wider society. It expands imagination and sympathy, cultivates
habits of tolerance, encourages a healthy competition between different
ways of life, adds colour and beauty to social life and deepens our appreciation of the nature and possibilities of human existence. Furthermore no
culture, however rich it might be, can ever embody all that is valuable in
human life. Since human capacities, values and aspirations conflict, every
culture realises some of them and neglects, marginalises or suppresses
others. Different cultures thus correct and complement each other, help
each become aware of its strengths and weaknesses, and encourage critical
self-reflection and mutual borrowing. In short, cultural diversity is a necessary condition and component of human freedom and well-being, and
represents a vital public good.

V

Although the bifurcationist model avoids many of the mistakes of the
assimilationist and has much to be said in favour of it, it suffers, as we
briefly noticed earlier, from two major defects.

First, every political community that has lasted a while develops a
widely shared body of values, practices, institutions, myths, conception of
its past and future, a mode of public discourse and so on, all of which
constitute its shared political culture or identity. Although the political
culture is deeply inscribed in its way of life and is the basis of its unity, it is
neither monolithic nor beyond criticism. It reflects and registers a historical
moral consensus and it needs to be reassessed when the consensus ceases to

exist. The dominant values and practices might discriminate against or bear unduly heavily on those who are new to it, or whose historical experiences are different, or who have long been marginalised and ignored. These groups might therefore rightly question their content or inner balance, and seek their redefinition. This is what women have done, and there is no reason why cultural minorities should be denied the right. If their criticisms of the political culture are justified, we need a public and open minded dialogue. To deny the dialogue on the ground that the revision of the community's political values threatens its stability or identity is both to misconceive their nature and to be unfair to their critics. The dialogue in such cases is never easy, both because the parties involved are likely to talk past each other on matters of deep differences, and because one or both parties are likely to prove intransigent on subjects of great moral and emotional significance to them. However, it cannot be avoided. And even if the dialogue does not always result in an agreement, it serves the vital purpose of giving the minorities a fair hearing, highlighting the limitations of the prevailing political culture, increasing mutual understanding and deepening the democratic process.

This is what happened in Britain and France respectively during the Rushdie and the *foulard* affairs. British Muslims asked why freedom of expression should be given a highly privileged status, why it should include the right to mock sacred beliefs, and why the prevailing balance between freedoms of speech and religions should not be reconsidered. The French Muslims questioned the *laicite* of the French state school, and wondered why the cross was allowed but not the headscarf and why the schools should deny harmless forms of cultural self-expression. In each case the wider society proved uncompromising and refused to reopen the questions it regarded as settled. Over time and after much democratic protest, a dialogue ensued, rendered difficult in Britain because of the unacceptable threat on Rushdie's life. Although it led to no changes in Britain and only to minor ones in France, it did generate debates both within and between the majority and minority communities, deepened their understanding of both themselves and each other, softened rigidities on both sides and placed new issues on the public agenda.

What is true of the community's values is also true of its political symbols, images, myths, ceremonies, view of its history and so on. They too reflect and reproduce a specific historical consensus, and need to be suitably revised when they are shown to misrepresent, distort or ignore the presence, experiences and contributions of marginalised groups, or to be out of step with the changes in the social composition of the community. Old and marginalised as well as newly arrived groups may rightly ask that the wider society should grant them suitable public recognition by incorporating their symbols, ceremonies, views etc. into the collective expressions of national life. Such recognition confers public legitimacy on their presence, recognises them as valued members of the community and facilitates their integration.

The second major defect of the bifurcationist model is that its attempt to combine a monocultural public realm with a multicultural private realm tends to subvert the latter. In every society the public realm enjoys considerable dignity and prestige, which generally far outweigh those of the private realm. When one culture is not only publicly recognised but is also embodied in political institutions and practices, it seems to be seen as the official culture of the community, an expression of its collective identity, and commands considerable state patronage, power and access to public resources. By contrast the excluded cultures come to be seen as marginal, peripheral, even deviant and inferior, only worth practising outside the public gaze of society and in the privacy of the family and communal associations. When the public realm prizes uniformity, diversity tends to be devalued throughout society.

Lacking prestige, power, resources and collective encouragement, minority cultures suffer from often unintended structural disadvantages and can only survive with the greatest of effort. Their members, especially the youth whose roots in their parental cultures are precarious and shallow, tend to feel nervous and take the easy path of uncritical assimilation. The older generation of Jewish immigrants have remarked that many of them used to feel deeply embarrassed when their parents spoke in Yiddish, dressed differently, wore yarmulke or performed their traditional religious, wedding and other ceremonies in public, and that over time they lost their language and suppressed public expressions of their culture. The sad phenomenon is still pervasive, as many minority parents and their children testify. A couple of years ago when I was travelling by train from London to Hull, I was sitting opposite an elderly Pakistani couple and next to their adolescent daughter. When the crowded train pulled out of King's Cross station, the parents began to talk in Urdu. The girl felt restless and nervous and began making strange signals to them. As they carried on their conversation for a few more minutes, she angrily leaned over the table and asked them to shut up. When the confused mother asked for an explanation, the girl shot back: 'Just as you do not expose your private parts in public, you do not speak in *that* language in public.' Though no one had presumably taught that to her, she knew that the public realm belonged to whites, that only *their* language, customs, bodily gestures and ways of talking were legitimate within it, and that ethnic identities were to be confined to the private realm. In a society dominated by one culture, tolerance alone is not enough to sustain diversity. Without necessarily endorsing all their values and practices, the wider society needs to find ways of welcoming and cherishing its minor cultures, giving them self-confidence and offering them such moral, cultural and material help as they need and cannot otherwise obtain. Since the bifurcationist model is generally inhospitable to all this, and leaves cultural diversity to survive precariously in the overpowering shadow of the dominant culture, the cultural minorities do not feel secure enough to interact with the dominant culture and retain, revise or reject their ways of life. They are left with only two alternatives, uncritical assimilation and an equally uncritical adherence to their traditional culture. Both are born out of fear and raise problems, and neither has much to commend itself.

VI

The pluralist model which affirms and encourages multiculturalism in both the public and private realms is free from the defects of its bifurcationist rival. It cherishes both unity and diversity and privileges neither. It also appreciates their interplay and does not assign them to separate and unrelated realms. The multicultural public realm that it seeks to create publicly recognises minority cultures as a legitimate and valued part of the community, and makes it easier for them to identify with it. In so doing it acquires both the right to demand their loyalty and support, and the power to mobilise their moral and emotional energies.

The multiculturally constituted public realm institutionalises and embodies diversity in the very self-conception of the community, making it as normal and valued a part of collective life as unity. By creating a climate conducive to diversity and by giving minority communities such help as they need and merit, the pluralist model minimises assimilationist pressures and enables them freely to negotiate their relations with the dominant culture. Some minorities might wish to assimilate completely; some might do so partially; yet others might prefer to experiment with different forms of intercultural synthesis. Whatever their decision, they arrive at it freely, without duress and coercion, and at their own pace. Since they do not feel nervously protective about their identity, they are likely to enter into a dialogue both with each other and with the majority culture. The dialogue requires them publicly to defend their beliefs and practices, thereby encouraging internal debates, making them more open and reflective, and promoting intercultural understanding and exchange. This helps create a rich, shared and multicultural private realm capable of underpinning an equally rich and multicultural public realm.

In the pluralist model unity and diversity are not confined to two separate areas of life but are dialectically related and reinforce each other.

When unity and diversity are disjoined, unity remains abstract and devoid of energy, and diversity, lacking a regulative principle, encourages fragmentation and isolation. The pluralist model avoids this mistake. The unity of the community here is not formal and abstract and located in a transcendental public realm; rather it is grounded in a multiculturally constituted public realm which both sustains and is in turn sustained by a multiculturally constituted private realm. There is no hiatus, no clash of organising principles, between the two realms. Both alike cherish diversity and unity, and the spirit of multiculturality effortlessly flows from one to the other within the framework of a shared and plural collective culture.

The pluralist model is not without its difficulties. It is based on a vision of society in which different cultural communities, interacting with each other in a spirit of equality and openness, create a rich, plural and tolerant collective culture affirmed alike in all areas of life, including and especially the political. The vision is not easy to realise and has its own problems. Some cultural communities might not be open and experimental and might jealously guard their inherited identities; for example, the Amish in the United States and some aboriginal peoples in Canada, Australia and elsewhere. A multicultural society should respect their wishes, for they generally cause no harm, do not threaten political unity and in their own different ways add a valuable dimension to social life. Their values and practices differ from and sometimes offend against those of the majority, but they should be tolerated subject to such collectively agreed minimum principles as respect for human life and dignity. Even those communities that are more hospitable to intercultural interaction do not always find it easy to accept the choices of their members. They might frown upon dissenters and even subject them to social sanctions. The wider society needs to respond to the resulting tension in a judicious and balanced manner. It cannot ignore the dissenters altogether, but nor can it allow their rights always to trump the community's desire to preserve itself. This is a difficult issue, and no plural society has as yet found ways of resolving it.

The pluralist model presupposes that individuals not only do not feel culturally threatened by differences, but take positive delight in them and resist the temptation to seek premature closure and consensus. This in turn calls for tolerance, love of diversity, willingness to enter into a dialogue with other beliefs and practices, absence of dogmatism and a measure of self-criticism. These and related virtues, which lie at the very basis of the pluralist model, are not widely found even in mature liberal societies. Their cultivation requires a radical restructuring of educational, political, cultural and other institutions – not an easy task.

VII

We may now turn to the millet model, whose defects are too obvious to need elaboration. It rests on the belief that human beings are culturally embedded and find their fulfilment in their membership of specific cultural communities. This is a highly static and impoverished view of human beings, for they need access not only to a stable cultural community but also to a variety of cultures in order to appreciate the specificity and correct the inadequacies of their own. That in turn requires a democratic political community accommodating diversity within a framework based on common citizenship, shared values and so forth. Since the millet model fragments society into neatly isolated communities, reinforces their inherited prejudices and mutual suspicions, and prevents the emergence of a shared collective life, it rules out an interactive democratic community and is inherently unsatisfactory. The Ottoman millet system worked for centuries only because the imperial form of government ruled out a shared public life and treated non-Muslims as second-class citizens. It had great virtues, including a remarkable record of religious toleration that put Europe to shame, but it also froze religious communities, rigidified their internal structures and arrested the growth of common bonds and a shared political life.

The millet model suffers from other defects as well. Individuals belong to several communities, such as the ethnic, the religious and the cultural, which do not necessarily coincide, thereby making it difficult to decide which community to protect. Even when a cultural community can be individuated, its members rarely take an uniform view of its identity. Protecting its autonomy often institutionalises the rule of the dominant elite and denies the dissenters redress. Again, the millet model might make some sense in an undeveloped agricultural economy but none in an industrialised society, whose requirements of constant mobility and close interactions between groups break through the communal barriers and necessitate a common body of rules, norms and practices. To grant a measure of self-government to such cohesive communities as the aboriginal peoples and the Amish is one thing; to make this the organising principle of the entire political community is altogether different.

VIII

In the light of our discussion it should be clear that in my view the pluralist model better reconciles the legitimate demands of unity and diversity than the others, and is best suited to a multicultural society. The proceduralist view offers an incoherent account of the unity of the state and leaves

diversity to the precarious mercy of the dominant culture. The assimilationist model ignores the cultural claims of minorities, takes an impossibly
stringent view of integration and threatens the unity of the state both by
locating it in a non-existent uniform national culture and by provoking
minority resistance. Since the bifurcationist model does nothing to relieve
the alienation of cultural minorities from the public realm, it is unable to
command their enthusiastic support and cannot provide a stable basis of
unity. And since it does nothing to reduce the structural disadvantages of
its minority cultures, it not only discourages diversity in the private realm
but also runs the risk of encouraging fundamentalism among its nervous
minorities. As for the millet model, it clearly offers the least coherent and
plausible account of the unity of the state. And although it appears to be
hospitable to diversity, that diversity remains static, frozen, isolated and
sometimes oppressive, and hence inherently fragile and irrelevant to industrialised democracies.

Although the pluralist model of integration is better than the rest, it
cannot be held up as a model for all societies. A society has to start from
where it is and choose a model that best coheres with its history, traditions,
self-understanding, moral and cultural resources, level of economic and
political development, the nature, number and demands of its cultural
minorities, and so forth. If a society consists of long-established and mutually suspicious communities with no tradition of co-operative action, it
might be wiser to opt for some version of the proceduralist or the millet
model, at least in the short run. Or if an otherwise open and plural society
includes an economically and culturally self-contained minority that does
not wish to integrate with the rest of society, as is the case with the Amish
in the United States and the aboriginal peoples in many parts of the world,
they should be left free to govern themselves subject to a body of minimum
and collectively agreed principles. Again, if an otherwise liberal society
were to include an insecure minority, as was the case with Indian Muslims
in the aftermath of the country's partition and as is the case with the Arab
minority in Israel, it makes both moral and political sense to win over its
trust by respecting its customs and practices, funding its educational and
cultural institutions, and in general protecting its cultural space within a
modified millet model. All these are obviously second best alternatives, and
the ultimate hope should be that the various communities would over time
feel relaxed and trust each other enough to evolve an appropriate pluralist
model in which they can freely retain, revise, enrich or reject their respective cultures as they please within an open, plural and commonly shared
collective culture.

IX

Although different multicultural societies need to evolve their own appropriate models of integration suited to their history, traditions, demographic composition, political requirements and so on, their decisions ought to be guided by two general principles, namely respect for cultural diversity and fostering a spirit of common belonging and citizenship.

As argued earlier, the case for respect for cultural diversity rests on three grounds. First, since individuals are culturally embedded and give meaning to and structure their personal and social lives in terms of the view of the world derived from their culture, respect for them entails respect for their cultures. Second, cultural diversity is valuable for the society as a whole. It adds a valuable aesthetic dimension to the collective life, widens the range of moral sympathy and imagination, corrects the inescapable biases of each culture, deepens appreciation of the nature and possibilities of human existence, encourages critical self-reflection, and in these and other ways promotes human freedom, rationality and well-being. Third, respect for cultural diversity gives the minority communities a sense of security, prevents a moral panic and creates a relaxed environment in which they can both affirm and revise their identities in their uncoerced interactions with others. It is generally the best way to avoid the twin evils of uncritical assimilation and mindless fundamentalism.

Respect for cultural diversity can take many forms. Minority communities may be allowed to run their internal affairs themselves and to set up appropriate cultural, educational and other institutions with such state help as they need and may legitimately ask for. Respect for cultural diversity also requires due recognition of cultural differences in the formulation and enforcement of public policies and laws. If a cultural community is territorially concentrated, its autonomy might require that it should enjoy rights and powers not available to other communities. When the Meach Lake Agreement in Canada acknowledged Quebec as a 'distinct society' and gave it powers not available to other provinces, when the constitution of Malaysia granted Borneo a 'special status', or when India conferred special powers and privileges on some north-eastern states and the state of Kashmir, the countries concerned showed considerable political wisdom. In terms of the standard theory of the state advocated by the European legal and political philosophers, these countries were open to the charge of violating the principle of equality. However, the authors of these provisions rightly concluded that formal equality sometimes led to substantive inequality and violated the principle of justice, and that even justice, though a very important political value, needed to be reconciled with such other political values as stability, civil order, promotion of diversity and giving the citizens a cultural stake in the state.[4]

While ensuring its constituent communities secure cultural spaces, a multicultural society also needs to develop a common sense of belonging and unity among them. Otherwise it lacks the capacity to act as a collective agent, resolve their inescapable conflicts, develop the necessary mutual trust and goodwill among them, and the confidence to tolerate and enjoy deep diversity. Paradoxical as it may seem, the greater the range and depth of diversity in a society, the greater is the need for a sense of unity and common belonging. Its citizens must feel sufficiently committed to each other to feel confident that, no matter what their differences, they wish to continue to live together and would do nothing to destroy the society. Unlike the nation state which bases its political unity on cultural uniformity, a multiculturally constituted state needs to base its unity on its diversity, to rest its singularity on its gracefully accepted multiplicity. This is a demanding task requiring a break with the habits of thought encouraged by the three centuries of the nation state and a bold and imaginative exploration of alternative ways of conceptualising and organising political life. Unless we face it with courage and wisdom, there is no hope for multicultural societies and, since most societies today are multicultural, for our volatile and violent age.

Notes

1 I am grateful to Dan Avnon, Avner de-Shalit and Rainer Bauböck for their helpful comments on this essay.
2 For Charles Taylor's 'The Politics of Recognition', see Amy Gutmann (ed.), *Multiculturalism and the 'Politics of Recognition'* (Princeton: Princeton University Press, 1922). See also Will Kymlicka, *Multicultural Citizenship: A Liberal Theory of Minority Rights* (Oxford: Oxford University Press, 1995); David Miller, *On Nationality* (Oxford: Oxford University Press, 1995); Rainer Bauböck, *Transnational Citizenship* (London: Edward Elgar, 1994); and Jeff Spinner, *The Boundaries of Citizenship* (Baltimore, Johns Hopkins University Press, 1994).
3 Under the millet system Muslims, Christians and Jews were self-governing units enjoying the right to impose their religious laws on their members, with the help of the state when necessary. The system lasted for nearly five centuries and was known for its humane toleration of group differences. Some of the Ottoman jurists and political theorists offered fascinating defences of the system and advanced ingenious theories of communal rights.
4 For a fuller discussion of national identity, see my 'Discourses on National Identity', *Political Studies* (September 1994), and 'The Concept of National Identity', *New Community* (April 1995).

Part III

Alternatives to liberalism

How feasible?

Introduction

Liberalism may not be a perfect theory. But is it not the best we have? The final part of this book discusses alternatives to liberalism. However, it is important to note that all the following discussions take place from within the liberal discourse. All three authors ask whether to redress weaknesses or injustices associated with liberal practices necessitates abandoning liberalism.

Frank Cunningham puzzles over the eruption of group hatreds in societies that have undergone democratisation. Without rejecting such core liberal values as pluralistic toler-ance and respect for individual autonomy, Cunningham considers mere advocacy of these values insufficient to address such major social problems as persisting ethno/national enmity and violence. Thus Cunningham adds a perspective not addressed by Stephen Holmes in his analysis of the impoverishment of liberal democracy in weak states. In approaching democracy Cunningham adopts a nuanced version of popular sovereignty.[1] Like Bhikhu Parekh, Frank Cunningham also places a premium on pluralism as the essen-tial feature of liberalism. However, he transfers pluralism from liberalism to democracy, especially in contexts of group hatreds. Cunningham's turn to democratic, rather than solely liberal, solutions is an extension of his emphasis on individuality as embedded in relationships, that is, groups. Indeed, close attention to specific social and political contexts, including community traditions, is required if we are to relate liberalism to the expansion of democracy. Therefore Cunningham resists a propensity within liberalism to set universal values against community-specific tradition. Indeed, he seeks those formal institutions and informal practices which stand the best chance of enhancing collective self-determination in specific circumstances. By emphasising the plurality of group attachments, Cunningham shares Moller Okin's criticism of autocratic groups and the reluctance of liberals to criti-cise these groups' ideas of the good. But unlike Moller Okin, who anchors her alternative to autocratic groups in a return to the classical liberal individual, Cunningham believes that it is possible to put forward a new notion of group affiliation, grounded in democratic internal organisation.

Ronald Beiner also wants to enhance political membership and citizenship. He thus shifts the focus on liberalism's weaknesses from discussion of economic inequality to questions of civic equality. He considers liberalism's primary weakness to be its diluting of the citizen's sense of responsibility to, and emotive solidarity with, fellow citizens. Liberalism at its worst is, for Beiner, a wasteland of sameness, of 'tastes, of cliched perceptions of the world, of the glum ennui, with which one reconciles oneself to the monolithic routines of our world'.[2] Beiner's advocacy of socialism as a viable alternative to liberalism is based on a redefinition of both liberalism and socialism. From liberalism he picks up its openness to participation and already established frameworks for channelling organised interests. From socialism he takes its sensitivity to the misery and tribulations of others, and, in addition, socialism's commitment to mobilisation over extended periods of time. So socialism can exploit the liberal democratic structure to enhance democratic participation, and consequently civic virtues. In this meeting of liberalism with socialism Beiner ends up anticipating a third form of political association, namely a new republicanism.

It is often thought that another alternative to liberalism is communitarianism. But David Miller thinks that communitarianism should not be distinguished from liberalism, but rather from individualism, because all communitarians claim that the individual cannot be detached from his or her social and other contextual affiliations. Thus the uniting element of all communitarians is that they are anti-individualistic in their philosophical anthropology. But Miller goes on to claim that the reason 'communitarianism' as such is not an alternative to liberalism, is that the concept is too wide, embracing too many and quite distinct notions of the good. Therefore he distinguishes between three versions of communitarianism, one of them being 'left communitarianism', commensurable with a community-based version of socialism. In the latter Miller finds a feasible alternative to liberalism. Left communitarianism is formed on the basis of egalitarianism, and in addition the community is self-determining rather than subject to the authority of tradition. As such he shares Cunningham's assumption, insofar as 'people flourish best when they are associated together on the basis of equality, and have a deep interest in shaping their environment collectively'.

Notes

1 See also C. B. Macpherson, *Democratic Theory* (Oxford University Press, 1973).
2 R. Beiner, *What's the Matter with Liberalism?* (Berkeley: University of California Press, 1992), p. 23.

8 Group hatreds and democracy[1]

Frank Cunningham

'Group hatreds' refers to situations where two or more groups of people, none of which is on the face of it objectively hateful, seem motivated by mutual hatred. Examples may be found among some of the Irish Protestants and Catholics, Hindus and Muslims in Southeast Asia, Bosnian Serbs, Croats, and Muslims, and Jewish and Arab antagonists in the Middle East. Sources of much pain and suffering, group hatreds also pose a severe threat to democracy. Group hatreds are marked by defiantly open and typically violent intolerance. Hence, they are inimical to pluralism, which nearly all democrats now see as an indispensable component of any modern democracy.[2] A major political-philosophical task, then, is to seek ways consistently with democratic practices, cultures, and institutions that group hatreds might effectively be confronted. This includes trying to head off hostilities (like those between Franco and Anglo communities in my own country) before they turn into full-blown hatreds.

Some philosophers have addressed virulent hatreds, and there is much to learn from philosophical enquiries regarding the Holocaust, anti-Black racism, sexism, or homophobia, to take prominent examples. The situations with which I am concerned are those where enmity is both mutual and, insofar as one is thinking of entire populations and not just individual villainous members, unjustified, but about these situations there is little specifically philosophical literature. To be sure, there is much social-scientific, political, and historical material. However, my philosophical biases lead me to think that conceptual interrogation of the terrain is required in order to make fruitful use of such studies. In what follows I shall analyse the topic into three (interpenetrating) components: identification of the phenomenon in question; approaches to explanation; and prescriptions. In each category I shall advance tentative hypotheses rather than defend fixed conclusions.

What is group hatred?

The first question to ask is how many phenomena we are confronting. On general Wittgensteinian grounds I am assuming that group hatred is a 'family concept' such that no two instances of it are identical. It might be further argued that there is not even a single family, that animosities between Irish Catholics and Protestants, Hutus and Tutsis, Jewish Israelis and Palestinians, and so on, have so little in common that they ought not to be considered together at all. But it seems to me that there are some core similarities. Hostilities are fuelled by melded appeal to real grievances and mythic constructions; religious traditions are invoked despite the sparse and never unequivocal justification for enmity in their central texts; small differences are exaggerated and large similarities are ignored; each involves a tragic element as people are drawn involuntarily into self-destructive combat; territoriality looms large; violence takes the form of desecration; children and women are special and intended targets.

Another important question is suggested by the rational choice theorist Russell Hardin who challenges the view that violent group conflicts involve hatred at all. The thesis of his *One for All* is that when people find themselves 'coordinated' in a religious, ethnic, linguistic, or national group, that is, when they are acting in concert and nonconflictually with others in the group, they come to identify with it. This is individually rational because coordination gives the group power in competition with other groups for desired resources. Often egged on or even initially coordinated by self-serving leaders in search of political or economic power, groups come into increasingly hostile conflict, and people find themselves drawn into violence as an unintended consequence of their rationally self-interested group identifications.[3]

Hardin may well be right to reject the view he attributes to Robert Kaplan that violent conflicts are nothing but expressions of primordial hatreds handed down through the generations.[4] But, in addition to other deficiencies in his alternative account,[5] Hardin fails to exorcize hatred from the field of violent conflict. Thus, discussing the fictionalized account by Prosper Mérimée of conflict between the Corsican della Rebbia and Bariccini families, he asks:

> Why did the two Corsican families become enemies? This is probably not as interesting a question as that of how their enmity was maintained and what course it took. Once they were coordinated on enmity by some more or less random event, they were likely to continue in the convention of enmity because neither could trust the other to write off past behavior in their culture of the vendetta.[6]

This complicates Hardin's account. Granting that initial familial identification is innocuous, once the enmity becomes itself a 'coordinating' feature of groups, it is implicated in the identities of the individuals in question, and hostility has returned to a central role.

A virtue I see in Hardin's theory is its caution against inferring from the fact that hatreds are to be found in the *descriptions* of violent group conflicts that therefore hatred must also be their basic *explanation*. Still, it seems to me that hatred – taken to involve intense and all-consuming animosity – must figure with other emotions, such as fear or vengefulness, as among the perpetuating causes of violent group conflicts. Otherwise it would be hard to explain how the violence is so pervasive and sustained and how it persists even when obviously destructive of perpetrators as well as recipients of violent behaviour. Recognizing a role for hatred, however, does not yet give us a characterization of its group nature or an understanding of the salient features of the attitude from the point of view of individuals themselves.

Unless a strange theory of social groups is embraced, it must be recognized that groups *per se* do not hate (or dislike, or fear, love, and so on). So to attribute hatred to a group must be to say that individuals in the group harbour attitudes of animosity towards another group. Since one is still confronting a social phenomenon, this need not mean that each and every member of a group exhibits such an attitude or that the attitudes are held with the same intensity. This raises some murky problems in the philosophy of the social sciences, but they are no more severe in the current case than in more mundane ones, such as in describing a group as traditional or anomic. I shall take it that a group displays hatred towards another group to the extent that those claiming to act on behalf of the group can count on sufficient popular support to sustain threatening or destructive activities over a prolonged period of time and in spite of the opprobrium of third parties or the dictates of self-preservation or common sense morality.

A more intriguing feature of the ontology of group hatred concerns its intensional object. Interviews with people implicated in violent conflict often elicit the claim that they do not hate this or that individual from an opposing group, or even that, with the exception of a minority of perpetrators of atrocities, they do not hate *any* of the individuals, with whom they may sympathize for the bad luck of having been born into their group. Rather, it is the group itself that is hated. In this respect group hatred resembles racism of the sort found, for example, in communities void of members from discriminated against people.

Finally, I think it useful to try identifying what I shall call a 'phenomenological centre' of group hatred. By this I mean something more attitudinal than the many ways that group hatreds may manifest themselves, such as those common elements listed above (exaggeration of differences, territoriality, desecration, and so on), and closer to ordinary consciousness than putative psychodynamic causes. Rather, a phenomenological centre will be the *explanandum* for which psychodynamic explanations are sought and in terms of which the many ways that group hatreds are expressed are organized into a world view. I recognize that phenomenological centres may be complex or different for different groups, but in the interests of generating a provisional hypothesis, I shall seek one such common centre.

A putative example gleaned from Hardin's account might be superciliousness.[7] Such an attitude may be a suitable candidate for a phenomenological centre of a racist world view, but I do not think it appropriate to group hatreds as here conceived. That racist-like feelings of superiority often accompany such animosities there can be no doubt, but the enmity could be just as strong and pervasive if the detested group was seen simply as alien – as a threatening other. I have the impression that superiority more typically figures in the rhetoric of justification for violent behaviour than as a point of reference around which such behaviour is made comprehensible to those engaged in it. Better candidates for this purpose are vengefulness and fear.

According to Réné Girard, a tendency towards mutually destructive cycles of revenge is at the heart of group conflict, and, indeed, of civilization itself. Sophistication of such things as scapegoating rituals combined with state control serve to contain downward spirals of vengeful violence, but the 'law of retribution' persists and if 'we are still strangers to this law it is not because we have managed to transcend it, but because its application to the modern world has been indefinitely postponed, for reasons unknown to us'.[8]

As I read Girard, revenge plays something like the role of what I am calling a phenomenological centre. In his *Violence and the Sacred*, Girard is less concerned to identify the deep causes of tendencies to violence than to address resulting vengeful stances, which, once recognized, make sense of a multitude of otherwise heterogeneous phenemena: rites and rituals, religion and magic, sacrifice, tragic literature, the rule of law, and more.[9] Whether this hypothesis does make all these things cohere is a matter of continuing debate especially among anthropologically minded classics scholars. Relevant to the current exercise, however, is whether or how it makes sense of a world of violent conflict to someone embroiled in it. Girard's most persuasive phenomenological descriptions are limited to primitive societies where the organizing principle is not strictly revenge but apprehension of mutually destructive revenge.[10]

This suggests to me that revenge is not quite suitable as a pervasive centre of conflictual world views. In the example, it figures not as an orienting attitude but as a cause of one, localized such attitude. Alternatively, it can be imagined that once a wrong has been committed, this might spark vengefulness, but it might also spark fatalistic submission or a high-ground attitude of turning the other cheek. In each of these cases it will be essential that the wrong, whether objectively based or imagined, is perceived *as* a wrong by the (self-designated) injured party. Similar considerations pertain to fear. It is true that the behaviour of people gripped by group hatreds often or perhaps always exhibits classic paranoia with its odd combination of narcissism and anxieties of impotence. But such attitudes are typically not transparent to the paranoic, much less points of reference for interpreting their social world. Straightforward fear of a loathed other is no doubt a major and often justified reaction to conflict once begun, but it need not be a proximate motivation, and fear alone is as compatible with a stance of flight or supplication as with one of combat.

My candidate for a phenomenological centre of group hatred – which might be taken alone or in combination with vengefulness and/or fear – is *blame*. People enmeshed in such relationships view the hated group as morally responsible and hence blameworthy for misfortunes they endure in common with other members of their own group: economic hardship, frustrated political self-determination, erosion of their culture, and the like. Revenge is not a response to specific slights or atrocities, but to a deliberate attack on one's whole way of life or at least to apathetic complicity in its demise. Fear is not for the well-being of individual group members but for the continuing existence of the group itself.

In most if not all instances of group hatred, power imbalances and histories of oppression provide a basis for resentment and fear by members of oppressed groups, and when animosities spark cycles of retributive violence, fear on the part of members of the more powerful groups is also partly justified. In these circumstances, blame may be entirely justified when it is directed towards activities and policies of group leaders or perpetrators of atrocities. However, when indiscriminately directed towards all the members of a group, blame becomes instead a perpetuating source of hatred.

Sometimes (nearly) entire populations *are* blameworthy, as when its members generally harbour racist or other discriminatory attitudes or facilitate atrocities. Whites in apartheid South Africa or populations which were at best culpably passive regarding the Holocaust or other genocidal campaigns come to mind as examples. Recognizing that the line between these situations and the mutually unjustified enmity I am addressing is not sharp, I believe that the two situations confront one with different problems and call for different analyses. In the apartheid and Holocaust type cases such things are required as assurance that criminals are brought to justice, provisions for redress, forums for acknowledgement of complicity, and criteria and means for appropriate forgiveness.

With respect to mutually unjustified indiscriminate hatred, focussing on blame as a phenomenological centre helps to explain extreme intolerance. Not only is it permissible, but intolerance is mandated. Since it is not immoral individuals from an opposing group that are blameworthy, but the group itself, care must be taken to distance oneself, both ethnically and geographically, from it and to attack the very essence of the 'criminal' group, just as it is attacking yours – hence the exaggeration of differences, desecration, expulsion, and cultural or even physical genocide. The self-destructive potential of conflict with blamed groups is to be expected, as are casualties in a crusade. Violations of common morality are justified by consideration of the immorality of the opposing group.

The explanation of group hatreds

One way of sorting putative explanations of violent group conflict is to figure out whether they fit into what I shall call a 'lid on the pot' paradigm, according to which eruptions of violent hatred are always seething beneath the surface of ethno-national communities waiting for the right conditions to emerge or, alternatively, into a 'combustion' paradigm, where such conflicts result from the coming together of independently innocuous elements which in combination have the disastrous results. Another sorting principle is methodological: are the conflicts results of dispositions of individuals, activated when they come together in groups, or do they result from features of groups which, in the manner described in Georgy LeBon's classic treatment of crowds,[11] transform otherwise pacific people into hate-inspired monsters?

Hardin's treatment is unequivocally on the combustion and individualistic side of these debates, while Girard's more easily matches the 'lid' paradigm and employs a holistic methodology. I have the impression that social-scientific approaches suppose alternative, mixed models. Sociologists like George Simmel or Erik Erikson look for group-specific sparks of action within a combustion paradigm.[12] Political scientists, even when they emphasize the machinations of group leaders, still take groups as primitive, describing them as if they were individuals. Standard political-scientific prescriptions, such as those of Donald Horowitz,[13] are institutional and suppose a 'lid' paradigm such that if proper institutional constraints are not found, ethnic violence is inevitable.

A luxury of addressing group hatreds specifically from the standpoint of democracy is that causal considerations need be taken into account only to the extent that one is seeking democratic solutions, which may free one from the obligation to expose deep causes. I wish now to suggest that such a strategy is possible in the present case provided that appropriate stands on the lid/combustion and individual-centred/group-centred questions can be defended. To this end I shall summarize another cluster of putative explanations, those of the sociobiologists.

On one sort of sociobiological explanation, violent group conflicts are a result of the survival value to humans of group coherence. Intergroup conflict is explained as functional to this end by providing a common enemy and/or by providing an out-group towards which aggression can be directed instead of disrupting the group.[14] A related explanation sees survival value to ethnocentric or xenophobic attitudes with their attendant protective stance towards groups with which one identifies and antagonism to those groups with which one does not.[15]

Sociobiologists have identified a problem in both sorts of explanation. If antagonism towards out-groups is to be explained by reference to its func-tion of protecting in-group cohesion, one needs to explain why there is such cohesion to be protected. The standard sociobiological explanation is that cooperation has survival value for the individuals who cooperate, but then it needs to be explained why this would not extend beyond limited groups. In attempting to offer such an explanation main differences among sociobiologists emerge.

Richard Alexander holds that culturally transmitted dispositions to rationalize racism and other forms of hostility always accompany a geneti-cally inherited disposition to cooperation which for its part is required for the sake of effective competition.[16] Ian Vine argues that cooperation requires cooperating agents to deceive themselves into thinking they are doing so out of altruism, but because altruism carried too far is dysfunc-tional for survival, it must come psychologically tempered with 'a weakly xenophobic tendency'.[17] Peter Meyer argues that 'affectivity' is a 'scarce resource', which can only be conferred on a limited number of people.[18] To my mind, these and other proffered explanations have a strained, hypothesis-saving character, as do the analogous efforts of those who start with the claim that what is basic is xenophobia and ethnocentrism. These latter must explain how it is that individuals are able to limit the bound-aries of their xenophobia so that there are groups beyond their immediate families, or, indeed, their individual selves, with whom to identify in an exclusionary way.

One reason for attending to sociobiological theory is that it might be considered the arch example of a lid-paradigmatic approach to group hatreds: genetically carried dispositions to violent group behaviour are essential to human survival. However, when pressed, it seems that what is essential for survival is the right *blend* of aggressive competition and cooperation and that if there is a fixed line between in- and out-groups, sociobiologists do not agree on where it is, or what features of human survival tools explain where cooperation must end and conflict begin. Dispositions to conflict or xenophobia thus coexist with dispositions to cooperation or fellow-feeling, and in the absence of either conclusive empirical evidence or convincing theory to the contrary, it must be assumed that how they combine and when or whether the one dominates are contingent matters.

This weakens a lid paradigm to the extent that it merges with its alternative. One might say that the 'default' disposition is conflict, but if this disposition always coexists with a cooperative one, and if the blend of cooperation and conflict is shiftable, the necessity of violent conflict is called into question. Of course, if a disposition to violence is always present, it is important to keep it constrained, but in practice this would not be different from a combustion-paradigm champion noting that it is important to inhibit the coalescence of elements which spark violence.

Another reason to consider sociobiological explanations is that this forces nuanced attention to the traditional distinction between group-centred and individual-centred accounts. Summarizing one version of the innate xenophobia thesis Johan van der Dennen writes:

> There is an analogy ... between immunological reactions of the body and the ethnocentric reactions of the individual or of a society. Just as the body is better prepared to avoid destruction by foreign substances, so an individual or a society may be better prepared to avoid destructions by aliens as a result of a generalized tendency to distrust, avoid, or reject foreign-seeming individuals.[19]

The repeated disjunction 'individual or society' highlights a difficulty in offering genetic explanations of group behaviour since it is individuals, not groups, who actually carry genes, and at least in human societies people in orthodox sociobiological theory aim at individual survival of which species survival is a product.[20] Hence some way must be found to give genetic description to the survival value of individuals *qua* members of groups, or, alternatively, to groups *insofar as* they depend on the attitudes of their member individuals. In either case, it would be strained to call the resulting stance either methodologically individualistic or holistic.

I wish now to suggest – and this is the principal hypothesis of this section of the essay – that these two features of sociobiological explanation can be generalized. Unless someone adopts the question-begging view that all apparently nonantagonistic or cooperative behaviour of humans are in fact disguised forms of acrimonious conflict, it must be allowed that group hatred, tendencies towards violence, and the like are dispositions which coexist with contrary dispositions. This is clearly the case in Girard's theory, since he himself is at pains to show how apprehension of revenge-motivated violence leads to a variety of strategies to avoid it. Similarly, even the most Hobbesian of political theorists recognize, as did Hobbes himself, that an element of pacific consensus is required to make institutions for constraining violence effective. This, I submit, gives the edge to a combustion paradigm of group violence, which, as will shortly be argued, offers hope for democratic political solutions.

As to the need for integrating group and individual orientations, this, too, seems to me mandated for theories beyond those seeking genetic explanations. The point is latent in the observations about the ontology of group hatred offered in the first part of the essay. It is individuals who hate, but groups whom they hate, and these groups are hated insofar as they are perceived as standing in a blameworthy, threatening relation to groups with whom the hating agent identifies. This already clouds an exclusively individual or group-centred dichotomy, and if one adds a view advanced at least since the time of Hegel and Marx, and repeated in each subsequent generation (by the Pragmatists, the Symbolic Interactionists, and now by the Communitarians and Discourse Analytic schools), that individuals are in Marx's phrase 'the ensemble of their social relations,' the distinction between the two orientations disappears altogether.

Let me now illustrate one way that an approach from within a 'combustion' paradigm, and combining (or superseding) individual and group orientations, suggests a democratic stance towards violently antagonistic attitudes. The approach (explicable from within one of several philosophical or social-theoretical perspectives)[21] begins with group identifications and assumes that individuals either importantly recognize themselves in terms of these identifications or, on the most radical versions, are entirely constituted by them. Since, however, no individual identifies with or is constituted by one group alone, various combinations are possible, and identifications can change over time. Thus one may identify with any combination of such things as an ethnicity, nationality, class, profession, religion, linguistic community, gender, generation, region, and so on, with varying priorities and in different combinations.

Clusters of identifications which persist over time and involve many people who share at least highly prioritized identifying elements count as (subjectively constituted) social groups. Members of groups may have a range of attitudes towards other social groups, from friendly feelings to indifference and hostility, and conflicts, for example over material or cultural resources, may be peacefully negotiated or addressed with violence. Also, groups may overlap or be relatively insulated from one another.

On a combustion paradigm, conflicts do not automatically turn to violence, but do so only in contingent contexts. In particular, the likelihood of violence will increase when appropriate terrain for peaceful negotiation among groups is denied. This means that while almost any combination of possible objects of identification or constitution may be compatible with peaceful negotiation,[22] certain such objects must be kept out of an identifying group cluster, namely those objects required for negotiation itself. I have in mind a geographic terrain physically inhabited by different groups and a political terrain wherein negotiation, whether at a constitutional or more local and informal level, may take place.

If the members of a group believe that either exclusive domination of a shared territory or a preponderance of state power is integral to its very group identity, this denies the terrains required for peaceful negotiation, leaving only violence. When territoriality is seen as integral to (or, in discourse-theoretical terms, 'sutured with') a centrally valued component of one's identity, such as nationality, for instance as in Anglo-Canadian and Franco-Quebec hostility to one another and to aboriginal land claims, or when, as in the case of a theocratic identity, religion and the state are sutured, extreme hostility – hatred – is a not unlikely result. Moreover, when one's nationality or religion is partly integrated with territory or the state but exclusive domination of these latter are challenged, this simultaneously thwarts national or religious projects and specifies the source of one's frustration, namely the challenging group or groups. It is thus that 'blame' becomes central to group hostilities.

The democratic fix

If this characterization of violent group conflict locates a proximate, if not a remote cause, then any strategy that might effectively impede violence-prone identifications should also constrain the resulting violence, and it may not be necessary to figure out putatively deeper lying origins to confront the problem of group hatreds. I shall conclude my remarks by suggesting that democratic practices and institutions are the best suited to this purpose, but first two disclaimers are in order.

First, it is unlikely that democratic measures could completely eradicate antagonistic attitudes and fractious conflict from human relations. If group identifications are implicated in the genesis of such conflicts, this will sometimes unavoidably involve self-definition by contrast or even in opposition to other groups. This feature of human self formation cannot be wished away any more than can the fact that groups find themselves in conflict over objectively scarce material or cultural resources. This is why the best to be hoped for is that negotiation can be prompted and appropriate spaces maintained by and in which it can take place.

A second caveat has to do with resources. It used to be popular in some Marxist circles to maintain that human antagonisms can be entirely overcome by transcending class conflict and egalitarian distribution of a superabundance of goods. I did not treat the first part of this claim in my comments about the causes of violent group conflict because it rests on what I take as a now generally recognized unsupportable class reductionist attitude, belied by the fact that extra-class conflicts (racial, gender-based, national, and so on) cut across class lines.[23] As to resources, I doubt that the elimination of scarcity or even the provision of plenty would result in a complete withering of antagonistic conflict, which, to the extent that it has to do with strongly held values implicated in people's self-identification, often feeds on extra-material symbols. Moreover, scarce cultural resources, such as limitations on the number of official languages possible in a country or region (a source of concern in highly multicultural societies like my own), cannot be overcome by purely economic measures.

Let me hasten to add that if socialist economic solutions are poor candidates for a complete solution to the problem of violent group conflicts, capitalist ones are even worse. I thus disagree with one of Hardin's suggestions. In keeping with currently popular neoliberal attitudes he calls for downsizing government, and citing Adam Smith for authority, argues that 'we make a better world by ignoring what kind of world we make and living for ourselves than if we concentrate first on the ethnic political structure of our world'.[24] Perhaps, if the world moneyed powers gave up their profitable dependence on local state powers in the interests of achieving pure competition, people would be too occupied with business to concern themselves with mere ethnic or national matters, but I doubt it. In any case it is worth noting that in the real world militant *laissez-faire* capitalism and hostility to big government are attitudes often expressed by champions of the sorts of intolerant ethnic groups that most worry Hardin, for instance, national chauvinists and members of the religious right wing in the United States. Also, the collapse of Communism was replaced simultaneously by Smithian capitalism and ethnic politics, often endorsed by the same people.

Class domination and ill-distributed material resources surely exacerbate violent group attitudes, and while I am contesting the view that such attitudes and resulting conflicts would disappear along with class distinctions and scarcity, I suppose that the severity of their effects would greatly diminish. Indeed, I think that these factors are so important that were scarcity and class domination eliminated, the conflicts that remained could probably be addressed well enough so that alternative solutions need not be sought. The problem, however, is that extra-class conflicts also impede efforts to address class domination, thus precluding a serial approach to different forms of conflict.

Structures of economic and class domination may well be omnipresent parts of a mix including ethno-national conflicts and group hatreds, and there is room for debate about dominant causal lines among these things, as well as about their relation to other structured oppressions, such as patriarchy. Regarded practically, however, the relation might be pictured as a triangle, the sides of which – structured oppressions, ethno-national conflicts, and group hatreds – at least reinforce one another. In this essay I am asking whether and how democratic practices might head off, reverse, or contain one of these components, namely group hatreds. To the extent that this or any other strategy succeeds, the other two sides of this 'triangle' would also be weakened.

What, then, about democracy? It might seem that this is an especially ill-timed recommendation. The violent ethnic strife we see in the former Soviet bloc *followed* democratization. In several places, political leaders who openly play to chauvinistic sentiment have won elections. As an orienting hypothesis one might press a theory which I have called that of the 'democratic fix'. This is the view that social and political problems, including those created by democracy, may be fruitfully confronted not by constraining democracy but by expanding it.[25] For example, faced with the election of chauvinists, an advocate of the democratic fix thesis will interrogate local electoral practices – the political party system including nomination procedures which determine what the choices will be, criteria for voter eligibility, media coverage, accountability of elected officials, levels of citizen apathy, availability of extra-parliamentary forms of democratic participation, and so on.

I recognize that application of the democratic fix to current situations of violent conflict and group hatred is risky, but what are the alternatives? In addition to the starkly socialistic or capitalistic economic alternatives already mentioned, I see four: authoritarianism, consociationism, individualism, and moral education. These are not meant to be strictly exclusive alternatives, since various mixtures of them with one another and with democracy are possible. The question is whether any of them could provide the pivot of a strategy.

Thus conceived the shortcomings of the alternatives are not hard to identify. A common view in the press and in many political-scientific circles, largely informed by the 'lid' paradigm, is that authoritarianism in the former Soviet bloc restrained ethnic violence. Perhaps it did restrain conflicts, but at issue in this essay is how to address the group hatreds which are, I have claimed, implicated in the most violent of them. Obviously, authoritarian restraint did nothing to dissipate the hatreds which have now found such terrible expression. In fact, a case can be made that socialist authoritarianism exacerbated hatreds.

This socialism, especially in its Soviet and Chinese incarnations, set itself the task of attacking the traditions of communities in civil society, which were seen as threats and as out of keeping with an image of the new socialist personality. Such attacks are, however, doomed to failure, and their effect was instead to drive the traditions underground into mutually isolating niches where their most intolerant dimensions were nurtured. When authoritarian constraints were lifted, this released onto one another people whose souls had been held together partly through desperate adherence to one of several traditions, but who had been denied the habits of pluralistic tolerance.

Less severe is a consociationist political alternative. On this model, elite members of ethnic, national, religious, and other such groups are encouraged to negotiate with one another to find *modi vivendi* for peaceful cohabitation of their groups. Except for the strongest advocates of direct, participatory democracy some such arrangement is recognized as an acceptable part of democratic politics, but only if it is integrated with democracy, that is, only if there is accountability of group leaders to group members and only if cross-group democratic checks are in place to inhibit the elites constituting a self-serving cabal. Without subordinating consociationism to democracy, it becomes a version of the authoritarian alternative. Some such mixed model existed in socialist Yugoslavia where after Tito's death it contributed to an exacerbation of ethnic strife, as national leaders exaggerated and even manufactured local intolerance in power politics among one another.[26]

By 'moral education' I mean the hope that a moral ideal, typically as personified in charismatic proponents of peace and toleration such as Mahatma Gandhi, will, by force of moral argumentation and example, induce people to pacific behaviour. The sad failure of the efforts of Gandhi himself and those who followed him indicates the shortcoming of such a prescription if followed alone. One problem with any attempt to combat group hatreds with moral argument is that, if the hypothesis about the centrality of blame to the hatreds is right, they are already themselves moralistic. It is hard enough for moral exhortation to overcome self-interest, but even harder when confronting people who firmly believe themselves wronged.

In addition, if I read the relevant history of South Asia correctly, the moral example offered by Gandhi, powerful as it was, could not overcome entrenched ethnic and religious suspicions in combination with narrow regional political and economic interests which, as in the Yugoslavian case, exacerbated and made use of them. Gandhi also spoke to the economically disadvantaged who constitute a large majority among all the groups in the region, and this might have helped to form bridges among their communities were it not for the fact that often privileged minority interests had a stake in maintaining the divisions. Hence the approach might have been more effective had it been combined with vigorous majoritarian politics, that is, with democracy.

In tension with his 'tend your own garden' prescription, Hardin recommends promotion of a world-wide ethic of universalistic individualism – for example, of the Kantian variety – as an antidote to 'particularistic' attachment to community norms, which he sees as being perniciously endorsed by contemporary communitarian philosophers.[27] Setting aside the current debate about whether such a universalistic ethic is desirable, there is a problem about its realism in the face of existing group identifications. It is hard to see what kind of educational campaign could make inroads in communities with strong bonds, where it would be the most needed.

Moreover, it is not clear that the only choices are between tolerance promoting individualism and intolerant communitarianism. Hardin ignores theorists in the latter tradition like Charles Taylor, Michael Walzer, or Shlomo Avineri who advocate critical respect for tradition of a sort that is pluralistically tolerant.[28] It is noteworthy that these theorists are also prodemocratic, thus suggesting that campaigns of moral education compatible with respect for community traditions might, like consociationist practices or Gandhiism, admit of integration with democracy. A main argument in favour of a democratic approach to the group hatred problem, then, is that this is required to take advantage of what virtues there are in other measures (minus the authoritarian one, of course). I also see four additional strengths to democratic prescriptions.

One of these pertains to international intervention. The principal means to date for confronting violent conflicts involving group hatreds (when they have been confronted at all) are by international diplomacy and pressure, including military intervention. On the democratic fix hypothesis, part of the explanation for the weakness or outright failure of such ventures is that they have lacked democratic support. Democratic institutions are almost exclusively confined within state boundaries, thus making international intervention structurally nondemocratic.

Political philosophers in recent years have been advancing a variety of ingenious proposals for cross-border democratic institutions, which would not only facilitate international intervention, but also bring decisions about when and how to intervene into publicly accessible forums, governed by formal decision procedures and the rule of law.[29] This would be superior to the present situation, where such decisions are made in an *ad hoc* manner by those government leaders who choose to play a role, and it would lend democratic legitimacy to intervention.

Other applications of the democratic fix theory address group hatreds within a state boundary. I mentioned earlier that not all members of groups in violent conflict need be motivated by hostile attitudes. It is not always obvious just how many people indigenous to such a group support bellicose activities, and those who do typically try to sustain 'bandwagon' support by inhibiting dissident expression. Provision of forums for expression of opinion on the part of those within a society who abjure attitudes of hatred may well reveal that ordinary citizens are not as seized with blood lust as their most vocal members or often self-appointed leaders maintain.

More ambitiously, the democratic hypothesis suggests that when people harbour violently intolerant or otherwise antidemocratic opinions, this is sometimes in *default* of democracy. One thesis of the late C. B. Macpherson was that when selfishness and consumerism ('possessive individualism') is widespread in a society, this is a result of severe constraints on people's ability jointly to shape the future they will share. Democratic empowerment, then, should counteract these dispositions.[30] Analogously, group hatred might be seen as at least partly a response to impotence and susceptible to counteraction in the same way.

A final consideration relates to group identities and territory or the state. To make clear how the democratic fix relates to this problem, I need briefly to explain how I am using the word 'democracy'. In keeping with the classical conception, I view democracy as rule by the ruled; however, departing from some deployments of this concept, I think it appropriate to seek democracy not just in formal government but also in informal settings. Moreover, there are no privileged means for democratic practice, which might involve majority voting, weighted voting, pursuing formal or informal means to reach consensus or to negotiate a compromise, or even delegating decision making to an acceptable, *pro temp* authority. Determining what means are the most democratic in specific circumstances is achieved by estimating which would best make progress towards an ideal democracy. In an ideal democracy either consensus has been attained among all affected members of the situation or a mutually acceptable compromise has been negotiated, provided that neither outcome jeopardizes pursuit of consensus-building or negotiation in the future.[31]

Thus conceived, it is in the interests of democracy to keep the geographic and political spaces for consensus-building and negotiation open. Abstractly considered, this creates a seemingly insurmountable dilemma: democratic forums are required in order for democratic measures to be employed to maintain such forums. However, when democracy is seen concretely and as a process, this dilemma becomes instead a project. If democracy has the advantages claimed for it, then, as people come increasingly to profit from such advantages, they will favour the strengthening and widening of democracy, which in turn will make democracy more secure and lay the basis for further advances.

Such a project might begin by exhibiting (in word and deed) the advantages for a single group to appropriate forms of democracy internal to the group in preserving its traditions and values. One such advantage is that internally autocratic group practices threaten group traditions themselves when their protection is entrusted to group leaders who are not recallable. (What happens when the traditions are themselves autocratic? Then choices need to be made and certain aspects of a group's traditions may be subject to alteration or even abandonment.)[32] Another advantage is that groups are seldom homogeneous. So internal conflict will always be a threat to their coherence, and democracy represents the best chance to confront such conflict in a way that will not tear apart the group.

Further, such a project should exhibit the importance of external democratic respect for the preservation of internal group democracy. The attitudes of pluralistic tolerance and respect required for democracy are not like tap water that can be turned on or off at will or confined within a single basin. Intolerance and disrespect directed towards other groups sets in motion processes – political, social-psychological, and, in the extreme case, military – that threaten internal democratic practices and culture. Thus, those who have come, on group specific grounds, to value democracy should also see hatred directed to other groups as inimical to this end. The fourth argument for democracy, then, is democracy itself.

Notes

1 Earlier drafts of this paper were read at the Radical Philosophy Association meetings at Purdue University, November 14–17 1996, and at a conference in honour of Shlomo Avineri, The Hebrew University of Jerusalem, December 16–18 1996.
2 I discuss the central role of pluralism in democracy in my *The Real World of Democracy Revisited and Other Essays on Democracy and Socialism* (Atlantic Highlands, NJ: Humanities Press, 1994), essay 5.
3 Russell Hardin, *One for All: The Logic of Group Conflict* (Princeton: Princeton University Press, 1955).
4 Ibid., pp. 160–61.
5 I criticize Hardin's approach in a critical review of his book, in *The Canadian Journal of Philosophy*, 27, 4 (December 1997), pp. 571–94.

6 Hardin, op. cit., n. 3, p. 121.
7 In his Chapter 4, Hardin identifies attitudes of exclusionary superiority as central to group animosities.
8 Réné Girard, *Violence and the Sacred* (Baltimore: Johns Hopkins University Press, 1979), p. 260.
9 Ibid., p. 316. On p. 33, Girard expresses agnosticism about the origins of vengefulness, but in *Deceit, Desire and the Novel* (Balitmore: Johns Hopkins University Press, 1965) and other works he advances an hypothesis to explain violence in terms of human insecurity and memetic desire. See the analyses by Paul Dumouchel and Jean-Pierre Dupuy, *L'Enfer des choses* (Paris: Seuil, 1979) and by Eugene Webb, *The Self Between* (Seattle: Washington University Press, 1993), chapters 3 and 5.
10 See, for example, Girard, op. cit., n. 8, p. 20: 'When the least false step can have dire consequences [a downward spiral of retributive violence], human relationships may well be marked by a prudence that seems to us excessive....It is in this sense that we must understand the lengthy palavers that precede any undertaking not sanctified by custom, in this sense that we must understand primitive man's reluctance to engage in nonritualized games or contests.'
11 Georgy LeBon, *The Crowd: A Study of the Popular Mind* (New York: Macmillan, 1986).
12 George Simmel, *Conflict and the Web of Group Affiliations* (New York: Free Press, 1966). A pertinent article by Erikson is 'Pseudospeciation in the Nuclear Age', *Political Psychology*, 6 (1985), 213–17.
13 See Horowitz's summary contribution, 'Democracy in Divided Societies', in Larry Diamond and Marc F. Plattner (eds), *Nationalism, Ethnic Conflict, and Democracy* (Baltimore: Johns Hopkins University Press, 1994), pp. 35–55.
14 R. S. Bigelow is one representative of the first approach, *The Dawn Warriors: Man's Evolution towards Peace* (Boston: Little Brown, 1969); L. A. Coser, *The Functions of Social Conflict* (New York: The Free Press, 1956), of the second. These and many of the other relevant sociobiological positions are conveniently summarized by Johan M.G. van der Dennen in 'Ethnocentrism and In-Group/Out-Group Differentiation: A Review and Interpretation of the Literature', in Vernon Reynolds *et al.* (eds), *The Sociobiology of Ethnocentrism: Evolutionary Dimensions of Xenophobia, Discrimination, Racism and Nationalism* (London: Croom Helm, 1987), pp. 1–47.
15 Edmond Wilson seems to hold one version of this view, as in his classic *On Human Nature* (Cambridge, MA: Harvard University Press, 1978).
16 Richard Alexander, *Darwinism and Human Affairs* (Seattle: University of Washington Press, 1979).
17 Ian Vine, 'Inclusive Fitness and the Self-System: The Roles of Human Nature and Sociocultural Processes in Intergroup Discrimination', in Reynonds *et al.*, op. cit., n. 14, pp. 60–80.
18 Peter Meyer, 'Ethnocentrism in Human Social Behaviour: Some Biosociological Considerations', in Reynonds *et al.*, op. cit., n. 14, pp. 81–93; Meyer somehow calculates that the optimal number of people to whom one's affection can be extended is thirty.
19 Van der Dennan, in Reynonds *et al.*, op. cit., n. 14, p. 8. He is summarizing a view of Paul Rosenblatt.

20 See the treatment of this problem, without offering a solution, by Umberto Melotti, 'In-Group/Out-Group Relations and the Issue of Group Selection,' in Reynonds *et al.*, op. cit., n. 14, pp. 94–111.

21 I am comfortable with the version of Ernesto Laclau and Chantal Mouffe, who, borrowing from post-structuralist and neo-Gramscian theory, first expressed it in *Hegemony and Socialist Strategy* (London: Verso, 1985), and later explicated and applied it to pluralist democracy in several writings. However, one can, I think, agree with the characterization below from within other perspectives and without agreeing with all the philosophical tenets of Laclau and Mouffe.

22 This is true, as well, of most situations where a group identity is partly constituted in contradistinction or even in opposition to another group, for example where part of what it means to someone to be a 'true Protestant' is not to be a Catholic. Violent conflict probably is unavoidable when violence is itself built into the opposition, for example where to be a 'true Protestant' is not to be a 'hated Catholic.' But all identities could not be of this form (under pain of the paradox of internal relations), and an hypothesis of this paper is that whether oppositional dimensions of group identities internalize hatred is itself a contextual matter.

23 I discuss this issue in 'Class Reductionism', Chapter 9 of my *Democratic Theory and Socialism* (Cambridge: Cambridge University Press, 1987).

24 Hardin, op. cit., n. 3, pp. 179 and 227.

25 I argue that this theory escapes the shortcomings of the 'technological fix', from which its name was taken in *Democratic Theory and Socialism*, op. cit., n. 23, pp. 65–7.

26 A summary of this history appropriate to the current exercise is by Svetozar Stojanovic, 'The Destruction of Yugoslavia', *Fordham International Law Journal*, 19, 2 (December 1995), pp. 337–62.

27 Hardin, op. cit., n. 3, Chapter 7. Consistently with his rational-choice theoretical perspective, Hardin is pessimistic that such a morality can in fact be achieved and is thus driven to the Smithian solution referred to above.

28 Pertinent treatments by Michael Walzer are *The Company of Critics* (New York: Basic Books, 1988) and *Thick and Thin* (Notre Dame: University of Notre Dame Press, 1994), see Chapter 3. Taylor exemplifies such a stance in his interventions to conflicts in Canada, *Reconciling the Solitudes* (Montreal: Queen's–McGill Universities Press, 1993). I read Shlomo Avineri's *The Making of Modern Zionism* (New York: Basic Books, 1981) as an exposition of a Zionist 'company of critics' whose traditionalism is democratically infused. Also pertinent by Avineri are his comments on a panel with Ghia Nodia and Francis Fukuyama, published in Larry Diamond and Marc F. Plattner (eds), *Nationalism, Ethnic Conflict, and Democracy* (Baltimore: Johns Hopkins University Press, 1994), pp. 28–31.

29 Relevant readings are David Held, 'Democracy, the Nation-State and the Global System', in D. Held (ed.), *Political Theory Today* (Cambridge: Cambridge University Press, 1991), pp. 197–235; Antonio Cassese, *International Law in a Divided World* (Oxford: Oxford University Press, 1987); Richard Falk, *The Promise of World Order* (Philadelphia: Temple University Press, 1987).

30 Pertinent works by Macpherson are *Democratic Theory: Essays in Retrieval* (Oxford: Oxford University Press, 1973), see essay 3, and *The Life and Times of Liberal Democracy* (Oxford: Oxford University Press, 1977). I update

Macpherson's views in my *The Real World of Democracy Revisited*, op. cit., n. 2, see especially essay 8.

31 *Democratic Theory and Socialism*, op. cit., n. 23, Chapter 3, and *The Real World of Democracy Revisited*, op. cit., n. 2, essay 3 explicate my understanding of democracy.

32 It is a main aim of Avineri, Taylor, and Walzer (in the works referred to in n. 28) to show that traditions can be internally challenged and changed from within. I treat this subject in *The Real World of Democracy Revisited*, op. cit., n. 2, essay 6, 'Community, Democracy, and Socialism'.

9   The civic argument for socialism

Ronald Beiner

> One may care less for the efficiency of the capitalist process in producing
> economic and cultural values than for the kind of human beings that it
> turns out and then leaves to their own devices, free to make a mess of their
> lives.
>
> Joseph A. Schumpeter

If liberalism cannot create political solutions to social and moral quandaries that are associated with it, is socialism a feasible alternative? And
even if socialism is considered an alternative to liberalism, is it indeed an
alternative, or is it simply an offshoot of liberal discourse? Put otherwise, is
socialism, or can it be convincingly conceived as, a genuinely postliberal
social-political philosophy?[1] The problem that we confront here is that
arguments on behalf of socialism are still largely framed within categories
that are of a piece with the terms of liberal discourse. To address this
problem, I will try sketching the lines of a possible alternative way of
formulating the case for socialism, one that I will label, for reasons that I
hope will clarify themselves in what follows, the *political* argument for
socialism. Whether socialist practice can surmount the quandaries of
liberal capitalism may, after all, depend decisively on the character of the
defining terms by which one fashions or refashions notions of socialism.

Socialism and citizenship

The standard case for socialism turns on an argument about distributive
justice, an argument concerning social and economic rights or entitlements, and it has the concept of equality as its defining term. In what
follows I shall merely put this argument to one side, neither discounting its
validity nor acknowledging its force; in other words, I suspend judgement
about the force of the standard argument. I wish to sidestep these issues,

for I believe it is possible to construct an alternative case for socialism that revolves around citizenship rather than social justice, around political enfranchisement rather than economic entitlements, and that substitutes the concept of solidarity for that of social equality as its pivotal term. It is an argument of which intimations may be drawn from Rousseau, J. S. Mill, and perhaps even Marx.[2] As I say, I want neither to repudiate nor to endorse the conventional argument, but merely to suggest other terms in which the question of socialism might be debated.

The question I want to ask is whether it is possible to elaborate a justification of socialism that does not depend upon principles of distributive justice. Michael Walzer, in the context of an argument for a more developed system of communal provision in the United States, notes: "One might also argue that American citizens should work to build a stronger and more intensely experienced political community. But this argument, though it would have distributive consequences, is not, properly speaking, an argument about distributive justice."[3] It is important to pose this question on account of the prominence lately accorded to theories of distributive justice within contemporary political philosophy.[4] The disproportionate attention devoted to questions of fair distribution and social justice make it necessary to consider the other argument that Walzer notes but does not pursue.

The problem with basing the argument for socialism strictly on the claims of social justice is that this way of proceeding runs the risk of getting enmeshed in the language of rights and entitlements that defines (and in my opinion disfigures) liberalism as a political philosophy, and is thus liable to distract from what Marx considered the key question about socialism, namely the quality of social relations between human beings. Let me refer here to a familiar case. Rawls's theory offers an extreme instance of what one may call socialism through the back door, that is, a possible justification of socialist measures by means of a theory of distributive justice that gives only the most minimal account of shared ends and does it on the basis of a thoroughly instrumentalist conception of rationality. I propose the opposite theoretical strategy, eliminating the intermediate problem of fairness of distribution and going straight to questions of shared ends and the basis of social solidarity (which is, at best, a derivative issue for Rawls).

Justice is of course a central and ineliminable term of political discourse. However, social justice does not exhaust our political concerns. It is questionable whether it is, as Rawls claims, the "first virtue" of social institutions, and it is certainly not the only virtue. Citizenship is also one of the essential needs that we have as political beings. When one argues for a given set of institutions, it is not immediately obvious how one should weigh these different claims. Perhaps it is unnecessary, since both require the same set of institutions (namely, socialism under some description). But it does not seem to me guaranteed in advance how the argument for distributive justice will be decided, and we would therefore be well advised to question whether considerations of social justice should have ultimate supremacy in case our need for justice and our need for citizenship should, perchance, conflict.

Suppose I could establish an irrefutable claim to various socioeconomic goods, based, say, on desert. Let us say that I can prove that I deserve a certain share of the social benefits and advantages available for social distribution. Suppose further that the cost of my obtaining what I actually deserve is that political activity and civic collaboration with others in my society is thereby impaired (because, for instance, the material conditions for replete political membership for those others are thereby denied, or because feelings of mutuality and fellow-feeling are damaged by the resultant inequalities). It seems quite reasonable to me, in such circumstances, to regard this as too high a cost for getting what I in fact deserve, in fulfillment of the principles of distributive justice. A public-minded citizen would wish to forgo his or her rightful entitlements in this case. Now I do not want actually to affirm the initial supposition. Rather, my point is that it is quite intelligible to assert the priority of politics over economics, which in this context means that as citizens we are prepared to subordinate questions of social and economic distribution to questions of political membership. Now of course it is possible that struggles over equalizing distribution may themselves actually forge bonds of political community and solidarity (we know that this often happens), and I certainly do not wish to exclude such possibilities. But I see no necessary relation between the two issues, and it seems to me important to establish an independent argument for egalitarian political commitments that does not rest upon the contingencies of economic distribution and the entitlement claims to which they give rise. In any case, one might want to establish the relative priority of economic parity and political democracy in defining one's idea of socialism. Does one seek social equality for its own sake, or in relation to a further end, namely that it makes us better citizens and promotes a shared experience of political community?

My contention, then, is that arguments about distributive justice do not exhaust the arguments for socialism, and that even if the former arguments were somehow definitively settled one way or the other, arguments that adduced other considerations could proceed nonetheless. This point is reflected to some extent in certain varieties of socialist rhetoric such as Bennite socialism in Britain, where the decisive arguments are often framed in terms of participatory democracy and, in particular, of radical democratization of the party system. (This, of course, does not deny the social-economic dimension of these arguments, related as they are to a struggle against a particular class system.) But even supposing that the two sets of concerns, socioeconomic and civic-political, could easily converge, the question remains whether we wish to conduct the argument for a socialist society within the language of economic rights or that of political goods, and this choice between one rhetoric or the other at the same time involves a choice of substance between rival conceptions of socialism.

Up to now, I have been presenting arguments to suggest why it would be unwise to limit the case for socialism to a derivation from social and economic entitlements, and why it would be sensible to introduce other considerations. It remains to indicate what would be the shape of an alternative argument. In barest outline, the claim would be that socialist arrangements would heighten political identity and enhance civic consciousness, and thereby reverse or at least mitigate the trend toward depoliticization and "civil privatism" documented by Habermas among others. Socialism, in short, would make us better citizens. This, of course, is an empirical claim, dependent on counterfactual projections about how a genuinely socialist transformation would affect the quality of political life. In the absence of solid empirical grounding for this claim, I shall content myself for now with some more casual observations that tend to support my case. My intention is more to intimate the lines upon which such an argument could be developed than actually to fill in its content in any detail.[5] There is one rather simple way to demonstrate that the advancement of socialism must go hand in hand with a much more active sense of citizenship. The societies with which we are here concerned are nonsocialist and appear to be little inclined to socialism. These societies are at the same time massively depoliticized. By socialism, of course, I do not mean merely the election of socialist parties committed to greater government spending. I mean a large-scale transformation of attitudes, institutions, and relationships in society with a view to the achievement of shared purposes and social justice through the public disposal of collective resources ("common ownership of the means of production" is the standard formulation). Such a transformation would be unthinkable without a general shift of consciousness throughout the society. This shift of consciousness, in turn, would presuppose a thorough politicization of the whole population. A major turn toward socialist ideals and the corresponding political objectives would not come about unless people in very large numbers took an extremely active interest in politics and seriously concerned themselves with problems of political change. In short, they would have to exercise citizenship in the fullest way. In the West, intimations of such a politicization have been witnessed, for example, in the black voter registration drive associated with the presidential campaigns of Rev. Jesse Jackson, and in certain aspects of the nuclear disarmament movement.

No doubt one could employ the same reasoning to argue that in systems of state socialism the natural means of politicizing people is through the mobilization of discontent and protest against the prevailing (that is, state-socialist) mode of social organization. In fact this is precisely what we have seen at the end of the 1980s throughout Eastern Europe, with results that, from the point of view of the concerns of this essay, have been very impressive. Therefore it seems hard to deny that the same argument that supports socialism in capitalist societies works in the opposite direction in the case of socialist (but, at least until recently, equally depoliticized) societies in the Eastern bloc. Perhaps the thesis here comes to no more than the self-evident observation that political change of any sort presupposes that the people who will undertake it have been politicized to the appropriate degree. But I think more is entailed; the societies in need of political change (whether West or East) are not simply unjust, oppressive, or prone to corruption but are also, and above all, depoliticized. When a community is mobilized to rectify injustices, whether economic or political, it is at the same time educated to citizenship. The most powerful example of this in our time has been the Solidarity movement in Poland.

This argument concerns the gains to citizenship that would accrue from working or struggling toward socialism, or participating in socialist movements, rather than from fully formed socialist institutions themselves. It would be easy to indulge in speculations about the flowering of political activity and civic involvement under socialism, but it is difficult to see any empirical grounds for assuming that the entrenchment of social equality would automatically lead to a full and active political life. It might simply lead to equal participation in consumerist indolence. Whether civic activity blossomed in a postcapitalist society would depend not on the achievement of social equality per se, but rather on how one defined and conceived socialism, whether within socioeconomic categories or in broader terms (and, needless to say, a radical democratization of active citizenship *would* be central to the version of socialism that I am advocating). If socialism is defined in terms of shared civic responsibility rather than economic justice, then the achievement of a socialist order will, by definition, usher in a new republicanism.

There is, however, one important respect in which egalitarian social conditions certainly do foster citizenship and civic solidarity. If there exist substantial disparities of wealth and opportunity, the common exercise of citizenship will be blocked by social divisions and feelings of relative deprivation. (In this connection, it should not be too difficult to speculate on the likely political implications of the significant erosion of the middle class, and the consequent polarization of rich and poor, that has been unfolding in North America over the last decades.) This is a theme familiar in republican political thought, for instance, in Aristotle, Machiavelli, and Rousseau.[6] And if inequalities impair the forms of mutuality required for the joint exercise of citizenship, it is reasonable to expect that the converse would hold as well, namely, that social equality would encourage forms of shared experience and common sentiment, which would in turn likely issue in richer political relationships.[7] It was this hope that prompted Aristotle and Rousseau, among others, to insist upon the easing of class divisions in a well-constituted society. It must be said again, though, that social equality would be no more than a necessary condition of good citizenship, not a sufficient condition. A socialism which resulted in a universal bourgeoisie – Sweden? – would remain subject to Rousseau's polemical opposition between *bourgeois* and *citoyen*.[8]

The argument that I am putting forward is neither classical liberal nor classical socialist. To show this, let us abstract two positions that lie at opposite poles. One line of argument would be that political and legal rights are all-important and that all attention should be directed at these rather than at social and economic disparities. Against this one can argue that legal-political freedoms are merely formal and that everything really hangs on whether the formal rights are given substance at the level of social and economic arrangements. This view is supported by the example of blacks in the United States, where their political power has grown in proportion to their social and economic gains, namely, the consolidation of a black middle class. But one could go on to argue (this is the second perspective) that political representation would be superfluous once social and economic equality had been firmly established, since the latter is, in any case, the real object of and rationale for the former. This line of reasoning, in my view, would be quite wrong. In fact, one of the main arguments for expanding social and economic entitlements is, precisely, in order to provide for the disenfranchised a meaningful enfranchisement. Again, it is not a question of the sense of solidarity being in the service of the passion for equality, but rather of social equality working to elicit greater political solidarity.

Thus far, the impression may have been conveyed that the struggle for equality belongs strictly within the sphere of social and economic competition. However, it would be wrong to assume that the concept of equality applies exclusively to the realm of social status and economic distribution. The concept of citizenship implies a conception of equality as well, and equality must prevail within the limits circumscribed by a given definition of citizenship. If we are regarded as citizens with respect to any legal and political rights or responsibilities, we must also be treated as equals within that same domain. Partial citizenship is an incoherent notion; the idea of unequal citizenship amounts to a contradiction in terms. If we are defined as citizens in any respect, we enjoy (or should enjoy) equality within the terms specified by that definition of citizenship. Therefore civic equality is synonymous with citizenship.[9] If the concept of equality can be given a political rendering distinct from its usual social-economic meaning, so too can the concept of justice. This calls for a further clarification of the relationship between the theory here sketched and standard theories of justice. Although my version of the socialist argument certainly has implications for the formulation of principles of distributive justice, it should be fairly clear from what I have already said that it is not centrally a theory *about* justice (or at least social justice). When we shift from equality for equality's sake to equality for citizenship's sake, the primary concern is no longer with what is just (for individual citizens) but with what is good (for the community as a whole); or rather, social justice is sought to the extent that it promotes political citizenship. A theory of social justice seeks to explain why the society should establish more or less distributive equality in terms of entitlement – what is due to individual members. Strictly speaking, my theory offers no such account. It seeks to argue for equality in terms of something else, something that transcends or supplements the claims and entitlements of individuals, namely political well-being. But citizenship, too, yields an account of justice, though not social justice. The claim to participate in general deliberation is also a claim to justice, to political justice; this is the sense that the term *justice* has in Aristotle's political philosophy. Justice, after all, is not exclusively a social concept; it also evokes a political meaning. When we refer to injustice in South Africa (during the apartheid era), for instance, we certainly do not refer only to social disadvantages; even if the levels of income among the races suddenly became equal, the nature of the political system would continue to violate our sense of political justice. Following Michael Walzer one might even include the latter dimension of justice under the heading of "distributive justice," for claims to participate in a political system necessarily call for principles of distribution for arbitrating among such claims. According to Walzer, citizenship, like social justice, is a distributive question.[10]

The point of my argument has been to show that one can have other than egalitarian reasons for embracing socialism and that one can support socialist goals without being already committed to social equality per se. (I am assuming that arguments about distributive justice are inherently murky and that the case for full-bodied political citizenship is more straightforward; though here too, undoubtedly, the desirability of the end will be severely contested.) To reformulate the problem along these lines carries the advantage that it shifts the focus to the distinctively political benefits of socialism and away from the theoretically confusing issue of economic costs.[11] In discussions of the relative merits of socialism and liberal capitalism, it is generally assumed that the relative inefficiency of socialist economies exhibits the political inferiority of socialism. It is hardly ever considered that it may in fact constitute a political advantage of socialism that such economies operate less efficiently and thus offer fewer goods to be distributed. If indeed economic disadvantages yield political advantages, the reason is, as political philosophers from Plato onward have always recognized, that too much affluence breeds poor citizens. This kind of reflection is integral to Rousseau's way of thinking, with its resolute subordination of the economic to the political. The same thought finds expression within more recent political thought in the work of Hannah Arendt (which likewise subordinates economics to politics): "Economic growth may one day turn out to be a curse rather than a good, and under no conditions can it either lead into freedom or constitute a proof for its existence."[12] It is fairly astonishing to what a small degree factors such as low crime rates, as well as low rates of unemployment, are considered suitable measures of political achievement in the evaluation of socialist societies. On the converse side, it is scarcely less stunning that pervasive drug taking, rampant sexual exploitation, the addiction to consumerist "lifestyles," and the ubiquity of the credit card in Western societies are not commonly taken as key indicators of political debility relative to other societies.[13] Or to pick another topical example, we could ask ourselves: Have we carried our identification of political freedom with consumer freedom so far that it is unthinkable to see the infinite availability of pornographic publications in West Berlin relative to East Berlin hitherto as at least one political advantage to be reckoned on the side of the latter?[14] Again, what seems to loom largest is the criterion of economic productivity; the truly political consideration – the question of what promotes good citizenship – appears less important.[15]

Some arguments for socialism regard politics as the means and economic equality as the end. Here this perspective is reversed: economic equality is the means and greater exercise of political citizenship is the end. At the outset I referred to my endeavor as the political argument for socialism in order to distinguish it from the social-economic argument. Of course, the latter is also a political argument, at least in the content of the commitment it elicits, if not in the quality of the grounds upon which it is based. Perhaps the contrast would be brought out more sharply by dubbing mine the "civic" argument for socialism. This theoretical strategy may be summed up in the notion that socialism should be pursued not on account of equality for its own sake, but because it makes us better citizens or promotes citizenship generally, or rather, that greater equality is justified insofar as it makes better citizens and encourages citizenship. My conclusion is that even those who are not persuaded that egalitarianism for its own sake is justified might nonetheless have good grounds for embracing socialism if they could be shown the truth of the civic argument.

Reconceiving socialism

We may well be disconcerted to find, on reflection, that we have considered as the most appropriate argument on behalf of socialism one that in significant measure abstracts from the actual content of socialist politics. This forces us to confront much more directly a problem we have so far avoided, and which is at the heart of the current crisis of socialism that all thoughtful socialists have acknowledged, namely that it is anything but clear on what bases we are, today, to attach a clear and compelling content to the socialist idea. My argument up to this point would seem to imply that a definite sense of what we all understand by socialism already exists. Yet it would not be surprising if the altered terms of my case for socialism at the same time produced important modifications in the very conception of socialism. For the sake of simplicity in the preceding argument I have presupposed a more or less traditional definition of socialism in terms of ownership of means of production, or public disposal of collective resources. However, the specific circumstances of our contemporary situation (not excluding widespread public skepticism about the efficacy of state ownership) may well force us to consider a redefinition of what socialism means, or of what core commitments constitute grounds for identifying oneself as a socialist.[16] In order to face up to this problem as directly as possible let me submit for consideration what we can call the three principles of moral economy in a postliberal state. For each of these principles some remarks are offered that are in keeping with the political argument presented thus far. As should already be apparent, the intention has not been to establish a compelling case for socialism, but merely to offer suggestions for how to conduct the political debate, an argument whose real point is to highlight problems in the ways the debate is usually conducted.[17]

Full employment

Even Western societies in the developed world have had sufficient experience of mass unemployment to measure how profoundly it demoralizes those who suffer it directly as well as the society as a whole. In the light of both the social realities of our century and the specific contours of our argument, it would thus be reasonable to say that the first precept of a redefined socialism ought to be an overriding commitment to the goal of full employment, backed up by the agency of state planning. To be sure, it would appear that the redefinition of socialism centering upon this particular goal leads to certain paradoxes. In China, by 1976 the policies of the Cultural Revolution had produced very high unemployment in the cities. An important motivation behind the move toward private enterprise by the Deng Xiaoping regime was to eliminate this unemployment. But given these facts, it seems odd to say that the development of a mixed economy in China since 1976 represents a betrayal of socialist aspirations. (The opposite conclusion must be drawn in Hungary, say, where, even before the upheavals of 1989, socialist economists were being tempted by their experiments with market socialism to experiment as well with Western-style unemployment, in order to spur efficiency and competitiveness.) In theory, of course, unemployment can be overcome without state planning, but those who put their faith in the market are not likely to view unemployment as necessarily an evil, nor full employment as necessarily a good. The British experience, in particular, shows how unemployment serves the market by disciplining workers to conform themselves to market imperatives.

The reason for regarding full employment as the foremost political priority for state action is that no one subject to chronic unemployment can consider himself or herself, or be considered by the society, as a citizen in any meaningful sense.[18] Thus this formulation of the present-day meaning of socialism (focused upon productive employment within the society, and not, say, nationalization of industries or public intervention in the economy per se) remains consistent with the preceding argument, that socialism should be defined and justified not in terms of amelioration of the social condition, but in terms of expanded citizenship. To put it in the form of a principle applicable to the policies of social democratic government: public intervention in the workings of the economy is politically desirable, *whether or not it is economically more efficient,*[19] when it tends to draw more members of the society into a stable sense of being full citizens, or gives those already citizens a deepened or enlarged sense of political membership. The same principle can be applied to the urgent problem of housing in capitalist societies. How could a society that permits, as North American society permits, countless people to remain homeless, flatter itself that it offers an experience of common citizenship for its inhabitants?[20] Without certain minimal conditions of membership, such as adequate shelter and a reasonable prospect of reasonable employment, the promise of citizenship shows itself to be the merest pretense.

Any argument on behalf of socialist transformation presupposes an answer to the question "What is socialism?" or "How ought socialism to be conceived in the given historical context?" By proposing that the goal of full employment be made central to the definition of socialism, I have sought to supply an answer to this question: socialism today must signify a determination to put people to work, by any available means, utilizing the full powers and resources of the state, and to see to it that no one is deprived of the dignity of employment. The argument for this interpretation of socialism can be made on civic grounds. Without work one possesses no stable location in the world, no proper locus for one's dignity as a member of the society; and without the latter there can be no citizenship. (Such assumptions about the relationship between employment and citizenship have prompted the recent development of workfare programs in the United States.[21]) If being a citizen is a basic good within a good society, then full employment, as the condition of full citizenship, has priority over other social purposes.[22] Today socialism must be defined, in the first instance, not in terms of nationalization or social equality as such, but rather in terms of a publicly organized resistance against the evil of unemployment; and this, as I have presented it, is an aspect of what I have called the civic argument for socialism.[23]

Decent employment

But what if – horrors! – capitalism turns out to offer the only prospect of meaningful full employment; what if it turns out to be not only the more efficient producer of goods but also the more efficient producer of jobs?[24] The critic of capitalism will of course reply that not just *any* jobs will do; that the kinds of jobs generated by contemporary capitalist societies are no better than, perhaps in fact worse than, unemployment. Yet this reply is not entirely satisfactory. On the basis of what historical experience of capitalist and socialist economies can we hope for any guarantee that every job will be decent and satisfying? Marx's vision of a society in which all forms of labor are individually and socially rewarding, because those that are not are rendered technologically redundant, appears to be not an inch closer to realization today, after a century of unmatched economic growth and technological progress. If such a thing were possible, why has not a single government, left or right, simply abolished drudgery?[25] Even a socialist might begin to suspect that drudgery is not, within the range of finite expectations, abolishable.[26]

On the other hand, nothing dictates that one cannot continue to include the demand for full *and rewarding* employment as a reasonable object of socialist aspiration. After all, my purpose here is to clarify the nature of coherent socialist ideals; and an ideal, by definition, defines the direction in which hopes transcend realities.

The Plato principle

The basic moral intuition underlying the commitment to some version of socialism is, of course, that it is offensive that certain members of society earn incomes that are grossly out of relation to their real contribution to the welfare of society (because of arbitrary aspects of the social system of one sort or another). When one reflects on the wealth accumulated by a Mick Jagger, or a Jane Fonda, or a Wayne Gretzky, this intuition seems eminently sound. And the arbitrariness of the social criteria that establish these gross disparities appears all the more outrageous when one considers how, humiliated by seeing the obscene forms of consumption around them, those who are most severely deprived are effectively excluded from the possibility of sharing in a real political community with those who are most privileged. It hardly requires a full-blown theory of distributive justice to see that gross inequalities are bound to spawn widespread perceptions of injustice that cannot help but do violence to sentiments of shared citizenship. While material incentives may be necessary for the efficient working of a modern economy, it is difficult to see why these incentives must be of the scale of the existing ratios between the wealth of the highest-paid earners and that of the lowest-paid earners. (Did the Soviet Union and Hungary really require Soviet and Hungarian multimillionaires in order to reform *their* economies?) One can certainly seek to alter the magnitude of the disparity without entirely eliminating private incentives. But it remains open to the political philosopher to endorse greater equality either on grounds of the unfairness of existing arrangement or on grounds of the consequences for possibilities of solidarity and a greater sense of commonality (insofar as a distribution of material resources that is manifestly inegalitarian tends to undermine the perception of shared citizenship).[27]

In Plato's *Laws*, we have an ancient precedent of a political philosophy that mandates publicly enforced equality not for the sake of equity in the social relations between individuals, but for the sake of social order and the health of the polity. In Book 5 (744d–745a), Plato introduces the principle that in order to avert the possibility of civil strife between rich and poor, which would be otherwise unavoidable, all citizens of the society must be guaranteed a basic minimum of property, and no one ought to be allowed to accumulate total property exceeding five times the original allotment. If someone does accumulate more, "by finding something or being given something, or by money-making, or some other such stroke of luck – let him dedicate the surplus to the city."[28] Applied to modern conditions, the Plato principle would yield the result that if a streetsweeper earned $25,000 a year, a corporate lawyer could not earn more than $125,000.[29]

While not perfectly egalitarian, the universal application of this five-to-one ratio would certainly have a revolutionary impact on capitalist societies as they now exist. Contemporary welfare states of course operate on a principle something like this, but with results that are less egalitarian. No one can question the feasibility of this proposal since (unlike certain other socialist projects), given the legislative will, it can be implemented instantaneously; at most, one can claim that putting it into practice would diminish economic efficiency. Yet, as I have suggested above, this possibility of lower economic prospects should not necessarily count against it as a political proposal.

Karl Marx was certainly right to criticize socialists for making fair distribution the be-all and end-all of a good society.[30] The question of just distribution ought to be strictly subordinate to the question of the richness or emptiness of the shared mode of life of a society. However, the width of disparities in wealth and income bears not a small relevance to the quality of social relations, as Marx could scarcely have denied. The same considerations apply to the problem of citizenship. Of course, it may be that equalization of material resources barely begins to go to the heart of what is required for sentiments of social and political solidarity within a political community. And there may be a whole multitude of possibilities for promoting such civic solidarity and bridging class boundaries that have little or nothing to do with income equalization.[31] On the other hand, it is difficult to see how one could truly speak about membership in a common political community when, to use Rousseau's phrase, citizens are increasingly divided into beggars who are forced to sell themselves and rich people who have the wherewithal to buy them.[32]

Liberal and socialist critiques of capitalism are typically founded on conceptions of distributive justice. However, as the very reference to Plato reminds us, there are other bases for a critical stance toward an economic system as inexorably dynamic and morally destabilizing as capitalism.[33] Regardless of one's idea of justice, another salient aspect of capitalism, noted with anxiety by conservatives as well as socialists, is its corrosive effect upon the moral order of a society and its tendency, at least in the long run, to undermine the sentiments of common purpose that are vital for a stable sense of citizenship.[34] (I say in the long run because, as Charles Taylor has argued, there is no problem of meaning in a capitalist civilization while it is in the process of building itself up. It is only later, when capitalism is "in the saddle," that the problem of sustaining the meaning of it all arises.[35]) This too entails a certain egalitarian commitment – a civic egalitarianism, that is, an egalitarianism of shared purpose.

Socialism?

Because socialism and liberal capitalism have presented themselves as the two principal ideological alternatives subsequent to the defeat of fascism, it is easy to exaggerate the contrasts between capitalism and socialism, and to understate the similarities. Yet one would have to be thoughtless indeed to go on assuming that socialism can be counted on to resolve all the predicaments of liberalism. Historically, and with increasing apparentness as we near the close of this century, socialist politics has been caught within the very same predicaments. Like liberalism, it is an ideology focused chiefly on building economic productivity and expanding opportunities for freedom in exploiting nature, not on building character or enriching the experience of citizenship.[36] Even the committed socialist would have to be rather foolish to feel any complacency about the superiority of socialism to liberalism in respect of the problems raised by critics of liberalism. As Alasdair MacIntyre quite correctly observes: "That a systematically lower standard of living ought to be preferred to a systematically higher standard of living is a thought incompatible with either the economics or the politics of peculiarly modern societies. ... A community which was guided by Aristotelian norms would not only have to view acquisitiveness as a vice but would have to set strict limits to growth."[37]

The reorientation of political thinking implied in MacIntyre's challenge lies outside the horizon of traditional socialism just as much as it lies outside the horizon of liberalism. Still, socialism may hold certain advantages that ought not to be overlooked. Daniel Bell cites an incisive remark by Schumpeter to the effect that "stationary feudalism was an historical entity, stationary socialism an historical possibility, but stationary capitalism an historical contradiction in terms."[38] What this implies for our argument is that because socialism contains at least the theoretical possibility of a stationary economy, it retains advantages over capitalism, owing to the mounting social and environmental problems spawned by limitless growth, that are yet to be fully appreciated in modern societies.

There is one last advantage to a socialist outlook that may bear mention. For anyone who has looked to socialism as the solution to history's riddles, a glance at most of the regimes that have called themselves socialist in our epoch should suffice to dispel one's imaginings. But it is not yet fully clear that the antidote to political hubris exists in the liberal West. It may well be that the Western liberal democracies, led by the United States, have won the Cold War, as some have recently claimed.[39] On the other hand, it might just as well be true that the gradual rapprochement between the two leading superpowers owes as much to the anxiety of the American nation concerning its fitness to maintain its position in the world as to the anxiety of the ex-Soviet Union concerning its position in the world. At any rate, it is hard to see how shifting global destinies, with all their uncertainty, could warrant self-satisfaction on either side. Nor should it be assumed that the events of 1989 mark the end of socialism. Indeed, it is reasonable to claim that the anti-Communist revolutions in Eastern Europe had the effect of redeeming the socialist ideal no less than the regimes they have displaced served to discredit that ideal. In particular, socialism may come to be newly appreciated by the politically emancipated themselves as they begin to experience the unemployment, high housing costs, and other forms of unpleasantness associated with a free market.[40] Let us hope that the nearing of the end of the second millennium brings a mood of political reflectiveness and reserve commensurate with the awesome responsibilities exercised by centers of political power today.

Let us now sum up the preceding discussion. The experienced economic inadequacies of command economies and state-run enterprises in mixed economies have left nondogmatic socialists in a state of some anxiety in regard to whether adjustments in socialist doctrine can be made that absorb these lessons of socialist experience and yet leave the socialist ideal with some meaningful content, so that it remains something more than an empty radicalism or an egalitarian rhetoric uttered in order to assuage middle-class guilt. I have proposed three specific principles or guidelines of socialist practice, none of which has anything to do with public ownership:

1   Every employable member of the society is to be guaranteed a job at the behest of public authority. A Western society that consents to, or promotes,[41] the unemployment of 10 per cent of its working population should come to be seen in the same light, and be subject to the same degree of moral censure, as a society that arbitrarily disenfranchises a tenth of its adult citizenry. The contemporary salience of this principle is related to the fact that as political regimes in Eastern Europe move in the direction of a free market system, they will almost certainly have to accept significant levels of unemployment. Capitalist societies, while they may not necessarily welcome unemployment, have shown themselves willing to tolerate it as a price of economic efficiency; and previously communist social orders may consent to pay the same price. It would not be a negligible contribution to socialist theory to clarify the nature of this price, namely debased citizenship for those who are displaced to the margins.

2   Public authority is obliged to do everything in its power to render it more likely that the kinds of jobs actually available to members of the society do not destroy the soul.

3   The ratio of the highest to the lowest income in the society shall not
    exceed, say, five to one. This ratio shall be implemented by a publicly
    enforced, non-loophole-ridden, redistributive tax system. In a just
    social order it should be impossible for anyone to say what Leona
    Helmsley reportedly said to her maid: "We don't pay taxes. Only little
    people pay taxes."

The purpose of these policies is not to maximize social equality for its own
sake, but to support and enhance a sense of citizenship and common
involvement in the doings of the society one inhabits. Thus my argument
remains, as it was intended to be, a civic argument for socialism.[42]
    It may be asked: Why call this a brand of socialism if it has nothing to
do with public ownership or socialized ownership of some kind? Indeed, in
the United States, where there has been less of a socialist tradition than in
other liberal democracies, many a theorist committed to these three ideals
would probably not identify himself or herself as a socialist. But I think it
may be conceded that the greater the public intervention in the workings
of the market, the more valid the socialist label; and by any standard, the
three proposals discussed involve a large degree of deliberate political
intervention in the economy. Also, with these proposals I am assuming the
retention of what the best welfare states already provide. Therefore, for
instance, the United States, lacking a system of socialized medicine, would
be required to provide one. I should hasten to add that nothing here rules
out socialized ownership. Naturally, any socialist will be sympathetic to
workers' cooperatives, public agencies to meet basic needs, and so on. My
point, rather, is that even if various experiments in noncapitalist ownership
prove unworkable in the face of imperatives of global competition, there
would still be ideals to which chastened socialists could and should remain
faithful. Is it possible that in a socialist society according to the civic model,
citizenship would be sufficiently robust, feelings of solidarity sufficiently
pronounced, and the commitment to care for disadvantaged members of
one's society sufficiently strong that the whole society would become like
one very large kibbutz? Not very likely; but to the extent that these socialist
ideals were realized, the super-kibbutz analogy would have some force in
this respect at least: that the regulation, by the collective decision making
of the society as a whole, of tolerable margins of relative income, security
of employment, and thus life prospects generally, would be in some way
analogous to the collective regulation within the kibbutz of the relative
income, job security, and life prospects of its members; and to this extent
the residual fact of private ownership would be of less relevance. Even if
there is no general socialization of property, there would be, one might say,
a socialization of the perils of living in a modern society.

Of course, liberals will protest that theirs is an egalitarian philosophy too. But the question to be raised is whether a neutralist metatheory permits them to give a sufficient account of their own egalitarianism. Are we offering merely a beefed-up welfare state? Perhaps; or let us say, a beefed-up welfare state plus a greater sense of political involvement, by all citizens, in its fate. For as we have seen all too clearly from the politics of the 1980s, one of the major political problems of the welfare state is that even where it continues to receive grudging support from taxpayers, it is vulnerable to attack so long as socially egalitarian policies of the state are seen by citizens as an imposition by an alien power. Perhaps the repudiation by socialists of the principle of state neutrality can help them to do a better job than liberals of upholding egalitarianism in the eyes of the political community that will decide its future.

For the state to take charge of restructuring the economy to ensure full employment (if necessary, through employment by the state), to maximize humanly rewarding employment, and to equalize the distribution of wealth and income, are large and ambitious public purposes. But the larger the undertakings of the state, the greater the demands placed upon citizenship. We can glimpse here intimations of a vicious circle. The state would have to act as the agent of a shared purpose embraced by the whole political community, supported by a general and generous civic identification felt by members of that political community.[43] So measures at the level of public policy intended to strengthen and expand the experience of citizenship would themselves require the support of an already consolidated commitment to the state as the locus of citizenship and the agent of shared purposes: a classic chicken-and-egg problem.

We have examined a variety of strategies by which one might develop a brief for socialism, with the purpose of expanding the assumed range of theoretical options. (In any case, the *last* argument by which to persuade anyone in the last decade of the twentieth century of the desirability of socialism is that of Karl Marx – namely, its vastly superior potential for economic efficiency.) One would hope that the proposed principles are sufficiently straightforward and mutually reinforcing to provide a clear and coherent direction; unfortunately, things are not as simple as one would wish. Some of the problems have already been touched on: What if the guarantee of a full-employment economy requires a level of economic activity so dynamic that it jeopardizes other concerns that tend to engage socialists, such as environmental problems? What if a stationary or no-growth economy (desired for the sake of establishing a saner form of social existence) entails that the goal of full employment could only be secured at the price of forgoing the goal of decent employment? What if the only way to guarantee full employment in an economic environment shaped by a highly competitive global economy is precisely by propagating soul-destroying, tedious work (for example, by placing everyone in front of a computer terminal from nine to five)? What if, as I mentioned earlier, the principle of full employment in practice means forced drudgery at low wages? All of these pose real political challenges. However, the question of what sort of public policy would guarantee both employment for all *and* kinds of employment that would not wreck the higher human capacities of those employed is not one that we can reasonably expect a political philosophy to answer.[44]

Notes

1 John Gray has recently described himself as committed to "post-liberal theorizing," but the kind of theory that he appeals to in this context, that of Hobbes, seems to me to be preliberal rather than postliberal. See his *Liberalisms: Essays in Political Philosophy* (London: Routledge, 1989), pp. 234–6.

2 Since the reference to Marx may elicit some surprise, let me mention one supporting text. In the *Grundrisse*, trans. Martin Nicolaus (New York: Vintage, 1973), pp. 487–8, Marx observes that for the ancients "the question is always which mode of property creates the best citizens," and that in this respect antiquity is loftier than modernity. This quotation is taken from James T. Knauer, "Rethinking Arendt's *Vita Activa*: Toward a Theory of Democratic Praxis," *Praxis International*, 5, 2 (July 1985), pp. 185–94. Knauer, on pp. 192–3, attempts to draw from the work of Hannah Arendt the outlines of a theory of social justice conceived as instrumental to political equality, i.e. political justice, a theory that agrees very well with the one I attempt to sketch in this essay.

3 Michael Walzer, *Spheres of Justice: A Defense of Pluralism and Equality* (New York: Basic Books, 1983), p. 85. Walzer himself offers a definition of socialism focused on the invigoration of participatory politics in "Civility and Civic Virtue in Contemporary America," *Social Research* 41, 4 (Winter 1974), pp. 609, 611.

4 As John Dunn well observes, one of the outstanding weaknesses of modern political understanding "is the absurd overemphasis in political philosophy, ever since the constitution of political economy and the formation in reaction to it of socialist theories, upon distributive justice. In any political society which permits the open discussion of political choices, justice in the distribution of material goods is an inevitable focus of dispute. But the degree to which modern philosophers, whether Marxist or liberal, concentrate their imaginative energies upon this problem reflects a quite ludicrous level of misjudgment," *Rethinking Modern Political Theory* (Cambridge: Cambridge University Press, 1985), p. 186.

5 Similar lines of reflection are pursued in Philip Green's instructive book, *Retrieving Democracy: In Search of Civic Equality* (Totowa, NJ: Rowman and Allanheld, 1985). In *A Preface to Economic Democracy* (Berkeley: University of California Press, 1985), pp. 94–110, Robert Dahl considers an argument of the same form on behalf of workplace democracy. He examines arguments for and against the view "that democracy within firms would improve the quality

of democracy in the government of the state by transforming us into better citizens and by facilitating greater political equality among us" (p. 94).

6 Cf. Robert A. Dahl, *Democracy and its Critics* (New Haven: Yale University Press, 1989), p. 333; and Dahl, *A Preface to Economic Democracy*, op. cit., n. 5, pp. 10, 68–70, 110. See also Cass R. Sunstein, "Beyond the Republican Revival," *Yale Law Journal*, 97, 8 (July 1988), pp. 1552–3.

7 Cf. John Dunn, *The Politics of Socialism: An Essay in Political Theory* (Cambridge: Cambridge University Press, 1984), p. 53: "The redistribution of all substantial aggregations of private wealth in a society like Britain (or even the United States) would make a relatively trivial once and for all contribution to the material welfare of the great majority. But to live in a society which contrived to preserve all the other merits of these countries, but which no longer set off the distress of their less fortunate members by the gross luxury of a tiny parasitic class would at least make it easier to see the society itself as a single community and membership within it as a human bond with some genuine moral significance."

8 Jean-Jacques Rousseau, *On the Social Contract*, ed. R. D. Masters (New York: St Martin's Press, 1978), p. 54 n. and pp. 137–8 n.32. It is an odd fact that both ends of this French dichotomy can be translated by the same German word: *Bürger*. (The German *Bürgerlich* at the same time annuls the English distinction between civil and civic.) This seems to indicate that the relation between *bourgeois* and *citoyen* contains aspects of convergence as well as of tension. Perhaps the explanation for it has to do with T. H. Marshall's suggestion that the rise of modern citizenship coincides with the bourgeois triumph over feudalism: "Citizenship and Social Class," in T. H. Marshall, *Class, Citizenship, and Social Development* (Garden City, NY: Anchor Books, 1965), pp. 92–3. Cf. Ralf Dahrendorf, "Citizenship and Beyond: The Social Dynamics of an Idea," *Social Research*, 41, 4 (Winter 1974), pp. 675–6.

9 As Michael Walzer points out, according to the usage of the French Revolution, the title *Citoyen* connoted a universal status in a way that the title *Monsieur*, at the time, did not. Walzer, "Citizenship," in T. Ball *et al.* (eds), *Political Innovation and Conceptual Change* (Cambridge: Cambridge University Press, 1989), p. 211. On "the equality implicit in the concept of citizenship," cf. Marshall, *Class, Citizenship, and Social Development*, op. cit., n. 8, pp. 92–3.

10 Walzer, *Spheres of Justice*, op. cit., n. 3, Chapter 12.

11 For a consideration of certain political advantages of "actually existing" socialist regimes – a treatment informed by the political thinking of Plato – see Hans Jonas, *The Imperative of Responsibility: In Search of an Ethics for the Technological Age* (Chicago: University of Chicago Press, 1984), pp.145–51.

12 Hannah Arendt, *On Revolution* (New York: Viking Press, 1965), pp. 219–20.

13 In a speech on 26 July 1986, Fidel Castro declared, not without justification, that widespread drug use in the United States served to demonstrate the inability of Americans to practice virtue. In my view Castro was quite right to point to narcotics abuse as among the appropriate terms of comparison by which to measure the moral and political qualities of socialist versus nonsocialist societies.

14 According to Alexander Solzhenitsyn, the invasion of Western-style "freedom" commenced even before the barriers between East and West were lifted. He writes: "The iron curtain did an excellent job of defending our country against everything good in the West ... but the curtain didn't quite go all the way

down, and allowed the liquid dung of a debauched and decadent 'pop mass culture' to ooze underneath." Quoted in Michael Scammell, "A Great Man Eclipsed," *Times Literary Supplement*, 16–22 November 1990, p. 1234.

15 It is striking that even the authors of the much-publicized manifesto of the "Movement for Socialist Renewal" (drafted in November 1985) restrict their critical analysis of the relative strength of East and West chiefly to economic comparisons, agreeing entirely with Lenin's view that the decisive test of the success or failure of socialism would be whether it could outstrip the productivity of labor in capitalist economies. (In retrospect, it is clear that this document was an early statement of "Gorbachevism.")

16 For a thoughtful attempt to redirect socialist thought away from its preoccupation with the question of ownership, see Robert A. Dahl, *After the Revolution?* (New Haven: Yale University Press, 1970), pp. 115–40. An invaluable guide to the sorts of rethinking that are required is Alec Nove, *The Economics of Feasible Socialism* (London: George Allen and Unwin, 1983).

17 For a tough-minded and grimly realistic challenge to conventional renderings of the socialist idea, see Dunn's *Politics of Socialism*, op. cit., n. 7. It should be added that Dunn would not view with any greater equanimity the kind of alternative conception formulated here. Ibid., pp. 56–7.

18 Cf. Dunn, op. cit., n. 7, p. 54: "The prospect of a capitalist economy permanently unable to supply a large proportion of the society's adult members with gainful employment is not a pretty one. What sense can such victims be expected to make of their membership in a society which remains complacently or maliciously capitalist in its values?"

19 Socialists have always made the sanguine assumption that the supersession of capitalism would be accompanied by a higher standard of living (having your cake and eating it). But this assumption has turned out to be eminently falsifiable. If the socialist ideal delineates an intrinsically worthwhile form of life, it is not unthinkable that the ideal might be embraced at the price of (heresy!) a *lower* standard of living.

20 See Mary Ellen Hombs and Mitch Snyder, *Homelessness in America* (Washington: Community for Creative Non-Violence, 1986), p. xvi, for a hair-raising estimate of the numbers of these subcitizens: 1 per cent of the population. In November 1988 the General Accounting Office of the US Government let it be known that it considered credible the possibility that the homeless might actually exceed 1 per cent. *The World Almanac and Book of Facts, 1990* (New York: Pharos Books, 1989), p. 37.

21 See Lawrence M. Mead, *Beyond Entitlement: The Social Obligations of Citizenship* (New York: Free Press, 1986). Mead's argument is that welfare policies that tie entitlements to obligations to the society (that is, work in return for welfare benefits) would do more to enhance equality, not simply in the sense of economic equality but in the deeper sense of shared citizenship, than policies that confer entitlements with no corresponding duties or obligations. The concerns that inform Mead's book also run through Morris Janowitz, *The Reconstruction of Patriotism* (Chicago: University of Chicago Press, 1983). For critical scrutiny of the prescriptions offered by Mead and Janowitz, see Robert K. Fullinwider, "Citizenship and Welfare," in Amy Gutmann (ed.), *Democracy and the Welfare State* (Princeton: Princeton University Press, 1988), pp. 270–78. On the possible political advantages of workfare, cf. Benjamin Barber, *Strong Democracy* (Berkeley: University of California Press, 1984), pp. 210–11.

22   The principle of full employment is, to be sure, very noble sounding. Put into practice, especially when conjoined to the notion that employment is not simply a right (i.e. an option) but a social obligation, it acquires perhaps a harsher ring. However, it may be argued that the presence of an enduring underclass in American society is a problem of such desperate urgency that, analogous to the forcing to be free of Rousseau's citizens, the members of this underclass can permissibly be forced to be more equal partners in the social and economic life of the whole society. The Soviets were evidently less compromising than Westerners on the relation between work and citizenship, though admittedly this was expressed fairly unpleasantly in the Stalinist constitution of 1936: "It shall be the duty and honor of every able-bodied citizen of the USSR to work, according to the principle 'he who does not work, does not eat'." Quoted in Mead, op. cit., n. 21, p. 214. The source of this Stalinist principle is, remarkably enough, St Paul (2 Thess. 3:10). These observations may well remove some of the moralistic luster of socialist rhetoric about full employment. In any case, it seems pretty clear that what full employment really meant in, say, Soviet society was precisely workfare – that is, compulsory menial labor at the minimum wage.

23   It is not only socialists, to be sure, who recognize the threat to citizenship posed by unemployment. For discussion by a leading liberal of the relationship between work and citizenship, see Judith Shklar, "American Citizenship: The Quest for Inclusion," in Grethe B. Peterson (ed.), *The Tanner Lectures on Human Values*, vol. 11, (Salt Lake City: University of Utah Press, 1990), pp. 413–39, especially pp. 433–9.

24   For some information concerning episodes of unemployment in socialist societies, see Michael Ellman, *Socialist Planning* (Cambridge: Cambridge University Press, 2nd edn, 1989), pp. 179–87.

25   Michael Ellman's conclusion seems pretty much on the mark: "The CMEA [Comecon] countries do not differ fundamentally from the capitalist countries with respect to the rationality of the economic system, the labour process, the division of labour, and the social ownership of the means of production. In both groups of countries, most of the population is forced to engage in dreary labour in an inefficient, stratified, unequal society in which the means of production are not in social ownership." Ibid., p. 325.

26   On some relevant problems, see Fred Hirsch, *Social Limits to Growth* (Cambridge: Harvard University Press, 1976), pp. 41–51, especially p. 42. Hirsch argues that better equipping people for more attractive jobs does not actually increase the supply of such jobs, but merely intensifies the competition in a zero-sum game. (In Hirsch's terminology, sought-after kinds of employment are positional goods.)

27   For some helpful reflections on the extremity of inequality in contemporary American capitalism and its adverse implications for democratic citizenship, see Dahl, op. cit., n. 16, pp. 105–15, and his *Dilemmas of Pluralist Democracy* (New Haven: Yale University Press, 1982), pp. 170–86.

28   Plato, *The Laws*, ed. Thomas L. Pangle (Chicago: University of Chicago Press, 1988), p. 132. Cf. Plato, *Republic*, 421d–422a, 552a–b. The same line of thought is to be found throughout the writings of Rousseau, and it forms the philosophical ground of his own egalitarian politics. For one among many relevant texts, see Rousseau, "Political Economy," in *On the Social Contract*, op. cit., n. 8, pp. 230–32. What I have called the Plato principle also finds expression in

the following passage from Book 2, Chapter 11 of the *Social Contract* (p. 75 n.): "Do you want to give stability to the State? Bring the extremes as close together as possible: tolerate neither opulent people nor beggars. These two conditions, naturally inseparable, are equally fatal to the common good."

29 In *A Preface to Economic Democracy*, op. cit., n. 5, p. 105, Robert Dahl refers to wage and salary differentials in the United States of ten to one, twenty to one, and even one hundred to one, among individuals employed within the same firm. For elaboration by a noted economist of a proposal very similar to the one I have drawn from *The Laws*, see Lester C. Thurow, *The Zero-Sum Society* (New York: Basic Books, 1980), pp. 200ff. Plato's proposal is actually considerably more radical than the one advanced here, for Plato proposed the equalization of total property holdings, rather than merely that of income. As J. M. Barbalet demonstrates convincingly in *Citizenship* (Milton Keynes: Open University Press, 1988), pp. 52–4, the reduction of income differentials may leave untouched substantial inequalities of wealth, with adverse consequences for the ideal of equal citizenship (cf. Thurow, *Zero-Sum Society*, pp. 168–77). In order to ensure that equalization of incomes was not rendered nugatory by advantages associated with established property, my version of the Plato principle would have to be supplemented by a severe inheritance tax and a severe capital gains tax, as well as devices to equalize access to credit between those with capital and those without it.

30 Karl Marx, "Critique of the Gotha Programme," in Karl Marx and Frederick Engels, *Selected Works* (New York: International Publishers, 1968), pp. 321–5.

31 A persuasive argument along these lines is sketched by Mickey Kaus (drawing upon some of Michael Walzer's ideas about equal citizenship) in "For a New Equality," *New Republic*, 7 May 1990, pp. 18–27. The same analysis, applied to the policies of the post-World War II Labour government in Britain, can be found in Marshall, "Citizenship and Social Class," op. cit., n. 8, pp. 101, 113–14, 132; "Equality of status is more important than equality of income" (p. 113).

32 Rousseau, *Social Contract*, Book 2, Chapter 12.

33 For discussion of one possible source of critical reflection on capitalism that is neither liberal nor socialist in inspiration, see my "Hannah Arendt on Capitalism and Socialism," *Government and Opposition*, 25, 3 (Summer 1990), pp. 359–70.

34 Irving Kristol accuses left-wing radicals of succumbing to "highly apocalyptic notions of the present." But Kristol's own assessment of the present is not much less apocalyptic: "The inner spiritual chaos of the times, so powerfully created by the dynamics of capitalism itself, is such as to make nihilism an easy temptation," *Capitalism Today*, ed. Daniel Bell and Irving Kristol (New York: Basic Books, 1971), pp. 11, 13. In a similar vein, see also Daniel Bell, *The Cultural Contradictions of Capitalism* (New York: Basic Books, 1976). The same ambivalence toward capitalism, and the gloomy pathos that accompanies it, is already to be found in Schumpeter's celebration of capitalism's achievements and dismay over its self-annulling tendencies. (This attitude is captured well in the title of Kristol's book *Two Cheers for Capitalism* (New York: Basic Books, 1978); the choice of title is explained in the book's preface.) Like the neoconservatives, Schumpeter scorns radicals for failing to appreciate the extent to which the greatest feats of the modern world are owing to mentalities fostered by capitalism, but at the same time adopts a critical perspective that suggests,

168   *Ronald Beiner*

no less than that of the radical, that capitalism is morally problematical to a
profound degree. See Joseph A. Schumpeter, *Capitalism, Socialism and Democracy*
(New York: Harper and Row, 1976), p. 129: the radical's "adverse verdict
about capitalist civilization rests on nothing except stupidity, ignorance or irre-
sponsibility....But a completely adverse verdict may also be arrived at on a
higher plane." Reading Schumpeter and his successors, one is tempted to ask
whether capitalism is more unloved by its enemies than by the enemies of its
enemies. Similar lines of thought on the moral conditions of capitalism's
capacity to sustain itself are pursued in Kristol, "A Reply," *The Public Interest*, 22
(Winter 1971), pp. 104–5; Kristol, "Capitalism, Socialism, and Nihilism," *The
Public Interest*, 31 (Spring 1973), pp. 3–16; and (from a point of view that seems
more receptive to socialist possibilities) Fred Hirsch, *Social Limits to Growth*, op.
cit., n. 26. For a helpful scan of these issues, see Raymond Plant, "Hirsch,
Hayek, and Habermas: Dilemmas of Distribution," in A. Ellis and K. Kumar
(eds), *Dilemmas of Liberal Democracies* (London: Tavistock, 1983), pp. 45–64.

35 Charles Taylor, "Interpretation and the Sciences of Man," *Review of
Metaphysics*, 25, 1 (September 1971), pp. 42–3. Max Weber, in a key formulation, stated: "Capitalism at the time of its development needed labourers who
were available for economic exploitation for conscience's sake. To-day it is in
the saddle, and hence able to force people to labour without transcendental
sanctions." But if transcendental sanctions are dispensable, by virtue of what
can capitalism be expected to remain in the saddle indefinitely? Can it not at
some point fall out of the saddle? Weber refers in the same passage to "the
impersonality of present-day labour...its joyless lack of meaning," without
considering the problems that this might pose for the self-maintenance of the
work ethic in the absence of a larger horizon of meaning. Max Weber, *The
Protestant Ethic and the Spirit of Capitalism*, trans. Talcott Parsons (London: George
Allen and Unwin, 1948), p. 282 n. 108.

36 For more detailed consideration of some of the affinities between socialism
and capitalism, see Beiner, op. cit., n. 33. Cf. Vaclav Havel in the title essay of
The Power of the Powerless, ed. John Keane (London: Hutchinson, 1985), pp.
26–7, 38–9, 45, 68, 89–92; and Havel, *Disturbing the Peace*, trans. Paul Wilson
(New York: Vintage Books, 1991), pp. 10, 13–16, 168. Also Alasdair
MacIntyre, *After Virtue* (Notre Dame, IN: University of Notre Dame Press,
1981), p. 33.

37 Alasdair MacIntyre, *Whose Justice? Which Rationality?* (Notre Dame, IN:
University of Notre Dame Press, 1988), p. 112. Cf. T. H. Marshall, "Value-
Problems of Welfare-Capitalism," in *The Right to Welfare and Other Essays*
(London: Heinemann Educational Books, 1981), pp. 120–21: "Materialism,
profit-seeking, quantity-worship and growth-mania are not characteristics of
capitalism alone, but permeate the whole of modern technological mass
society."

38 Bell, *Cultural Contradictions of Capitalism*, op. cit., n. 34, p. 240.

39 See, notably, Francis Fukuyama, "The End of History?," *The National Interest*,
16 (Summer 1989), pp. 3–18. For the most part, Fukuyama's argument is
suffused with obnoxious gloating, though it is punctuated by moments of
liberal self-doubt.

40 The situation of those in what was formerly East Germany (a wholesale
collapse of industry, and staggering rates of unemployment) bears a particular

pathos, given the cruel disparity between their expectations when they joined the West and their present plight.

41 While it might seem unlikely that any modern government would actually promote unemployment (as opposed to simply accepting it as the price of infla-tion-fighting measures in an unemployment-inflation trade-off), it is arguable that this was precisely the weapon deliberately used in the early years of Margaret Thatcher's government to discipline the trade union movement.

42 One should not overlook internal connections between the three principles. Thurow, op. cit., n. 29, pp. 203–6, draws out one such connection in arguing that the most effective means of narrowing differentials in income is by committing the state to the provision of universal employment.

43 The notion of citizenship bears a similar burden in David Miller, *Market, State and Community: Theoretical Foundations of Market Socialism* (Oxford: Clarendon Press, 1989), Part 3, especially Chapter 9. Miller, unfortunately, is still attracted to liberal neutralist metatheory.

44 Admittedly, socialism may present itself as a less than satisfying theory if it enumerates what all of us cherish – work, security, happiness, a sense of effi-cacy and empowerment, a decent life – while offering little definite guidance (certainly far less than it could once have confidently offered) on how to secure these good things. Why this is not the rightful task of theory, see R. Beiner, *What's the Matter with Liberalism?* (Berkeley: University of California Press, 1992), pp. 171–92.

10 Communitarianism
Left, right and centre

David Miller

My title is meant to suggest two things about communitarianism. The first is that there is a lot of it around. I am not sure which political philosopher was the first to say 'I am a communitarian' in the way that Pierre-Joseph Proudhon founded the (self-conscious) anarchist tradition when he wrote, in 1840, 'I am an anarchist', but what is certain is that by the mid-1980s it was becoming common to speak of communitarianism as an ideological rival to liberalism;[1] soon after that, indeed, with the political collapse of socialism, and the passage of most conservatives into the libertarian New Right, as the main or only ideological rival. In political philosophy we learnt to talk of a liberal–communitarian debate – an idea that I shall be looking at critically in a moment. Not long after, there appeared a political movement of communitarians. There was the Communitarian Network founded by Etzioni, with threads stretching outwards from Washington to connect to chapters in European and other liberal democracies.[2] Politicians of the centre-left – Clinton and Blair, for instance – began regularly to invoke community in their speeches. And this seemed to catch the spirit of the age, which was preoccupied with issues such as crime and social order, drug abuse, homelessness, problems for which 'more community' in some sense seemed to offer a solution.

Yet communitarianism considered as a political programme was and remains strangely amorphous. Does it really provide a new perspective on politics, or is it merely a rhetorical device by which fairly standard liberal (in the American sense) or social democratic (in the European sense) policies can be sold to the electorate? It is one thing to invoke community as a moral ideal, to encourage us all to be good neighbours, to keep our lawns neatly mown and try to ensure that children can walk safely to school along our streets. It is another thing to say that the state can legitimately enforce communal values, using the coercive apparatus at its disposal to oblige us to behave as good citizens. In avoiding the charge that they are moral totalitarians, communitarians seem to leave themselves open to the equally damaging charge, levelled by critics such as Stephen Holmes, that their attacks on liberalism are all hot air. 'Nebulousness about nonliberal politics,' Holmes says, 'is not an incidental feature of communitarianism; it is an essential one.'[3] The charge is that communitarianism cannot deliver an alternative political programme; it is made up merely of a series of rhetorical attacks on the alleged premises of liberal theory.

At this point I want to draw out the second idea contained in my title. Communitarianism as political theory comes in sharply different versions. There is a communitarianism of the left, an egalitarian communitarianism defended by many socialists and social democrats. There is also a communitarianism of the right, an authoritarian communitarianism less popular today than it was in the past, but still embraced by some conservatives. And finally – this suggestion may be a bit less familiar – there is a liberal version of communitarianism. I shall try to bring out as clearly as I can the crucial features that differentiate these three forms of communitarianism, and I shall also try to show that each taken by itself has fairly definite political implications. In other words, even if communitarianism as an umbrella term is politically amorphous, the three doctrines sheltering under that umbrella that I shall identify are not.

I draw the distinction between left, right and centre not just for the sake of intellectual clarity, but because I want to defend a form of left communitarianism. One unfortunate effect of the liberal v. communitarian framework is that people are put under some pressure to declare which team they support, to use Charles Taylor's metaphor. It is of some interest here that among the political philosophers who are usually nominated for the communitarian team, none has shown himself enthusiastic about wearing the team colours. Taylor and Michael Walzer have both offered subtle diagnoses of why there has been the appearance of a liberal–communitarian debate, avoiding in doing so the need to declare for either side.[4] MacIntyre roundly declares that he has strongly dissociated himself from contemporary communitarians whenever he has had the opportunity to do so.[5] Michael Sandel did self-apply the communitarian label in his introduction to *Liberalism and its Critics* – the book which probably did most to inspire the two teams model – but in his more recent work chooses instead to describe himself as a republican.[6] If my claim that communitarianism comes in radically different versions is correct, this reluctance is hardly surprising: no one wants to sign up to something which is liable to place them in the same camp as others whose political views they heartily despise – Michael Walzer with Roger Scruton, for instance. Once the relevant distinctions are drawn, however, each can unashamedly espouse and defend his or her favoured version of communitarianism without fear of confusion or misunderstanding.

Let me now say briefly why it was misleading to speak of a debate between communitarians and liberals. Any political theory, I want to suggest, contains two analytically separable elements: on the one hand a philosophical anthropology, a general account of the human person, of the conditions of moral agency, of the nature of human relationships and so forth. (This account may be implicit or explicit, but it is always there.) On the other hand, the theory will contain a set of prescriptive principles, principles specifying how social relationships are to be ordered, how the state is to be constituted and so on. The relationship between the philosophical anthropology and the prescriptive principles is one of support rather than entailment; the picture of human personhood helps to make plausible a certain political doctrine, but much additional legwork, often of a broadly empirical kind – claims about how different institutions are likely to function, for instance – needs to be done to back the doctrine up fully.[7]

If we apply this distinction between philosophical anthropology and prescriptive political doctrine to the case of communitarianism, we can see that what brings together those political thinkers who are called communitarians is primarily a convergence at the level of philosophical anthropology. As I shall argue in a minute, their political doctrines may be highly disparate. So what is the core element in a communitarian philosophical anthropology? It is a thesis about the social constitution of the self: the self cannot be understood apart from the social relations in which it is embedded. Putting this in different terms, the thesis is that we cannot understand human beings except against the background of social institutions, practices, forms of life which give them concrete identities. The contrast here is with individualism. For those who accept an individualist anthropology, the basic elements in the social world are individual human beings, each with the capacity to form their own beliefs, preferences and goals. The social world is made up of the practices and institutions that these individuals have created in order to pursue their aims in collaboration with one another. From a communitarian perspective, the individualist picture of the human condition is an incoherent one. It cannot make sense of the fact that we have identities that are not reducible to contingent matters of preference and belief: in other words that when I ask the question 'Who am I?', the answer I give does not merely list features of myself that I could change tomorrow, like my job or my taste in music, but unchosen characteristics deriving from the social setting in which I was formed – my ancestry, my gender, my ethnicity.[8] Equally, communitarians claim, an individualist anthropology cannot make sense of our ethical experience: our capacity to judge things, including our own tastes, right or wrong in some objective sense.[9] The claim is that this capacity can only be understood against the background of a community which provides us

with a language of shared evaluation. (Or, in the variant of this claim associated especially with Alasdair MacIntyre, it is that the relevant community
has largely disappeared – only fragments are left – so moral evaluation
collapses into subjective preference.[10])

So here then we have two broad philosophical anthropologies: the individualist picture which sees people as independent, freely choosing agents,
and the communitarian picture which sees them as essentially embedded
in communal relations. It is a difficult task to say exactly what is the nature
of the disagreement between the two pictures – how far the disagreement
is strictly philosophical, and how far it might be amenable to resolution by
appeal to empirical evidence, for instance – but fortunately for my present
purposes there is no need to pursue this question any further. What I do
want to argue is that when we use 'communitarianism' as an umbrella
term embracing a range of social theorists whose political outlooks are
often sharply at variance with one another, the proper contrast to draw is
with individualism and not with liberalism. Communitarianism in this
sense is a philosophical anthropology rather than a political doctrine.

So why did we start talking about a liberal–communitarian debate? The
answer, I believe, is that a certain widely held form of liberalism, which for
the sake of convenience rather than historical accuracy I shall call standard or mainstream liberalism, does have a natural affinity with
individualist anthropology. People who are liberals of this sort characteristically defend their political positions by invoking an individualist view of
the self. Mainstream liberalism typically involves such doctrines as the
priority of rights (rights as trumps), the notion that the principles of a just
social order should be established by reference to a hypothetical social
contract, and the idea that the state should preserve its neutrality as
between conceptions of the good life. These doctrines are very often
defended by appealing to the picture of the individual as a freely choosing
agent, and society as a set of arrangements designed or evolved to permit
such individuals to pursue their ends. We can fairly easily point to examples of political philosophies which move in this way from individualist
premises to mainstream liberal conclusions: Nozick's theory of rights, for
instance, Rawls' theory of justice (particularly in its original version when
the contractarian element was highlighted), Dworkin's theory of liberal
equality.[11] Those critics who get classified as communitarians take exception to this pattern of argument; they claim that the argumentative
assumptions, for instance Rawls' picture of individuals each with his or her
own conception of the good choosing principles of justice from behind a
veil of ignorance, fail to recognize the social preconditions for individual
agency. But they object much more to the pattern of argument than to the
conclusions reached. In that sense they are not critics of liberalism unless

we misleadingly enlarge the meaning of liberalism so that it includes not only a set of political doctrines but also a philosophical anthropology.

That, then, is my diagnosis of the so-called liberal–communitarian debate. Insofar as we can describe the miscellaneous set of political philosophers who are labelled communitarians as a group, what unites them are their anti-individualist philosophical anthropologies. They appear to be critics of liberalism only because there is some affinity between individualism and standard liberalism. (This affinity, by the way, is just that: an affinity, not a logical connection. Holding an individualist anthropology is neither a necessary nor a sufficient condition for adopting liberal political doctrines: to see that it isn't a sufficient condition, think of the case of Hobbes, who moved from individualist premises to authoritarian political conclusions.)

But if communitarians are not rightly understood as critics of liberalism, how are we to make sense of their political doctrines? If we begin from a communitarian anthropology, one that emphasizes the social constitution of the self and the embeddedness of the individual in social relations, what follows about the shape of our social and political institutions?

On the basis of what has been said so far about communitarian anthropology, the answer seems to be: nothing of very much substance. There are two paths along which we might try to move from the anthropological premise to some sort of political conclusion. On the one hand, we might argue that, because our identities are socially constituted, and therefore shared with others, it is both legitimate and desirable for these identities to be reflected in the way that our institutions are constructed and our policies are designed. The public sphere should express those aspects of the self that we hold in common with others. If that common identity involves adherence to a particular religion, for example, then our political institutions should be guided by the principles and symbolism of that religion. On the other hand, the claim may be that our communal identities cannot survive without political support; that we are in danger of becoming deracinated unless public policy is directed towards strengthening and reproducing these identities, for instance through the education system. As they stand, however, these claims are remarkably unspecific; they do not go very far in specifying how the public sphere should be constituted. It looks as though Holmes' charge that communitarianism as a political doctrine is essentially nebulous has been vindicated.

What I should like to suggest, however, is that it takes on much more definite shape when we distinguish left, right and centre variants. I want now to provide brief sketches of each, though I should say right away that the three versions are not exhaustive of communitarian political theory.

There are communitarianisms of the far right and the far left that I shall not consider: I am identifying forms of communitarianism that have at least some prospect of taking hold as the public philosophy of one of the technologically advanced liberal democracies. I'll start in the centre, with liberal communitarianism.

Liberal communitarians, among whom Jo Raz and Will Kymlicka are distinguished representatives in recent political philosophy, hold two central convictions that are characteristically liberal.[12] One concerns the irreducible plurality of individual values or 'conceptions of the good': there are many valuable ways of life which people may choose to pursue, and these cannot be derived from any single model or more fundamental principle. The other concerns the importance of autonomous choice: whichever way of life a person follows, it is important that he or she should have chosen to follow it after reflection on alternatives, rather than simply having been inducted into it, through a Jesuitical upbringing, for instance. These, as I said, are fairly standard liberal convictions. The communitarian twist occurs when it is argued that both the availability of a spectrum of ways of life and the capacity for autonomy depend upon a communal background. People can't engage in practices such as family life, religious observance or musical performance unless there are groups of people in their society who engage in such practices; moreover the capacity for autonomous choice – the capacity to stand back from and reflect critically upon any particular way of life – is not something that people are natively endowed with, but is a capacity that is nurtured by autonomy-supporting practices and institutions whose existence cannot be taken for granted.

The key idea in the liberal communitarian vision of things is that a political society should be made up of a plurality of communities which ought as far as possible to have the character of voluntary associations. That is, they are communities which individuals are free to leave, and which they therefore remain within by voluntary consent. The liberal communitarian does not deny that, as a matter of fact, individuals are born into some of these communities, and acquire their memberships not by choice but as a matter of brute historical fact. But ideally each person should reflect upon, and freely reaffirm, his or her membership of each of the communities with which he or she is associated. This is made possible by the fact that typically each person belongs to several such communities – say family, ethnic or religious group, work association, neighbourhood – and can criticize the norms and values of one group from the perspective of the others. Thus pluralism becomes a condition of autonomy, and recognition of the role of communities is squared with the liberal emphasis on autonomous choice.

How does this translate into liberal politics? On the one hand, standard liberal commitments – to individual rights, freedom of movement and association, the rule of law – can be defended as providing the conditions under which communities can flourish, while at the same time ensuring that as far as possible they take on the character of voluntary associations. On the other hand, the liberal communitarian is prepared to depart from what I earlier called standard liberalism in certain areas in order to recognize or foster community. One lively area of controversy here is the role of the state in relation to cultural groups of various kinds. How far is it justified to offer additional resources or special protections to such groups in order to support them against erosion by influences stemming from the wider society? On the other hand, how far should the state go in insisting that groups must adopt liberal norms such as freedom of expression internally?[13] These debates are familiar ones, but they are inevitable given the liberal communitarian assumptions, a) that group membership provides members with valuable forms of life and the resources to become autonomous; but b) that autonomy cannot be fully achieved unless members are able to reflect critically upon the assumptions and ethos of any particular group to which they belong.

This, then, is the liberal form of communitarianism. Let me turn now to communitarianism of the right, which can be introduced most easily by seeing what its advocates would see as the deficiencies of liberal communitarianism. As a representative of this position I shall take the conservative philosopher Roger Scruton.[14] What, according to Scruton and those who think like him, is wrong with liberal forms of communitarianism? The first deficiency of liberalism is that it fails to address the problem of social unity: what ties together all the various associations and sub-groups into a cohesive whole? The liberal looks to the state itself to perform this unifying function: we are held together by our mutual subscription to the authority of the state and its laws, but on the conservative view this is a shallow answer. Political legitimacy depends upon a pre-political sense of common membership. We have to feel that we belong together in a common society before we can address the question of the political institutions that will govern us.

So the first distinguishing mark of right communitarianism is that it looks to inclusive community as a source of social union. The second point is that it sees community as a source of authority. In identifying with a community, I subject myself to the customs and conventions that it embraces. Whereas the liberal sees communities as facilitating choice, on the conservative view, the point of communal identification is precisely to foreclose choice and provide people with a substantive way of life to adopt. And communities have to have a certain character if they are to do this.

'The real price of community', Scruton says, 'is sanctity, intolerance, exclusion, and a sense that life's meaning depends upon obedience, and also on vigilance against the enemy.'[15] Clearly if communities are like that they cannot be voluntary associations. They should be authoritatively structured, hard to leave and preferably hereditary in character. Using a loose metaphor, if the liberal ideal of community is something like a Quaker meeting, the conservative idea is something like the Roman Catholic Church.

If the two keynotes of right communitarianism are unity and authority, it is fairly easy to see why pride of place in conservative thinking should be given to nationality as a form of community. A national community by definition unifies those within the boundaries of the nation; and its nature is such as to exercise a deep influence on the characters of the people who belong to it. Scruton lists a shared language, shared associations, a shared history and a common culture as factors typically contributing to nationality, and clearly these are features that are pervasive and virtually impossible to shed: you cannot escape the fact that you were born in a certain place, into a certain culture, speaking a certain language and so forth. The conservative recipe thus calls for the nation-state – a state whose boundaries coincide with that of the nation – as the basis for political order. From this there follow a number of policy prescriptions which distance communitarianism of this sort from the liberal version – for instance, a highly restrictive approach to immigration, which is seen as diluting the common culture which supports the authority of the state; a more directive approach to education, part of whose function is to transmit the established cultural identity to the new generation; and so forth.

Let me turn by way of contrast to communitarianism of the left. Again we can most easily grasp this by seeing first of all how it is distinguished from the right communitarianism that I have just outlined. The two identifying features of the left communitarianism that I want to capture are that the community it seeks to preserve or create should be one formed on the basis of equality, and that the community should be actively self-determining rather than subject to the authority of tradition. Let me elaborate a little on these features. First, left communitarians look for communities in which each member enjoys equality of status. What does this mean? It means that although members may enjoy unequal standing in certain particular respects – one is regarded as more expert than another at solving engineering problems, one is seen as more capable than another at holding positions of responsibility and so forth – overall they regard and treat one another as equals. There are, in other words, no hierarchical class divisions such that one could say that, regarded simply as persons, Smith enjoys a higher status than Jones.[16] As to the second feature, although the community may have a special ethos that distinguishes it from other communities, this is not seen as sanctified by past tradition, but as open to revision when the members deliberate collectively about their aims and purposes. Thus it is essential that the community should have some mechanism to allow this deliberation to proceed – some form of democratic self-government. The anthropological assumption is that people flourish best when they associate together on the basis of equality, and have a deep interest in shaping their physical and social environment collectively.

Now the left communitarianism that I have in mind here is not the radical version, espoused by many communists and anarchists, which looks for an all-embracing form of community; which seeks to re-order society so that people are related to one another entirely through small encompassing communities – a world of friendly kibbutzim, if you like. This I take not to be a live political option in the world we live in. My interest is in the more moderate version espoused by many socialists and social democrats which recognizes that community has to compete with other forms of affiliation. It is perhaps best expressed through a doctrine of strong citizenship: this says that though people may choose to relate to one another in many different ways, their most basic form of association must be as equal citizens engaged in collective self-determination. Michael Walzer has perhaps expressed this most eloquently in the chapter of *Spheres of Justice* where he argues that equal membership of a political community is the precondition for all the more specific practices of distributive justice that citizens may engage in.[17]

I have pointed out what differentiates left communitarianism from right. What do left communitarians have to say about liberal communitarianism? Two things, mainly. First, if people define their identities through a plurality of specific communities without at the same time giving priority to an inclusive politically organized community, there is a danger that the social fabric will begin to unravel, with the different communal groups becoming increasingly alienated from and hostile to one another. This, if you like, is the left critique of multiculturalism: an exclusive emphasis on the celebration of specific cultural identities may be incompatible with preserving just that form of political community which allows such separate identities to co-exist in relative peace.[18] Second, there is no general reason to think that liberal communitarianism will be egalitarian. Communities may adopt hierarchical structures internally, which may be morally offensive in their own right – if they are sexist or racist, for instance – but even if they are not, may tend to undermine people's equal standing as citizens. Furthermore, allowing full autonomy to each community may produce inegalitarian outcomes overall, even if the various groups are democratic and egalitarian internally. Consider, for instance, a system of private schooling based on religious groups in a society where by and large the Protestants are rich and the Catholics are poor; or consider a system where ethnic groups run their own housing associations and there are big differences in the economic standing of different groups. From a left perspective, inequalities of this kind pose a grave danger to equal citizenship, and can only be combated if members of the various groups – Catholics and Protestants, blacks and whites – see themselves as belonging to the same inclusive community, which can then be organized politically to combat group inequalities in life-chances.

This completes my sketch of the three versions of communitarianism: there is a liberal communitarianism which seeks to create and support a plural society whose very pluralism, by the possibilities it offers for turning your back on one group and joining another, provides the conditions for individual autonomy. There is a conservative form of communitarian which argues that preserving the authority of a single inclusive community is the precondition for social cohesion and a legitimate state. And there is a left communitarianism, which also looks to an inclusive community, but wants it to be egalitarian and self-determining in a fairly strong sense.

If we reflect a bit on these three models, one thing we can see is that the anthropological idea of the social constitution of the self takes on a rather different meaning in each case. For the liberal communitarian the self is socially constituted in the sense that people acquire their conceptions of the good and their capacity for autonomy from their membership, typically, of several social communities; in other words a flourishing set of cross-cutting communities provides the soil from which the autonomous self springs. For the conservative communitarian, by contrast, what matters is that we should identify with, and recognize the authority of, an inherited way of life. The proper relation between self and community here is one of willing subjugation. The left communitarian has a different view again. Communities matter because each of us seeks recognition from those around him, and so the quest is for a form of community that unites us as equals, with every member being regarded as of equal standing and worth. But there is nothing sacred about the inherited culture or ethos of any particular community; this is a proper matter for collective deliberation and reform. The left communitarian, like the liberal communitarian and unlike the right communitarian, values personal autonomy, but whereas the liberal picture is of each individual choosing which way of life to adopt after encountering several possibilities, the left picture is of us choosing our way of life together, through critical reflection on the one we now have in common. Autonomy here has a political character that is missing from the liberal version. So my earlier suggestion, that communitarians converge at the level of their philosophical anthropology but then diverge at the level of prescriptive political doctrine, turns out to need qualification. There is some convergence, certainly, particularly if we juxtapose any of the positions I have just sketched with a crudely individualistic view of the self. But what emerges from my analysis is that claims such as 'community is constitutive of personal identity' which are loosely bandied about in discussions of communitarianism actually need a good deal of unpacking before it is clear what they mean; and in the course of the unpacking we discover some major ambiguities about what precise relationship between self and community is being envisaged.

So far my argument in this chapter has mainly been diagnostic. But behind this there lies a more practical question: what are the political prospects of communitarianism, and in particular a communitarianism of the left? At the moment the debate about community tends to oscillate between the centre and the right versions. One way of putting the challenge of Holmes and other liberals sceptical of communitarianism would be as follows: either communitarianism takes an innocuous form in which it departs from standard liberalism only in minor ways, for example in arguing for policies to help support cultural groups under threat of collapse; or it becomes authoritarian and involves using the state to impose a received set of moral values on unwilling subjects. This way of putting the challenge assumes that there is no feasible communitarianism of the left. Now what is certainly true is that whereas we can readily imagine what right communitarianism might look like in practice – we can point to states like Singapore or other places in Asia which approximate to the model – and we can equally imagine how liberal communitarianism would work by extrapolating a bit from the policies of multiculturalism that are currently practised in North America and elsewhere – it is harder to envisage how left communitarianism might take shape in the real world. Even though I have distanced it from radical communism, it might still seem to fall below the horizon of feasibility, so that the real communitarian options are either Asian authoritarianism or multicultural America. So what are the main problems that left communitarianism has to face? I think that there are three, but here I can only signal very briefly the solutions that I should want to propose.

The first is whether it is plausible to suppose that people can identify strongly with an inclusive political community as left communitarianism demands. Or is it the case that the identities that really count when we ask what constitutes the person are much more localized – are they ethnic or religious identities, for instance? It is in response to this problem that I have argued elsewhere[19] that in today's world strong citizenship can only be made to work when it is supported by a shared national identity, and that the left must therefore reconsider its traditional intellectual hostility to ideas of nationhood (I say 'intellectual' here because in practice the political left has always been willing to invoke national solidarity to help win support for its policies). The problem, then, is how to recast national identities so that they can both include everyone who is a member of the political community, and yet be strong enough to bind people together in a form of citizenship that can override sectional loyalties based on class, profession, locality, ethnicity, etc.

The second issue is whether citizenship alone can support a form of equality that is sufficiently robust from a left communitarian perspective. Citizenship is expressed concretely in the form of equal rights and principles of equal treatment. In the face of the substantial economic and other material inequalities that seem to be endemic in market societies, is this sufficient to create a community whose members genuinely regard themselves as one another's equals? You will recall Marx's charge, in his early essay on the Jewish question, that citizenship as a form of community must remain illusory in face of the divisions of civil society, where in Marx's view people's real life is led.[20] So how can we bolster the formal rights of citizenship in order to secure an equal status for each member of the relevant political community? Here I believe we must draw inspiration from Michael Walzer's idea of complex equality, the idea, to put it very briefly, that in a society which recognizes many separate spheres of distribution, inequalities in one sphere can be offset by countervailing inequalities in other spheres to sustain an overall equality of status.[21]

The third issue springs from the requirement that the values which animate the community should be adopted or re-adopted following collective deliberation on the part of the members – in other words that they should not merely be accepted as a received tradition, but they should be subject to critical scrutiny at regular intervals. How can this be achieved in a large society where face-to-face discussion between all members is out of the question? Is it not inevitable that the values which are adopted to govern policy decisions should be the values of the political elite, or of white heterosexual males? In other words, how can we achieve democratic deliberation of the kind that the left communitarian picture requires, if it is to be genuinely distinct from the right communitarian picture of an inherited national identity imposed on outsiders? Here I believe we need to explore new forms of democracy that take us beyond representative assemblies and conventional parties – for instance local forums, citizens' juries, deliberative opinion polls, referendums and other mechanisms which can draw ordinary citizens into the political dialogue.[22]

These three problems – how to generate a strong but inclusive political community, how to defend equal citizenship in face of economic inequality, how to ensure that the self-governing community is genuinely democratic – are all hard ones. What I find so unsatisfying about contemporary communitarianism *qua* political movement is that it addresses none of them. By remaining vague about the actual locus of community, it avoids taking a stand on the issue of nationality. It has almost nothing to say about increasing material equality or more generally issues of distributive justice (Etzioni is candid about this: 'What is the communitarian economic agenda? The short answer is, there is none.'[23]), and in this way it avoids the crucial issue of how community can be sustained at all in the face of market-driven economic inequalities. Finally it does not argue for changing political structures to enhance democracy, seeking instead to moralize existing representative systems by combating the corruption of legislators by special interest groups.[24] In short, then, the communitarian political movement, avoiding controversial political issues in order to appeal to as wide a range of constituents as possible, ends up as little more than a moral appeal to us all to behave better: take more responsibility for our social environment, avoid corruption, etc. etc. My argument in this chapter has been that communitarians must come off the fence: a politically relevant form of communitarianism may be a communitarianism of the left, the right or the centre, but it cannot be all of these at once.

Notes

1   See, in particular, A. Gutmann, 'Communitarian Critics of Liberalism', *Philosophy and Public Affairs*, 14 (1985), pp. 308–22, reprinted in S. Avineri and A. de-Shalit (eds), *Communitarianism and Individualism* (Oxford: Oxford University Press, 1992).

2   For its guiding ideas, see A. Etzioni, *The Spirit of Community* (London: Fontana, 1995).

3   S. Holmes, *The Anatomy of Antiliberalism* (Cambridge, MA: Harvard University Press, 1993), p. 178.

4   C. Taylor, 'Cross-Purposes: The Liberal–Communitarian Debate', in *Philosophical Arguments* (Cambridge, MA: Harvard University Press, 1995); M. Walzer, 'The Communitarian Critique of Liberalism', *Political Theory*, 18 (1990), pp. 6–23.

5   A. MacIntyre, 'A Partial Response to My Critics', in J. Horton and S. Mendus (eds), *After MacIntyre* (Cambridge: Polity Press, 1994), p. 302.

6   M. Sandel (ed.), *Liberalism and its Critics* (Oxford: Blackwell, 1984); M. Sandel, *Democracy's Discontents* (Cambridge, MA: Belknap Press, 1996).

7   Charles Taylor draws a rather similar distinction between 'ontological issues' and 'advocacy issues' in 'Cross-Purposes', op. cit., n. 4. See also S. Caney, 'Liberalism and Communitarianism: A Misconceived Debate', *Political Studies*, 40 (1992), pp. 273–89, and A. Buchanan, 'Assessing the Communitarian Critique of Liberalism', *Ethics*, 99 (1988–9), pp. 852–82.

8   For this argument, see, for instance, M. Sandel, *Liberalism and the Limits of Justice* (Cambridge: Cambridge University Press, 1982), Chapter 1.

Communitarianism: left, right and centre 183

9 This claim is developed in, for instance, C. Taylor, *Sources of the Self* (Cambridge: Cambridge University Press, 1989), Part 1.

10 A. MacIntyre, *After Virtue* (London: Duckworth, 1981), esp. chapters 1–5.

11 R. Nozick, *Anarchy, State and Utopia* (Oxford: Blackwell, 1974); J. Rawls, *A Theory of Justice* (Cambridge, MA: Harvard University Press, 1971); R. Dworkin, 'Liberalism', in *A Matter of Principle* (Oxford: Clarendon Press, 1986).

12 See J. Raz, *The Morality of Freedom* (Oxford: Clarendon Press, 1986), chapters 14–15; J. Raz, 'Multiculturalism: A Liberal Perspective', in *Ethics in the Public Domain* (Oxford: Clarendon Press, 1994); W. Kymlicka, *Liberalism, Community and Culture* (Oxford: Clarendon Press, 1989), chapters 7–9; W. Kymlicka, 'Liberal Individualism and Liberal Neutrality' *Ethics*, 99 (1988–9), pp. 883–905 (partially reprinted in S. Avineri and A. de-Shalit (eds), *Communitarianism and Individualism* (Oxford: Oxford University Press, 1992)).

13 See the debate on these questions between Chandran Kukathas and Will Kymlicka: C. Kukathas, 'Are There Any Cultural Rights?', *Political Theory*, 20 (1992), pp. 105–39; W. Kymlicka, 'The Rights of Minority Cultures: Reply to Kukathas', *Political Theory*, 20 (1992), pp. 140–46; C. Kukathas, 'Cultural Rights Again: A Rejoinder to Kymlicka', *Political Theory*, 20 (1992), pp. 674–80.

14 See R. Scruton, *The Meaning of Conservatism* (Harmondsworth: Penguin, 1980); 'In Defence of the Nation', in *The Philosopher on Dover Beach* (Manchester: Carcanet, 1990).

15 Scruton, 'In Defence of the Nation', op. cit., n. 14, p. 310.

16 I have explained the idea of equality of status more fully, and explored some of its empirical preconditions, in 'Complex Equality', in D. Miller and M. Walzer (eds), *Pluralism, Justice and Equality* (Oxford: Oxford University Press, 1995). See also D. Miller, 'What Kind of Equality Should the Left Pursue?', in J. Franklin (ed.), *Equality* (London: IPPR, 1997).

17 M. Walzer, *Spheres of Justice* (Oxford: Martin Robertson, 1983), Chapter 2.

18 I have argued this at greater length in *On Nationality* (Oxford: Clarendon Press, 1995), Chapter 5.

19 In *On Nationality*, op. cit., n. 18, chapters 4–5, and in 'Bounded Citizenship', forthcoming in K. Hutchings (ed.), *Cosmopolitan Citizenship*.

20 K. Marx, 'On the Jewish Question', in T. B. Bottomore (ed.), *Karl Marx: Early Writings* (London: Watts, 1963).

21 Walzer, op. cit., n. 17, Chapter 1; I have tried to expand upon and defend Walzer's idea in 'Complex Equality', op. cit., n. 16.

22 There is a large and growing literature on deliberative democracy which includes: B. Manin, 'On Legitimacy and Political Deliberation', *Political Theory*, 15 (1987), pp. 338–68; J. Cohen, 'Deliberation and Democratic Legitimacy', in A. Hamlin and P. Pettit (eds), *The Good Polity* (Oxford: Blackwell, 1989); J. Drysek, *Discursive Democracy* (Cambridge: Cambridge University Press, 1990); J. Fishkin, *Democracy and Deliberation* (New Haven: Yale University Press, 1991); D. Miller, 'Deliberative Democracy and Social Choice', *Political Studies*, Special Issue, 40 (1992), pp. 54–67; A. Gutmann and D. Thompson, *Democracy and Disagreement* (Cambridge, MA: Belknap Press, 1996).

23 A. Etzioni, 'Common Values', *New Statesman and Society*, 8(352), 12 May 1995, p. 25.

24 See Etzioni, op. cit., n. 2, Part 3.

Further reading

Instead of providing a redundant and possibly boring list of references, we want to suggest a list of books related to the topics discussed here, books that we personally find thought-provoking, interesting and helpful.

To those who are interested in the historical roots of the difficulties in implementing liberalism in practice, we would like to suggest a number of books. The first is Michael Freeden's book, *The New Liberalism: An Ideology of Social Reform* (Oxford: Clarendon Press, 1978) in which Freeden puts the liberal ideas in the historical context and examines how they did change at the turn of the century. Richard Bellamy's *Liberalism and Modern Society* (Cambridge: Polity Press, 1992) extends the discussion of changes in liberal ideas to what happened on the continent. James Young's *Reconsidering American Liberalism* (New York: Westview, 1996) is a timely rethinking of Louis Hartz, *The Liberal Tradition in America* (New York: Harcourt, Brace and Co., 1955). Young's book also has the additional merit of including a detailed and careful discussion of most of the relevant thinkers in contemporary North American liberal discourse, focusing on the relation between democracy and liberalism in American theory and practice. In *Democracy's Discontent* (Cambridge, MA: Harvard University Press, 1996), Michael Sandel examines the development of liberal and democratic ideas in the USA. He argues that part of the frustration that Americans feel with government and their feeling that they lose the 'moral fabric of community' is due to defects in the public philosophy by which Americans live. An earlier attempt to analyse the American difficulties with making sense of moral and public life and to relate it to the liberal idea of individualism, has been described by Robert Bellah *et al.*, in their influential book *Habits of the Heart* (Berkeley: University of California Press, 1985).

We recommend to our readers three books that represent opposing interpretations of liberalism's relation to the historical and philosophical traditions of Western political theory. These studies are interesting because they exemplify the variety of alternative understandings of 'liberalism at its best', and demonstrate the meeting of political commitments and scholarly analysis that is characteristic of so much of contemporary scholarly studies about liberalism. Harvey C. Mansfield, Jr, *The Spirit of Liberalism* (Cambridge, MA: Harvard University Press, 1978), presents a spirited attack on 'today's cucumber liberalism', suggesting that liberalism turn to classical conservatism as the source of inspiration to determine what should be done by 'true' liberals. An opposite interpretation of the merits of liberalism is developed in Robert Hollinger, *The Dark Side of Liberalism: Elitism vs. Democracy* (Westport, Conn.: Praeger, 1996). Tracing the aristocratic roots of liberal thought and practice, Hollinger suggests that liberalism should be oriented towards a more participatory form of democracy, a direction suggested by a number of authors included in our volume. Finally, Isaiah Berlin's *Four Essays on Liberty* (Oxford: Oxford University Press, 1969) has become a classical text, in terms of its impact on both liberal and non-liberal thinkers.

Controversies over multiculturalism and education, public television, same-sex politics, abortion and so on are all moral as well as political. Since our book analyses them philosophically, it seems that readers interested in the sociological and political aspects of these cases should read James Nolman, Jr (ed.), *The American Culture Wars* (Charlottesville: University Press of Virginia, 1996). For those interested in widening their knowledge of the multicultural question, we strongly recommend Bhikhu Parekh's book *The Politics of Multiculturalism* (London: Macmillan, 1996) and Amy Gutmann and Charles Taylor, *Multiculturalism and the Politics of Recognition* (Princeton, NJ: Princeton University Press, 1992). Will Kymlicka's book, *Liberalism, Community and Culture* (Oxford: Clarendon Press, 1989) is a theoretical study of the issue of liberalism in multicultural societies. A more anthropological study is Michael Walzer's *On Toleration* (New Haven: Yale University Press, 1997), which is an attempt to analyse several different political arrangements and see whether they can enable various ethnic and cultural groups to live together within a liberal framework.

The reader who is interested in the quest of national self-determination in liberal societies may consult two books: starting with liberalism, Yael Tamir's *Liberal Nationalism* (Princeton, NJ: Princeton University Press, 1993) is mainly an attempt to hold together national values and liberal beliefs. David Miller, *On Nationality* (Oxford: Clarendon Press, 1995) starts from defending nationality, only then seeking how to manifest the principle of nationality in ways which will not contradict liberal values.

Securing liberty in semi-liberal and recently becoming liberal societies is a key issue discussed in the essays in this book. Lord Dahrendorf's *The Modern Social Conflict: An Essay on the Politics of Liberty* (Berkeley: University of California Press, 1990) raises many questions with regard to humans' capability of securing liberty, though the book is a rather optimistic one. Ronald Beiner's *What's the Matter with Liberalism?* (Berkeley: University of California Press, 1992) is more critical and perhaps less optimistic about the scope of liberalism, especially if it does not revise itself to become less 'neutral' and more politically oriented. Stephen Holmes' *Passions and Constraints: On the Theory of Liberal Democracy* (Chicago: Chicago University Press) continues the line of argument of this author in our book, according to which protecting liberties implies a strong liberal society which also implies a strong state.

Finally, we must emphasize that all of the above works are written by scholars who are thoroughly immersed in the works of classical liberal philosophers. We believe that a reading of the original philosophers is a *sine qua non* for any serious study of matters relating to political theory and its practice. We won't list the works of these thinkers (Locke, J. S. Mill, T. H. Green), but would like to suggest that the standard list of classical liberal texts should be extended to include the writings of Baruch Spinoza, because we find the depth of his philosophical insight unparalleled in modern discussions of the meaning and experience of liberty and of toleration. Spinoza represents a unique meeting of biography, philosophy and practice that is simply wonderful. A recent study of Spinoza's role as a founder of modern liberalism is in Steven B. Smith, *Spinoza, Liberalism, and the Question of Jewish Identity* (New Haven: Yale University Press, 1997).

Index

features 17; origins 3; tension
between democracy and 13
liberty 5–6, 7, 29, 44; balancing of with
prosperity and civility 17–18, 21–30
Locke, John 110
Loewith, Karl 74
Luksic, Andrónico 56

MacIntyre, Alasdair 159, 171, 173
Macpherson, C.B. 141
Madison, James 28, 34–5
Malaysia 123
Mandeville, Bernard 65–6
Mann, Thomas 31
Margalit, Avishai and Halbertal, Moshe
89, 90–1, 91–2
market economy 17, 18
marriages, coerced 93
Marx, Karl 108, 135, 147, 156, 158,
162, 181
Marxism: and overcoming of group
hatreds 137
Meach Lake Agreement (Canada) 123
Mercurio, El 56
Meyer, Peter 133
middle class 23
Mill, J.S. 113
millet model: concept of citizenship
113; defects 121, 122; features
111–12
minorities: integration of *see*
integration, models of; and respect
of cultural diversity 123
multiculturalism 1, 79–124; as a
challenge to liberalism 4–7, 11, 13,
79; contexts and meanings 81–2;
factors distinguishing contemporary
106–8; and feminism 81–100; and
globalisation 107; and group rights
see group rights; left critique of 178;
models of integration *see*
integration, models of; need to
reconcile conflicting demands of
diversity and unity 109; and
pluralism 4–7, 11; and the state 108
Muslims 41; in Britain 6, 117; Indian
122

nationalism: and Russia 32–3

nationhood 181
Nazi Germany 27
neutrality, state 9–12
New Right 170
Nozick, Robert 52, 109, 173

Oakeshott, Michael 109
Olsen, Laurie 98–9
Ottoman empire 113, 121

personhood 3, 4, 172
Pinochet, Augusto 50, 51, 52, 54
Plato principle 157–8
pluralism: and democracy 13; and
group hatreds 127; internal and
external 3, 8–9, 10–11, 12, 13; and
multiculturalism 4–7, 11; and state
neutrality 9–12; theses of 7–9
pluralist model 122; advantages
119–20, 121; concept of citizenship
113; defects 120; features 111, 112
Poland 150
Popper, Karl 28
Poulter, Sebastian 88
poverty 23; in Latin America 61
private property 48
proceduralist model: concept of
citizenship 113; defects 113–14,
121–2; features 109, 112
Program for Action 85
property rights 41, 48
prosperity 2; balancing of with civility
and liberty 17–18, 21–30
Proudhon, Pierre-Joseph 170

racial discrimination 37, 129, 130
rational choice theory 128
Rawls, John 94, 110–11, 147, 173
Raz, Jo 175
reason: Hayek on limitations of 67–8;
Hegel's notion of cunning of 64–5,
67, 72–5
reasonableness 11–12
Reich, Robert 23
republicanism 126
right communitarianism 171, 176–7,
179, 180
rights 17, 173; dependence on the state
36–7, 38–9, 40–1; unenforcement in